Palgrave Studies in the History of the Media

Series Editors
Bill Bell
Cardiff University
Cardiff, UK

Chandrika Kaul
University of St Andrews
Fife, UK

Alexander S. Wilkinson
University College Dublin
Dublin, Ireland

Palgrave Studies in the History of the Media publishes original, high quality research into the cultures of communication from the middle ages to the present day. The series explores the variety of subjects and disciplinary approaches that characterize this vibrant field of enquiry. The series will help shape current interpretations not only of the media, in all its forms, but also of the powerful relationship between the media and politics, society, and the economy.
Advisory Board: Professor Peter Burke (Emmanuel College, Cambridge), Professor Nicholas Cull (University of Southern California), Professor Bridget Griffen-Foley (Macquarie University), Professor Monica Juneja (Heidelberg University), Professor Tom O'Malley (Aberystwyth University).

More information about this series at
http://www.palgrave.com/gp/series/14578

Bridget Griffen-Foley

Australian Radio Listeners and Television Viewers

Historical Perspectives

Bridget Griffen-Foley
Macquarie University
Sydney, NSW, Australia

Palgrave Studies in the History of the Media
ISBN 978-3-030-54639-7   ISBN 978-3-030-54637-3 (eBook)
https://doi.org/10.1007/978-3-030-54637-3

© The Editor(s) (if applicable) and The Author(s), under exclusive licence to Springer Nature Switzerland AG 2020
This work is subject to copyright. All rights are solely and exclusively licensed by the Publisher, whether the whole or part of the material is concerned, specifically the rights of translation, reprinting, reuse of illustrations, recitation, broadcasting, reproduction on microfilms or in any other physical way, and transmission or information storage and retrieval, electronic adaptation, computer software, or by similar or dissimilar methodology now known or hereafter developed.
The use of general descriptive names, registered names, trademarks, service marks, etc. in this publication does not imply, even in the absence of a specific statement, that such names are exempt from the relevant protective laws and regulations and therefore free for general use.
The publisher, the authors and the editors are safe to assume that the advice and information in this book are believed to be true and accurate at the date of publication. Neither the publisher nor the authors or the editors give a warranty, expressed or implied, with respect to the material contained herein or for any errors or omissions that may have been made. The publisher remains neutral with regard to jurisdictional claims in published maps and institutional affiliations.

Cover illustration: INTERFOTO / Alamy Stock Photo

This Palgrave Pivot imprint is published by the registered company Springer Nature Switzerland AG.
The registered company address is: Gewerbestrasse 11, 6330 Cham, Switzerland

A Note on Australian Callsigns

Radio callsigns feature a numerical prefix indicating the state or territory in which the station is located: 2 (New South Wales and Australian Capital Territory), 3 (Victoria), 4 (Queensland), 5 (South Australia), 6 (Western Australia), 7 (Tasmania) and 8 (Northern Territory).

The first two letters of television callsigns are selected by the licensee, and the third letter indicates the state or territory in which the station is located: N (New South Wales), V (Victoria), Q (Queensland), S (South Australia), W (Western Australia), C (Australian Capital Territory) and D (Darwin, Northern Territory).

Acknowledgements

I am indebted to the Australian Research Council for funding research for this book under the Future Fellowship scheme. The Faculty of Arts and central research offices at Macquarie University ably backed up my research on this book and related publications. I extend sincere thanks to supportive colleagues in the Department of Media, Music, Communication and Cultural Studies, and the Centre for Media History, at Macquarie University, including Professor Nicole Anderson, Dr Jeannine Baker, Dr Virginia Madsen, Dr Willa McDonald and Professor Joseph Pugliese.

I am grateful to a network of archive and library professionals. At the National Archives of Australia, I was again fortunate to be aided by Darren Watson and Edmund Rutledge and their colleagues in the Melbourne and Sydney reading rooms. Dr Rachel Franks provided a constant source of help and encouragement at the State Library of New South Wales, and her colleague Linda Brainwood provided invaluable assistance with illustrative research in the latter stages of the book. I also drew on the long expertise of Guy Tranter at the ABC Document Archives.

Early research assistance for this project was provided by Dr Kyle Harvey. More recently, I am indebted to Dr Kylie Andrews and Dr Michael Thurlow for their patient and enthusiastic help. Kylie was of particular help with illustrations, and Michael compiled the index and shared his research on television clubs with me.

For assistance with illustrative permissions, I thank Loui Silvestro; Josie Mack; Linda Curry; Kathy Hobson; Lindsay Foyle; Ian Grieve; Claudia Funder at the Arts Centre Melbourne; Janine Crichley at ABC Commercial;

Glen Menzies at the Copyright Agency; Alessandra Steele and Katie Jameson at Nine Radio; Nicholas Vinen at *Silicon Chip Magazine*; and Jamie Lee at Condé Nast Licensing.

I am grateful to Dr Chandrika Kaul for helping to shepherd through this book proposal, and the team at Palgrave Macmillan: Emily Russell, Joseph Johnson and Jasper Asir.

Thank you to my other gal pals, including Maree, Trish, Jennifer, Margaret, Liz and Alison, for their patience as I wrote this book during often challenging circumstances. And finally, thanks to my husband Dr Craig Munro for care, counsel and COVID-19 companionship.

Contents

1 Introduction 1

2 Aunts, Uncles and Argonauts 7

3 Club Loyalty 29

4 The Fan Mail Trail 51

5 Outrage and Complaint 75

6 Viewing Television by Committee 105

7 Matchmaking 127

8 Conclusion 153

Index 157

Abbreviations

ABC	Australian Broadcasting Commission/Corporation
ABT	Australian Broadcasting Tribunal
AWA	Amalgamated Wireless Australasia Ltd
BAPH	Brisbane, Adelaide, Perth and Hobart
BBC	British Broadcasting Corporation
DoI	Department of Information
FARB	Federation of Australian Radio Broadcasters
IMT	*In Melbourne Tonight*
NSW	New South Wales
PMG	Postmaster-General
PSCB	Parliamentary Standing Committee on Broadcasting
SBS	Special Broadcasting Service
YWCA	Young Women's Christian Association
WA	Western Australia(n)

List of Figures

Fig. 2.1	*Radio Pictorial of Australia*, September 1939. (By Brodie Mack. Copyright Josie Mack)	15
Fig. 2.2	3AW Birmacley Pet Club certificate, n.d., Nancy Lee Collection, Arts Centre Melbourne. (Copyright Nine Radio)	18
Fig. 3.1	The Argonauts Club 'Order of the Dragon's Tooth', certificate, c. 1965. (Copyright Linda Curry ('Oricus 28'))	38
Fig. 4.1	'Favourites of the air get fan mail', *Wireless Weekly*, 10 July 1936. (Copyright Silicon Chip Publishing)	55
Fig. 5.1	*Wireless Weekly*, 26 December 1930. (Copyright Silicon Chip Publishing)	77
Fig. 5.2	*Wireless Weekly*, 9 December 1932. (Copyright William Edwin Pidgeon/Copyright Agency, 2019)	78
Fig. 6.1	*Australian Women's Weekly*, 19 September 1956. (Courtesy of Stan Hunt estate)	110
Fig. 7.1	*Australian Women's Weekly*, 19 November 1938. (Copyright Nine Radio)	129
Fig. 7.2	From *Grundy Entertainment's Perfect Match* (1985). (Copyright Loui Silvestro)	138

CHAPTER 1

Introduction

Abstract This introductory chapter outlines the book's focus on how Australians have consumed and engaged with radio and television—public (Australian Broadcasting Commission) and commercial—since the 1920s. It explains the book's approach, which is to present a series of historical 'perspectives' based on fine-grained empirical research across Australia. Each chapter recovers and explores some of the lived experiences of Australian radio listeners and television viewers. The introduction also briefly summarises some key approaches to the study and history of media and broadcast audiences.

Keywords Media audiences • Radio • Television • Broadcasting • Australia

Australian Radio Listeners and Television Viewers: Historical Perspectives is about how Australian audiences have consumed and engaged with broadcast media over the last century. It considers radio since the 1920s and television since the 1950s, covering both public (Australian Broadcasting Commission) and commercial broadcasters. Moving away from a traditional focus on what the media has produced by way of texts and images, this book explores how radio and television content has been received, debated and engaged with, as well as the off-air role of radio and television stations and programs in the lives of Australian listeners and viewers.

© The Author(s) 2020
B. Griffen-Foley, *Australian Radio Listeners and Television Viewers*,
Palgrave Studies in the History of the Media,
https://doi.org/10.1007/978-3-030-54637-3_1

This book presents 'perspectives' on the topic, recovering and exploring some of the lived experiences of Australian broadcast audiences. The six chapters are based on a diverse range of primary sources from around Australia, many used here for the first time, including fan mail, complaints files, regulatory records, the private archives of radio clubs and the agendas and minutes of ABC Advisory Committees.

Chapter 2 explores the dynamic world for children created by the on-air and extracurricular endeavours of commercial stations and the ABC (including its famous Argonauts Club) in the years before World War II. Chapter 3 examines the emergence of other radio clubs—particularly attached to commercial stations—across Australia, and moves on to the role of television clubs. Chapter 4 intercepts some of the fan mail received by the ABC and commercial broadcasting stations and networks. Chapter 5, which is closely related to Chap. 4, is based on complaints received by radio and television broadcasters, as well as the Australian Broadcasting Control Board (1949–77), responsible mainly for the commercial sector. Chapter 6 turns its focus back to the ABC, tracing the role of the public service broadcaster's Advisory Committees before uncovering the operations of its state-based Television Viewers' Committees between 1959 and 1965. Chapter 7 considers programs about romance and dating since the 1930s, paying particular attention to participants and audience involvement in two creations of the 1980s: *Midnight Matchmaker* on Sydney radio and *Perfect Match* on network television.

In *The Practice of Everyday Life* in 1980, sociologist Michel de Certeau examined the ways in which people altered and individualised forms of mass culture in order to make them their own.[1] Scholars increasingly challenged the view, drawn largely from the 'effects tradition', that media consumers were passive, teasing out notions of the passive and the private, the active and the public.[2] By the mid-1990s scholars, including Australians Virginia Nightingale and Elizabeth Jacka, were comparing differing approaches to audience research in the social sciences.[3] Barrie Gunter and David Machin edited a four-volume work on media audiences, displaying the diversity of theoretical and methodological approaches to history, measurement and effects, in 2009.[4] This was followed by Nightingale's *The Handbook of Media Audiences*.[5]

There was an increasing realisation, as Richard Butsch put it, that '[p]opular and scholarly discussions of audiences have long lacked historical context'.[6] As Sonia Livingstone remarked, 'it is all too easy to make the ahistorical assumption that present theory and findings apply equally well to past or future periods'.[7]

My book seeks to uncover and explore some of the traces of the 'temporary communities'[8] formed by Australian broadcast audiences and broadcasting institutions themselves. It is informed by major historical studies over the last 30 years including American work on audiences for entertainment and radio[9]; essays in Michele Hilmes and Jason Loviglio's *Radio Reader*[10]; Kate Lacey's study of listening as a cultural practice;[11] and Paddy Scannell's exploration of the communicative experience in modern life.[12] It also builds on Australian studies including Kate Darian-Smith and Sue Turnbull's edited collection, *Remembering Television*[13]; Mark Balnaves, Tom O'Regan and Ben Goldsmith's book on audience measurement[14]; Michelle Arrow's studies of listeners to *Blue Hills*;[15] and work on *Perfect Match* by cultural studies scholars.[16]

It would be difficult, if not impossible, to write the definitive history of Australian broadcast audiences given the challenges of finding systematic sources created by, and about, listeners and viewers, and the multiplicity of individual experiences. Based on fine-grained empirical research, this book is instead a series of perspectives on aspects of the broadcasting experience.

Notes

1. Michel de Certeau, *The Practice of Everyday Life* (Berkeley: University of California Press, 1984).
2. Richard Butsch, *The Making of American Audiences: From Stage to Television, 1750–1990* (New York: Cambridge University Press, New York, 2000), pp. 3, 7–8; Sue Turnbull, 'Imagining the audience', in Stuart Cunningham and Sue Turnbull (eds.), *Media and Communication in Australia* (Sydney: Allen & Unwin, 2014), pp. 68–69.
3. For example, Virginia Nightingale, *Studying Audiences: The Shock of the Real* (London: Routledge, 1996); Elizabeth Jacka, 'Researching audiences: A dialogue between cultural studies and social science', *Media International Australia*, (73) (August 1994), pp. 45–51.
4. Barrie Gunter & David Machin (eds.), *Media Audiences*, vol. 1, *History of Audience Study*; vol. 2, *Measurement of Audiences*; vol. 3, *Aggregated and Disaggregated Audiences*; vol. 4, *Audiences and Influences*, (London: SAGE, 2009).
5. Virginia Nightingale, *The Handbook of Media Audiences* (Chichester, U.K.: Wiley-Blackwell, 2011).
6. Butsch (2000, p. 2).

7. Sonia Livingstone et al., 'Audiences for crime media 1946–91: A historical approach to reception studies', *Communication Review*, 4(2) (2001), p. 166.
8. Melvyn Stokes and Richard Maltby (eds.), *American Media Audiences: From the Turn of the Century to the Early Sound Era* (London: BFI, 1999), p. 9.
9. Butsch 2000; Ray Barfield, *Listening to Radio, 1920–1950* (Westport, C.T., Praeger, 1996); Elena Razlogova, *The Listener's Voice: Early Radio and the American Republic* (Philadelphia, P.A.: University of Pennsylvania Press, 2011).
10. Michele Hilmes & Jason Loviglio (eds.), *Radio Reader: Essays in the Cultural History of Radio* (London: Routledge, 2002).
11. Kate Lacey, *Listening Publics: The Politics and Experience of Listening in the Media Age* (Cambridge: Polity, 2013).
12. Paddy Scannell, *Radio, Television and Modern Life: A Phenomenological Approach* (Oxford: Blackwell, 1996); Jacka 1994, pp. 35–36.
13. Kate Darian-Smith and Sue Turnbull (eds.), *Remembering Television: Histories, Technologies, Memories* (Newcastle upon Tyne, U.K.: Cambridge Scholars Publishing, 2011).
14. Mark Balnaves, Tom O'Regan and Ben Goldsmith, *Rating the Audience: The Business of Media* (London: Bloomsbury Academic, 2011).
15. Michelle Arrow, '"Good entertainment & good family life": Listener readings and responses to Gwen Meredith's *The Lawsons* and *Blue Hills*', *Journal of Australian Studies*, 22(58) (1998), pp. 38–47 and '"The most sickening piece of snobbery I have ever heard": Race, radio listening, and the "Aboriginal question" in *Blue Hills*', *Australian Historical Studies*, 38(130) (2007), pp. 244–60.
16. Some of this work was published in *Australian Journal of Cultural Studies*, 4(2) (May 1987).

Bibliography

Arrow, Michelle. '"Good entertainment & good family life": Listener readings and responses to Gwen Meredith's *The Lawsons* and *Blue Hills*', *Journal of Australian Studies*, 22(58) (1998), pp. 38–47.

Arrow, Michelle. '"The most sickening piece of snobbery I have ever heard": Race, radio listening, and the "Aboriginal question" in *Blue Hills*', *Australian Historical Studies*, 38(130) (2007), pp. 244–60.

Australian Journal of Cultural Studies, 4(2) (May 1987).

Balnaves, Mark, Tom O'Regan and Ben Goldsmith. *Rating the Audience: The Business of Media* (London: Bloomsbury Academic, 2011).

Barfield, Ray. *Listening to Radio, 1920–1950* (Westport, C.T.: Praeger, 1996).

Butsch, Richard. *The Making of American Audiences: From Stage to Television, 1750–1990* (New York: Cambridge University Press, New York, 2000).

Darian-Smith, Kate and Turnbull, Sue (eds.). *Remembering Television: Histories, Technologies, Memories* (Newcastle upon Tyne, U.K.: Cambridge Scholars Publishing, 2011).

de Certeau, Michel. *The Practice of Everyday Life* (Berkeley: University of California Press, 1984).

Gunter, Barrie and Machin, David (eds.). *Media Audiences*, vol. 1, *History of Audience Study*; vol. 2, *Measurement of Audiences*; vol. 3, *Aggregated and Disaggregated Audiences*; vol. 4, *Audiences and Influences* (London: SAGE, 2009).

Hilmes, Michele and Loviglio, Jason (eds.). *Radio Reader: Essays in the Cultural History of Radio* (London: Routledge, 2002).

Jacka, Elizabeth. 'Researching audiences: A dialogue between cultural studies and social science', *Media International Australia*, (73) (1994), pp. 45–51.

Lacey, Kate. *Listening Publics: The Politics and Experience of Listening in the Media Age* (Cambridge: Polity, 2013).

Livingstone, Sonia, Jessica Allen and Robert Reiner. 'Audiences for crime media 1946–91: A historical approach to reception studies', *Communication Review*, 4(2) (2001), pp. 165–92.

Nightingale, Virginia. *Studying Audiences: The Shock of the Real* (London: Routledge, 1996).

Nightingale, Virginia. *The Handbook of Media Audiences* (Chichester, U.K.: Wiley-Blackwell, 2011).

Razlogova, Elena. *The Listener's Voice: Early Radio and the American Republic* (Philadelphia, P.A.: University of Pennsylvania Press, 2011).

Scannell, Paddy. *Radio, Television and Modern Life: A Phenomenological Approach* (Oxford: Blackwell, 1996).

Stokes, Melvyn and Maltby, Richard (eds.). *American Media Audiences: From the Turn of the Century to the Early Sound Era* (London: BFI, 1999).

Turnbull, Sue. 'Imagining the audience', in Stuart Cunningham and Sue Turnbull (eds.). *Media and Communication in Australia* (Sydney: Allen & Unwin, 2014), pp. 59–72.

CHAPTER 2

Aunts, Uncles and Argonauts

Abstract This chapter considers the emergence and role of radio 'Aunts' and 'Uncles' in cities and towns across Australia as the industry worked to foster a sense of intimacy and engagement and build communities of young listeners. It explores the dynamic world for children created by the on-air and extracurricular endeavours of commercial stations and the Australian Broadcasting Commission in the years before World War II. The chapter examines the launch of the ABC's ambitious Argonauts Club, which grew to be one of the biggest and most successful children's radio clubs in the world.

Keywords Broadcasting • Children's radio • Commercial radio • Australian Broadcasting Commission • Argonauts

Beginning with the 'Aunts' and 'Uncles' that appeared on radio stations around Australia in the second half of the 1920s, this chapter considers how an impersonal mass medium sought to foster intimacy and create communities of young Australian listeners in the years before World War II. Australia's radio industry consisted of 'A-class' (public service) stations, which were consolidated into the Australian Broadcasting Commission (ABC) in 1932, and B-class (commercial) stations. Both sectors created specific sound worlds for young listeners, and generated on-air and extra-curricular activities through membership certificates, birthday calls, film

© The Author(s) 2020
B. Griffen-Foley, *Australian Radio Listeners and Television Viewers*,
Palgrave Studies in the History of the Media,
https://doi.org/10.1007/978-3-030-54637-3_2

screenings, parties and excursions. The chapter examines the first incarnation of the ABC's Argonauts Club (1933–1935), concluding with its relaunch in 1941.

In the 1920s, for many listeners the great fascination of wireless lay in outside broadcasting, in the bringing of the wider world into the privacy and comfort of the home. But, as the broadcasting historian Lesley Johnson shows, by the end of the decade, Australian industry leaders and periodicals were convinced that radio was most successful when intimate, human and personal.[1]

The radio 'Uncle' and 'Aunt' were a feature of Australia's A- and B-class stations by the mid-1920s. One of the earliest was simply styled 'Uncle Radio', who was heard on 5CL Adelaide from 1924 to 1928.[2] This A-class station inaugurated the Twinklers' Boys Club, as an adjunct to the Scouting movement, in 1926. Enjoying vice-regal patronage, it was one of the earliest children's radio clubs in Australia[3] and was followed by the 5CL Bluebird Girls' Club.[4]

Sydney's *Wireless Weekly* reported in 1926 on the surreptitious visits of parents to radio offices, dropping in little gifts that Uncles and Aunts could send 'over the air' to children. 'Uncle George' (George Saunders) of A-class station 2BL was said to be amused by the letters he received, including one from a girl saying that although she knew that he was an old man (he was aged in his 30s), she hoped he would be spared to tell bedtime stories for many years to come.[5]

Queensland Radio News photographed the 'bright and cheery' 'Uncle Ben', who appeared on 4QG's Saturday evening bedtime story session, alongside a 'vivacious little lady' assistant, 'Miss Mabel Sunshine' (teenage elocution student Mabel Cormac). The periodical dedicated a regular page to 'Uncle Ben's Corner', relaying behind-the-scenes news, encouraging children to write in, conducting competitions, and publishing photos of children listening to the Brisbane A-class station.[6] The man behind Uncle Ben, printer Leonard L. Read, also produced a book of verses sung on his program, and *Uncle Ben's Book-o'-Fun* for boys and girls.[7] By December 1926 there were several 'Bed-time Storytellers' on 4QG in addition to Uncle Ben and Mabel (now known as 'Little Miss Sunshine').[8]

Several radio Uncles were also heard presenting programs for adults. A former army officer, J.M. Prentice, delivered lectures over 2BL, in addition to reading bedtime stories as 'Uncle Jack' and engaging in staged quarrels with 'Uncle George'.[9] 2SM's 'Uncle Tom' (John Dunne), 2UE's 'Uncle Lionel' (Lionel Lunn) and 'Uncle Bob' (Russell A. Yeldon) on

2WL Wollongong also held important positions behind the scenes.[10] Eric Bessemer had a curious journey at 4BC, joining as a junior engineer, becoming a popular breakfast personality as 'Sunshine Sam', and then being appointed chief-of-staff of the Brisbane B-class station.[11] Norman W. Simmons moved from being 'Uncle Cuthbert' at Hobart A-class station 7ZL to manager and engineer at Kalgoorlie B-class station 6KG.[12]

Some Aunts were married to station managers. In Adelaide, Stella Hume appeared on 5DN—a B-class station operating out of the house she shared with her husband Ernest—as 'Miss Leonora Starr', as elocutionist and as 'Auntie Stella'.[13] In Broken Hill in far-western New South Wales, 20-year-old 'Cousin Denny' (Denny Marshall), who hosted the *Tiny Tots* session on 2XL, was the daughter of the engineer on the short-lived B-class station.[14] Although women performed in dramas and comedies, many were confined to the role of 'Aunt' in sessions aimed at women and children,[15] or appeared as sidekicks.

Uncles and Aunts were joined by people whose radio names drew inspiration from Australian flora and fauna, including 'Bobby Bluegum' (Frank Hatherley), 'Kanga' (Frank W. Gorman), 'Billy Bunny' (Maurice Dudley) and 'Little Miss Kookaburra' (Hazel Maude). A-class stations reportedly struggled to cope with the volume of children and parents who requested calls to be relayed to individual children on their birthdays.[16] Sometimes announcers, having been tipped off by parents, explained where presents could be found. Several A-class stations asked for a donation to charity, with 2HD Newcastle one of a handful of B-class stations to charge a small fee for birthday calls.[17]

Barbara Corbett writes of her father building a wireless set in 1927, the first one in the area near Lake Macquarie north of Sydney. She recalls listening to the 'Hello Man' (A.S. Cochrane) every morning on Sydney's 2FC: 'He was like God. He knew everything. He knew all about birthdays … there was a deep-seated thrill when you heard your own name called over the wireless.'[18] One night in May 1928 he called up no fewer than 129 children who had written to him. Cochrane also discovered that his listeners remembered his own birthday from the previous year when he arrived at the studio to find letters and gifts awaiting him, including a dressing gown knitted for his mother.[19]

The Children's News Radio Birthday Club, run by department store Farmer & Co. through their station 2FC, started hosting an annual swimming party on Sydney Harbour in 1927.[20] 2BL was staging children's parties each Saturday morning in the hall of another retailer, Anthony

Hordern, by 1928.[21] Singing, lucky numbers and novelty competitions were accompanied by 'moral talks' from 'Uncle Bas', with a newspaper noting the 'effective way which Radio is entering into the life of the very young citizen'.[22] That Christmas Day, 2BL orchestrated the landing of Santa Claus at Manly beach. He spent the morning on a platform performing high jinx with Aunts, Uncles and Cousins in bathing suits, in one of Australia's most ambitious outside broadcasts to date.[23]

Noting how well children were catered for, *Wireless Weekly* attempted to list all 'THE WIRELESS UNCLES, AUNTS, BIRDS, DOGS, ETC.' heard across Australia in 1928.[24] Soon after, the *Evening News* reported that there were some nine members of the family—Uncles, Aunts, Cousins and the Hello Man—broadcasting on 2FC alone.[25] One of them was 'Aunt Willa', who recorded juvenile cantatas like 'Sing a Song of Sixpence', and took her listeners on magic carpet rides to 'Fairyland', 'Doll Town' and (in a nod to Australia) 'The Bush' on Tuesday evenings.[26]

Radio stations and networks worked hard to turn their personalities and endeavours into popular social movements. The creation of a 'Fairy Godmother' (Margaret Herd) by Sydney B-class station 2CH suggests that the radio family performed benevolent, as well as social and promotional, functions. Radio was represented as a means of escape and fun, of solace and support.[27] Readers of the first edition of Melbourne's *Listener In* for 1930 were advised to pull together and help each other in the face of the Great Depression, and to use radio to 'tune out the gloom'. In her Christmas message that year, 'Auntie Goodie' (Goodie Reeve) of 2GB's *Tiny Tots* session urged her nieces and nephews to 'specially appreciate your presents ... because most Mummies and Daddies have not had too many pennies'.[28]

In these experimental early years of broadcasting, children's personalities, and even clubs themselves, moved around. Reeve had first made her name at 2FC before it became part of the ABC. Farmer & Co. switched its allegiance from 2FC to a B-class station, 2UW, where the retailer established a Children's Radio Birthday Club under Uncle Jack, formerly of 2BL.[29] A.S. Cochrane was in 1932 lured to Sydney's newest commercial station, 2CH, operated by Amalgamated Wireless Australasia Ltd (AWA) on behalf of the NSW Council of Churches, as chief announcer. He took the Hello Man character with him, writing of his appearances at a city store each Saturday morning, when he would be greeted by a rush of 'little ones' with 'their eyes full of excitement and love'. Every child had to be 'noticed', if not personally addressed. Cochrane would lead the children in singing 'Advance Australia Fair', make a jovial speech, conduct a quiz, convey birthday greetings, show an absurd silent film and conclude with singing 'Auld Lang Syne' and 'Happy Days are Here Again'.[30]

That the children's radio clubs that emerged in Australia were generally free to join took on an extra significance during the Depression. As we shall see in Chap. 3, film and radio interests set up clubs for fans—including children—during the interwar years in order to enhance the industries' civic reputability, engender goodwill and facilitate tie-ins with businesses. Children were rewarded with events, and membership certificates and badges.[31]

By the early 1930s wireless and electrical interests were staging Australian radio exhibitions. At a major one held at Sydney Town Hall in March 1932 (the month the ABC launched), 2UW's contribution was 'Station T.O.T.' Hundreds of children, parents and teachers sent in entries to the 'station', with those selected presented in a novelty broadcast each night.[32] At an exhibition in Perth a few weeks later, Uncles and Aunts from 6WF and two B-class stations, 6LM and 6PR, joined forces for a Saturday afternoon appearance.[33]

The appeal of such programs and presenters is evident from the ABC's first annual report, which advised that some 57,601 letters had been received from children in 1932–33. ABC historian Ken Inglis notes that the number of children who contacted stations increased so rapidly that presenters had to stop making individual birthday calls. The ABC also reported that 'Children's Hours' were broadcast in each capital city, making up 4.6 per cent of total broadcasting time.[34] Copied from the BBC, the *Children's Hour* was based on the idea of a real hour mothers spent with their children 'between tea-time and bed-time'.[35]

'Experimental work' in children's programming was being carried out 'all over the world and not least in Australia', the ABC's annual report went on.[36] As early as 1927 BBC executives had begun objecting to radio Uncles and Aunts,[37] and Inglis explains that the new Commissioners did not think much of the Uncles and the Aunts they inherited.[38] In Melbourne, 3LO's manager, T.W. (Bill) Bearup, was mindful of competition from commercial stations 'which could always beat us at this game because they were able to give away concessions, chocolates and theatre tickets. I began to think seriously about the children's session because here we had a chance to do something for the listeners of the future.'[39]

Bearup and 3LO studio manager Frank D. Clewlow wanted the new ABC to create a children's session more serious and enterprising than any so far attempted on either A- or B-class stations. Clewlow, in consultation with the children's writer Nina Murdoch, conceived the idea of an Argonauts Club whose members, allocated to ships with Greek names, would unite under the mythological figure of Jason in a search for the Golden Fleece. Argonauts were to be known only by the name of their Greek ship and their oar number, assigned by the ABC, and to sign a pledge written by Murdoch. As a reward for sending in drawings, stories and poems that were marked and could be read out on-air, they would earn points to be admitted to 'Order of the Dragon's Tooth' and then the 'Order of the Golden Fleece'.[40]

Murdoch, known on the air as 'Pat', took over the Melbourne *Children's Hour* in August 1932. As she prepared to launch the Argonauts she altered the tone in a direction not enjoyed by all listeners. One parent wrote to the *Listener In* asking how to explain the changes:

> Billy Bunny is scarcely heard, the kookaburra laughs no more. ... Our children go to bed dissatisfied, saying there is nothing to tune in for, only someone called Pat, every night, who talks and talks and talks a lot of piffle. ... We get all the education we want at school; we only want amusement at the Children's Hour.

Murdoch replied that her policy was simply 'to treat children as intelligent young people'. Bearup was keen on the idea of the Argonauts but the ABC's general manager, W.T. Conder, was amongst those who thought it too highbrow. 'All that children want are Punch and Judy shows', he huffed, advocating instead for a national children's club. In a memo to Conder in June 1933, Bearup wrote that he had been comparing the 3LO *Children's Hour* with the ABC's interstate offerings: 'I invite anyone interested to do the same and I have no fear as to the result'.[41]

Finally, in mid-1933, the Argonauts got underway on 3LO.[42] A call was put out for members, with the promise of a special badge for the first city and the first country child to join. Each youngster who applied to join the 'Band of Happy Rowers' signed a pledge vowing to 'stand faithfully by all that is brave and beautiful'. Nearly 3000 young rowers enrolled within the first year. 'We have given up the idea of being gratuitous Aunts and Uncles to our listeners', Murdoch wrote. Her recruits did not even score personal appearances, as legend has it Murdoch was so timid she would run away and hide if any children came to the studio.[43]

Meanwhile, other states had their own ideas about children's clubs. The ABC's NSW office pressed hard for the Bobby Bluegum Sunshine Soldiers, a club for children dedicated to bringing 'sunshine' to parents and to less fortunate children. Around 4000 members who enrolled were sent certificates, and could listen in to club broadcasts on 2FC on Monday and Tuesday evenings.[44] Tasmania had the popular 7ZL Children's Radio Club, whose personalities—'Uncle Ben' and 'Aunt Topsy'—hosted community singing, parties and film screenings (including *Robinson Crusoe*).[45] These ABC endeavours were more along the lines of traditional Australian radio children's offerings.

South Australia's 5CL and 5CK had the Australian Boys' Club, with 13,000 members by late 1934. Under the leadership of 'Uncle Bert' (Bert Wooley), it had its own session on Monday nights. The Club aimed 'to promote the physical, mental and moral development of Australian boys, to extend their love for King and country, to secure funds and gifts for various charities and relief for poor and afflicted children' and, in a vague echo of the Argonauts, to 'encourage a love for music and literature and encourage and assist young artists, and generally develop the talents of the boys'.[46]

When Murdoch left the 3LO children's session in 1934 to live and write in Adelaide, her place was taken by Isobel Ann Shead. The following year, Conder countermanded an order for more Argonauts Club certificates and badges. Without money, the enterprise was for all practical purposes sunk, although the 'Argonauts Theatre' continued as part of the Melbourne *Children's Hour*.[47]

Commercial efforts, both metropolitan and regional, proceeded apace. In Newcastle, 'Cousin Joy' (Ivy Wood, who seems to have been the daughter of 2HD manager E.A. Wood) ran the Joy Club, which met weekly and had 6000 members by 1934.[48] Six months after its formation in 1933, the 2GF Smile Club in Grafton had 1800 young members, all of whom pledged to smile three times, and make someone smile, every day. The Club's Saturday-morning broadcasts, including a juvenile orchestra, were followed by child performers appearing at a local store. The Club staged pet parades, swimming carnivals, a cycling race and evening 'frolics', and raised funds for the local hospital and charities. 'The Smileman' (AWA executive Roger Fair) went on to introduce the Smile Club to two other regional AWA stations, 2AY Albury and 3BO Bendigo.[49] AWA's flagship metropolitan station, 2CH, then introduced its own Smile Club, with Charles Stanley as 'Chief Smiler'.[50]

One of the earliest programs on 2SM, a Catholic station launched in Sydney in 1932, was hosted by 'Uncle Tom'. Soon after he began reading stories to children, it occurred to John Dunne that children themselves could be heard on-air. And so he had five children come into the studio to sing. These children sent out calls to their pals, and before long 70 or 80 children were being ushered into 2SM for each hour-long children's session. From this initiative emerged Uncle Tom's Gang, boasting 50,000 members by 1935. Some were listed and photographed in issues of the *Wireless Weekly*. As the children aged the Punch Club emerged, with a Wednesday-night program showcasing their talents (Fig. 2.1).[51]

There was competition between capital city stations, as we can see from activities in Brisbane 1933–1934, and in Adelaide a little later. 4BC's children's session—headed by 'Aunt Marie' (Marie Landon), 'Uncle Rod' (Rod Gainford) and 'Sunrise Sam'—at 5.30 pm weekdays was revised in 1933 to feature a new club, the 4BC Happiness Club. Each Saturday morning the station staged a 'monster' children's party at McWhirter's department store, with performances by the Sunshine Kiddies.[52] After Aunt Marie left the station, the women's announcer Mary Elizabeth introduced a children's choir. The 4BC Bunny Club for younger children (aged four to six) was launched, with a 'King' and 'Queen Bunny' crowned each month by the Chief Bunny, 'Aunt Eva'.[53]

Members of 4BH's health and entertainment clubs for boys and girls were invited to a Saturday afternoon at Moreton Bay. A specially charted steamer conveyed 1500 children (for free) and some accompanying parents (for a small fee). They were entertained by donkey rides on the beach, wheelbarrow races and sporting activities, and served lemonade and cake. The 'jolly picnic' seems to have become an annual event.[54]

4BK tried something a little different, launching the Dixie Radio Club to provide 'clean healthful entertainment' for children aged between 4 and 14, cultivate a 'deeper sense of moral obligation', and assist deserving charities. It was helmed by 'Master Dixie' (Arthur L. Dixon, the station's manager and engineer) and the 'Reverend Dixie' (Wilfred Magor of the Brisbane City Mission). Although envisaged as being for children, the Club and members of the Dixie 'family' became associated with a musical revue and light entertainment session run each Saturday evening until midnight.[55]

Soon after becoming general manager of Hume Broadcasters in 1935, Gordon Marsh established the Kipling Boys' Club as part of a drive to make 5DN the leading station in South Australia. The Club adopted as its

Fig. 2.1 *Radio Pictorial of Australia*, September 1939. (By Brodie Mack. Copyright Josie Mack)

creed Rudyard Kipling's poem 'If', with no less than Donald Bradman as president and Kipling himself as patron. It acquired 16,000 members in its first year, with boys raising money for stoves, pianos, prams, clothing, wheelchairs and radio sets for the needy.[56] With Uncle Bert (formerly of the ABC) at the helm, Kipling Club broadcasts on Tuesday evenings were also heard over 5RM Renmark.[57] By 1937 another Adelaide station, 5DN, had formed the Kangaroo Club.[58] More than 65,000 'Kangas' were to be enrolled over the life of the Club, headed by 'Uncle Dick' (Richard Moore), and it raised more than £30,000 for charity.[59]

Meanwhile, some listeners came to tire of birthday calls, with E. West from Tamworth in north-east New South Wales dismissing them as an 'ear-sore' in a letter to *Wireless Weekly* in 1933. Her complaint about 'baby prattle' was endorsed by another correspondent in 1935, who on behalf of housewives expressed a desire for music while preparing dinner, rather than content for 'kiddies' across all Sydney stations.[60] In a 1934 'ballot' of 4BK listeners by the station's stablemate, the *Courier-Mail*, birthday greetings scored 68, compared with 926 at the top of the table (popular concert items). 'Hooray, birthday calls dropped dead by the wayside' was one response.[61] 2UW, 2GB and the ABC suspended the practice the following year, arguing that birthday calls interested only the children being called. But many stations continued the calls, in line with John Dunne's reasoning: 'Call a youngster and that kiddy remains a listener for life.'[62]

Interestingly, the Australian Broadcasting Control Board (established in 1949) was also ambivalent about the practice. With broadcasting stations intended to transmit matter for reception by the general public, the Board, like the Postmaster-General's Department, permitted 'personal messages' only in certain circumstances. Birthday and cheerio calls, the ABCB reiterated in 1953, were permitted only during times specified by stations for the purpose. However, it conceded the value of programs in which a link existed between a station and particular listeners, principally children and women.[63] 5AD's Kangaroo Club was amongst those clubs still sending out birthday calls into the 1950s.[64]

Western Australia, where the sense of isolation was acute, overflowed with children's personalities. In Perth, 6WF had 'Uncle Paul' (Paul Daly) and 'Aunty Peggy'.[65] 'Uncle Peter' (Harold Lalor and then Alwyn Kurts) and 'Pongo' (Jim Grant) presented the state's most popular children's session over 6PR. The station also had a birthday club with 15,000 members managed by 'Auntie Isla' (Isla Hayles). 6ML had 'Uncle Eric' (Eric L. Donald), 'Aunty Laurel' (Laurel Berryman) and 'Aunt Mary' (Joan

Allen), as well 'Sambo' (a 'Blackface', a fairly common caricature of the time) and the Junior Cheerio Club with 10,000 members. 'Aunt Judy' (Jessie Robertson) was at 6ML's sister station, 6IX. Children heard 'Uncle Rag' (Harold Wells) on 6AM Northam. That station's Saturday-morning Kiddies' Kommunity Koncerts were so popular that to avoid overcrowding, local health authorities capped attendance to 800. 6KG had 'Uncle Dan and Dusty', 'Uncle Jim' (C.J. Cross) and 'Auntie Amelia', as well as a Goldfields Boys' Club, with aeroplane and cricket sections.[66]

Then there was 'Nicky' and 'Nancy Lee' with their *Chatterbox Corner* on Melbourne's 3AW.[67] Clifford Nicholls Whitta ('Nicky'), a musician who had been working with 3LO, joined Fred Tupper ('Tuppy') in 1932 to host 3AW's breakfast show. The following year, singer and ukulele player Kathleen Lindgren was brought in to host the commercial station's children's show. She evolved from 'Ukulele Lady' to 'Nancy Lee', a name chosen by listeners themselves. Nicky hosted *Chatterbox Corner* with Nancy, starring as a naughty but loveable boy the Chums and their mums took to their hearts. The session had a wildly popular theme song, 'Being a Chum is Fun', and hosted parties, juvenile balls and Christmas fetes. Every Saturday-morning party was booked out for months ahead. There were events for invalid children, and hospital and Christmas appeals with goods donated by sponsors. A specially monogrammed 'Chatterbox Corner Plane' conveyed the personalities around Victoria. By 1936 the team needed a police escort, with Nicky on one occasion running around Melbourne Zoo desperately holding on to his trousers which were in danger of being torn off him by ardent admirers. 'Grown up Chums' had Nicky and Nancy Lee paired off right from the start, so the public fascination with the pair grew when it emerged that they had quietly married in 1935. They consistently won 'most popular' contests staged by Melbourne radio periodicals. 3AW's children's and breakfast sessions had sponsors lined up to buy space (Fig. 2.2).[68]

Children's personalities such as these were so ubiquitous that by 1937 *Radio Pictorial of Australia* was running one or two full pages per month entitled 'When Uncles and Aunts Appear'. Featuring updates on the activities of personalities from Sydney's six commercial stations, the periodical also included coupons for competitions for prizes ranging from darts to pet animals.[69] In 1940 a documentary company made a short film, *Children's Hour*, focused on Sydney and narrated by the Macquarie Network's Jack Davey. It began with a recreation of the early endeavours

Fig. 2.2 3AW Birmacley Pet Club certificate, n.d., Nancy Lee Collection, Arts Centre Melbourne. (Copyright Nine Radio)

of Uncle George at 2BL and ended with scenes of Uncle Tom's Gang, with members carefully rehearsed by John Dunne.[70]

These endeavours were important to commercial stations, networks and sponsors. The general manager of the powerful Macquarie Network (which included 3AW) focused on them in a 1940 letter 'To Every Advertiser Who is looking for Sales'. Amongst other things, it revealed how active children's personalities and clubs were in Tasmania, Australia's smallest state. There was Bob Lange, a young breakfast host who also broadcast to the 7HO Pals Club in Hobart each Thursday evening; 'Mary Lou' (Mary McEachern), who presided over the 7QT Queenstown *Children's Hour* and its Chums Club; 'Uncle Cliffe' (H.R. Parish) and the 7DY Sunpolishers' Club in Derby; and 'Aunty Betty' (Betty Raymond) and the 7BU Sunpolishers' Club in Burnie.[71]

Back at the ABC, children's radio was floundering. Dr Keith Barry, the ABC's Controller of Programs, had concluded in 1936 that there was an 'enormous opportunity to make lifelong friends of those who are to choose their stations later in life'. Two years later, however, he felt forced to confess to Charles Moses, Conder's successor as general manager, that 'we have no policy'.[72] Visiting Perth, Frank Clewlow, now Controller of Productions, reported back to Moses that while the *Children's Hour* there was popular, it contained too many 'cheerio' calls and patronisingly addressed children as 'little ones'.[73]

Deciding that the way forward was to pool talent, the ABC created a national *Children's Hour* in April 1939 for 5.30 pm weekdays. A familiar song, with the refrain 'it's time for the fun', was the signal for children across Australia to run to the radio to listen to 'Elizabeth' (Ida Osbourne).[74] Children were encouraged to contribute news, stories and poems to 'Mike', a weekly magazine of the air. The *Children's Hour* provided an anchor for children whose homes and families were disturbed by war.[75] Early in 1940, it was overhauled to further encourage 'girls and boys themselves [to] take part'. Certificates of different colours, signed by Elizabeth and denoting points for the type and merit of contributions, were despatched to children.[76]

Executives also worked up a plan to relaunch Jason and his fleet. The enterprise, and the *Children's Hour* more generally, was entrusted to 23-year-old Osbourne. She aimed to produce a bright and entertaining daily program that would stimulate children to do creative work and recruit them as future adult listeners.[77] As part of what was now being called the 'National Children's Session', the Argonauts Club reappeared on 7 January 1941 with Elizabeth at the helm.[78] Argonauts received an enamel badge and membership certificate with the pledge from a decade earlier. Within three weeks there were 3500 members aged from seven to 17; by June the ABC was receiving 600 letters a week. Clewlow, who saw the Club as based on 'the search for adventure and beauty', contended that even if only 20 per cent of the members emerged with 'improved taste and desire for fine things, the Commission's work in programmes will be greatly helped in the future'. The anonymity of a child's on-air identity supplied an atmosphere of mystery and adventure, and the privacy to attempt something—say poetry or music—that might otherwise have caused embarrassment. Children sent in contributions to the 'Argosy' magazine, which was read out on Fridays.[79]

Well-known personalities added quality and interest. 'The Melody Man' (Lindley Evans) looked after the music contributions, 'Anthony Inkwell' (the poet A.D. Hope) dealt with poems and stories, and Dr A.J. Marshall was 'Jock the Backyard Naturalist'. Ruth Park wrote a series of stories about a bunyip which later evolved into a 'muddle-headed wombat' and a series of best-selling books.[80]

The Argonauts, with 43,000 members by 1947,[81] grew to be one of the biggest and most successful children's broadcasting clubs in the world. It was the most creative and imaginative outlet for children's talent in writing, music, drawing and painting on Australian radio.[82] Commercial stations continued with their children's endeavours, with a show called *Peters Pals* on-air in four cities by 1945 to accompany the popular Pals Clubs.[83] Stations ran regular events for Pals, such as quarterly Saturday-morning parties in Hobart, and a ball marking Launceston's fiftieth jubilee in 1951 that attracted nearly 2000 children.[84] On the death of 'Nicky' in 1956, more than 150,000 people lined the streets of Melbourne to watch his funeral procession.[85]

Back in 1941, 2GB's general manager H.G. Horner, announcing that 17-year-old Joy Nichols and her 19-year-old brother George would help to present the station's children's session, had ventured to suggest that the days of Aunts and Uncles in children's sessions was coming to an end.[86] He may have been at least partly inspired to say this due to the ABC's move away from Aunts and Uncles and its recent successful relaunch of the Argonauts. 2CH's 'Fairy Godmother' Margaret Herd was amongst those radio personalities who defended the old children's radio model, pointing to the popularity of her Crusaders' Club, which aimed to do anything to help bring happiness to the world, including collecting pennies to help war victims.[87] Australian radio stations continued to have Aunts and Uncles into the 1950s, when the rollout of television spelled the gradual decline of radio's grand children's undertakings. Some younger children's personalities, such as Bert Newton, moved seamlessly to television, but illusions which cost next to nothing on radio were suddenly too expensive for the Argonauts to maintain in a visual medium. By the 1960s the number of new recruits was slowing; Argonauts broadcasts were confined to Sundays in 1969 and dropped in 1972.[88] This rupture symbolised the end of the dynamic world created by public and commercial radio stations for hundreds of thousands of Australian infants, children and teenagers children since the 1920s.

NOTES

1. Lesley Johnson, 'The intimate voice of Australian radio', *Historical Journal of Film, Radio and Television*, 3(1) (March 1983), pp. 43–47.
2. *News*, 25 May 1928, p. 8.
3. Peter Strawhan, 'Mills, Frederick John', *Australian Dictionary of Biography* (*ADB*), National Centre of Biography (NCB), Australian National University (ANU), http://adb.anu.edu.au/biography/mills-frederick-john-11131/text19823, published first in 2000, accessed 11 June 2019.
4. *Register*, 21 June 1928, p. 14.
5. *Wireless Weekly* (*WW*), 10 September 1926, p. 10. See also Dennis Francis, 'Memories of Mosman' (2013), http://mosmanmemories.net/story/269/dennis-francis-memories-of-mosman, accessed 11 June 2019.
6. *Queensland Radio News*, 1 June 1926, pp. 38–39; *Bowen Independent*, 21 June 1927, p. 2.
7. *Courier-Mail* (Brisbane), 8 November 1941, p. 5; *How Do You Do* (Brisbane: 4QG, 1926); Uncle Ben, *Uncle Ben's Book-o'-Fun: For Boys and Girls* (Brisbane: Read Press, 1926 and 1928).
8. *Queensland Radio News*, 1 December 1926, p. 72; 2 April 1928, p. 45. See also 'Notes from 4QG', *Telegraph*, 12 October 1927, p. 3.
9. *Northern Star*, 10 November 1926, p. 14; *WW*, 26 October 1928, p. 10.
10. Bridget Griffen-Foley, *Changing Stations: The Story of Australian Commercial Radio* (Sydney: UNSW Press, 2009), p. 119; https://www.radioheritage.net/Story222.asp, accessed 29 February 2020.
11. *Telegraph*, 28 February 1939, p. 12.
12. *Who's Who in Broadcasting in Western Australia* (Perth: Patersons Printing Press, 1933), p. 27.

13. Nancy Robinson Whittle, 'Hume, Stella Leonora', *ADB*, NCB, ANU, http://adb.anu.edu.au/biography/hume-stella-leonora-10571/text18775, published first in 1996, accessed 3 June 2019.
14. *WW*, 4 March 1932, p. 23.
15. Griffen-Foley 2009, p. 119.
16. K.S. Inglis, *This Is the ABC: The Australian Broadcasting Commission, 1932–1983* (Melbourne: Melbourne University Press, 1983), p. 15; Jacqueline Kent, *Out of the Bakelite Box* (Sydney: ABC, 1983), p. 104.
17. *WW*, 5 July 1931, p. 6.
18. Barbara Corbett, *No Ordinary Childhood: Barbara Corbett's Celebration of a Charmed Life in the 1920s* (St Lucia, Qld: University of Queensland Press, 1994), p. 103.
19. *Richmond River Herald*, 25 May 1928, p. 3; *Goulburn Evening Penny Post*, 1 June 1939, p. 1.
20. Farmer & Co. Children's News Radio Birthday Club, Third Annual Swimming Party, Rose Bay Baths, 8 March 1930, http://photosau.com.au/WoollahraImages/scripts/ExtSearch.asp?SearchTerm=pf004609, accessed 11 June 2019.
21. *Sun*, 1 March 1928, p. 17.
22. *Richmond River Herald*, 23 March 1928, p. 5.
23. *Daily Telegraph*, 26 December 1928, p. 7.
24. R.E. Corder, 'Catching up with the wireless world', *WW*, 20 April 1928, p. 4.
25. *Evening News*, 10 September 1929, p. 7.
26. *Western Mail*, 19 September 1929, p. 15.
27. Lesley Johnson, 'Images of radio: The construction of the radio audience by popular radio magazines', *Melbourne Working Papers* 4 (1983), p. 45 and *The Unseen Voice* (London: Routledge, 1988), pp. 88, 110–11, 196, 203. For Herd, see *Daily Telegraph*, 13 February 1932, p. 7.
28. L. Johnson 1983, p. 45; *Wireless Weekly*, 26 December 1930, p. 6; Joan Clarke, *All on One Good Dancing Leg* (Sydney: Hale & Iremonger, 1994), p. 121.
29. *Sun*, 5 November 1932, p. 7; *Truth*, 2 June 1935, p. 24.
30. *Sun*, 4 February 1932, p. 19; *WW*, 15 July 1932, p. 18.
31. See also Mark Taylor, *2017 Australian Radio, TV Stations, Newspapers & Theatres Australian Badge Guide* (2nd edition, 2017).
32. *WW*, 4 March 1932, p. 22.
33. *West Australian*, 6 April 1932, p. 15 and 23 April 1932, p. 7.
34. *Australian Broadcasting Commission 1st Annual Report* (Sydney: ABC, 1932–33), p. 9; Inglis 1983, pp. 8, 15; Alan Thomas, *Broadcast and Be Damned: The ABC's First Two Decades* (Melbourne: Melbourne University Press, 1980), pp. 39–40.

35. *BBC Year Book* (London: BBC, 1933), p. 21. For the United States, see Marilyn Lawrence Boemer, *The Children's Hour: Radio Programs for Children, 1929–1956* (Metuchen N.J. and London: Scarecrow Press, 1989), pp. 1–2.
36. *ABC 1st Annual Report* (1932–33), p. 9.
37. Asa Briggs, *The Golden Age of Wireless* (London: Oxford University Press, 1965), p. 33. Boemer 1989, p. 4 refers to the popularity of 'storytelling and the "Uncle" shows' in the United States.
38. Inglis 1983, p. 35.
39. T.W. Bearup quoted in Clement Semmler, *The ABC—Aunt Sally and Sacred Cow* (Melbourne: Melbourne University Press, 1981), pp. 171–72.
40. Inglis 1983, p. 35; Rob Johnson, *The Golden Age of the Argonauts* (Sydney: Hodder Headline, 1997), pp. 3–8; Ida Elizabeth Jenkins, *Good Rowing!* (Sydney: ABC, 1982), pp. 32–33.
41. Inglis 1983, p. 35; R. Johnson 1997, pp. 4–6; Thomas 1980, p. 40; Semmler 1981, p. 172.
42. *WW*, 21 July 1933, p. 40 and 28 July 1933, p. 62.
43. R. Johnson 1997, pp. 7–8; Jenkins 1982, p. 32.
44. Jenkins 1982, p. 33; R. Johnson 1997, p. 6; Frank Hatherley, 'The original Frank Hatherley' (2006), http://www.frankhatherley.com/the-original-frank-hatherley, accessed 21 June 2019; *Tweed Daily*, 15 August 1933, p. 5; *Newcastle Sun*, 23 February 1935, p. 3.
45. *Huon Times*, 6 April 1932, p. 4; *Mercury*, 8 November 1933, p. 11 and 29 August 1935, p. 7; *Teleradio*, 18 November 1933, p. 70 and 9 December 1933, p. 69.
46. *Teleradio*, 15 July 1933, p. 3 and 3 February 1934, p. 71; *Albany Advertiser*, 9 April 1934, p. 2; *Southern Argus*, 6 December 1934, p. 3
47. Semmler 1981, pp. 172–72; Jenkins, p. 33; R. Johnson 1997, pp. 8–9; Thomas 1980, p. 65.
48. *Newcastle Morning Herald*, 7 September 1933, p. 14; Taylor 2017, pp. 22–23.
49. *WW*, 20 April 1934, p. 9; *Daily Examiner*, 22 August 1934, p. 4; Ron Bell, *The History of Radio 2GF 1933–1997* (Grafton, NSW: Bell Publishing: n.d. 1997), pp. 127–32.
50. *WW*, 4 February 1939, p. 13.
51. *West Australian*, 21 February 1935, p. 7; *Radio Pictorial of Australia* (*RPA*), 1 June 1938, p. 39; *Catholic Press*, 19 October 1939, p. 37; *WW*, 27 September 1941, p. 23.
52. *Telegraph*, 26 April 1933, p. 8 and 10 May 1933, p. 6; *Teleradio*, 13 May 1933, p. 3, 10 June 1933, p. 71 and 29 July 1933, pp. 3, 7 and 24.

53. *Teleradio*, 4 November 1933, p. 6, 6 January 1934, p. 6, 10 March 1934, p. 9, 24 March 1934, p. 22 and 31 March 1934, p. 26; *Telegraph*, 14 February 1934, p. 8.
54. *Teleradio*, 24 February 1934, p. 16 and 7 April 1934, pp. 3, 16–17.
55. *Telegraph*, 17 May 1933, p. 17 and 2 August 1933, p. 8; *Teleradio*, 10 June 1933, p. 70.
56. *News*, 7 August 1935, p. 4; *WW*, 27 September 1935, pp. 16 and 21; *Southern Cross*, 10 July 1936, p. 9; *5DN 21st Anniversary, 1924–1945* (Adelaide: Hume Broadcasters, n.d. 1945); D.J. Towler, *The First Sixty Years 1924–1984, 5DN 972* (Adelaide: 5DN, 1984), pp. 43–45; National Film and Sound Archive: 5DN Records, Kipling Boys' Club records.
57. *Murray Pioneer and Australian River Record*, 5 March 1936, p. 4; *News*, 24 July 1935, p. 1.
58. *Northern Argus*, 8 January 1937, p. 3.
59. https://www.radioheritage.net/Story210.asp, accessed 29 February 2020.
60. *WW*, 14 July 1933, p. 17; 8 February 1935, p. 21.
61. *Courier-Mail*, 28 August 1934, p. 12.
62. *WW*, 8 February 1935, p. 23 and 27 September 1935, p. 23.
63. *Australian Broadcasting Control Board 5th Annual Report* (Canberra: Commonwealth of Australia, 1952–53), p. 26.
64. Eoin Cameron, *Rolling into the World: Memoirs of a Ratbag Child* (Perth: Fremantle Arts Centre Press, 2003), pp. 82–83.
65. *West Australian*, 23 April 1932, p. 7; *Telegraph*), 15 June 1932, p. 7.
66. *Who's Who in Broadcasting* (1933 and 1936); P. Hallahan, 'The Evolution of Radio Broadcasting in Western Australia, 1924–1958, thesis (Teachers' College Claremont, WA, 1958), Chapters 5–6; https://www.radioheritage.net/Story151.asp, accessed 29 February 2020.
67. The following is drawn from Arts Centre Melbourne (ACM): Nancy Lee Collection. See also *Argus*, 13 September 1956, p. 14; Nancy Lee, *Being a Chum was Fun* (Melbourne: Listen & Learn Productions, 1979); Dally Messenger, 'Whitta, Clifford Nicholls', *ADB*, NCB, ANU, http://adb.anu.edu.au/biography/whitta-clifford-nicholls-12023/text21543, published first in 2002, accessed online 24 February 2020. Nicky and Tuppy were amongst the personalities to appear in the *Radio Fun Book* (Melbourne: Allan & Co., n.d.), a musical compilation published between 1930 and 1939.
68. *Age*, 26 August 1935, p. 15.
69. For example, *RPA*, 1 August 1937, pp. 37–38, 1 April 1938, p. 37 and 1 July 1938, pp. 37–38.
70. *WW*, 7 September 1940, p. 11; 21 December 1940, p. 29. It has not been possible to locate a copy of the film.

71. ACM: Lee Collection: Box 1L9, Macquarie Network letter, 1940. See also *North-Eastern Advertiser*, 22 February 1938, p. 2.
72. R. Johnson 1997, p. 11; Semmler 1981, p. 172; Inglis 1983, p. 56; *ABC 7th Annual Report* (Sydney: ABC, 1938–39), p. 37.
73. National Archives of Australia (NAA)/NSW: C678/2, National Children's Session, memos from Clewlow to Moses, 26 October 1938, and Moses to ABC Manager for Western Australia, 31 October 1938.
74. Patti Crocker, *Radio Days: A Personal View of Australia's Radio Heyday* (Brookvale, NSW: Simon & Schuster Australia, 1989), pp. 46–47; Bridget Griffen-Foley, '"Let's Join In": Children and ABC radio', *Historical Journal of Film, Radio and Television*, 40(1) 2020, p. 190.
75. *ABC 7th Annual Report* (1938–39), p. 37; Geoffrey Dutton, *Snow on the Saltbush: The Australian Literary Experience* (Ringwood, Vic.: Viking Press, 1984), 85; NAA/: SP1762/1, 1058352, Ida Elizabeth Jenkins interview, 1968, p. 8.
76. Griffen-Foley 2020.
77. Inglis 1983, pp. 56, 90–91; R. Johnson 1997, pp. 15–19; Jenkins 1982, pp. 14–15; *ABC Weekly*, 2 March 1940, p. 54.
78. *ABC Weekly*, 28 December 1940, pp. 4–5.
79. R. Johnson 1997, pp. 35–37; Lindley Evans, *'Hello, Mr. Melody Man': Lindley Evans Remembers* (London, Sydney and Melbourne: Angus & Robertson, 1983), pp. 131–33; *ABC 9th Annual Report* (Sydney: ABC, 1940–41), p. 31; Griffen-Foley 2020.
80. Semmler 1981, p. 173; Inglis 1983, p. 166; Kent 1983, pp. 112–13.
81. *Sydney Morning Herald*, 19 November 1953, p. 7.
82. Kent 1983, p. 115.
83. *Broadcasting Business Year Book of Australia* (Sydney: Australian Radio Publications, 1938), p. 163; https://www.onlymelbourne.com.au/peters-ice-cream, accessed 21 June 2019.
84. *Mercury*, 21 March 1949, p. 12; *Examiner*, 29 September 1951, p. 9.
85. Lee 1979, p. 180.
86. *WW*, 21 June 1941, p. 10.
87. *WW*, 9 August 1941, p. 21.
88. Griffen-Foley 2020.

Bibliography

ABC Weekly.
Advertiser (Adelaide).
Age (Melbourne).
Albany Advertiser.
Arts Centre Melbourne (ACM): Nancy Lee Collection.

Australian Broadcasting Commission (ABC) 1st Annual Report (Sydney: ABC, 1932–1933).
ABC 7th Annual Report (1938–1939).
ABC 9th Annual Report (1940–1941).
Australian Broadcasting Control Board 5th Annual Report (Canberra: Commonwealth of Australia, 1952–1953).
BBC Year Book (London: BBC, 1933).
Bell, Ron. *The History of Radio 2GF 1933–1997* (Grafton, NSW: Bell Publishing: n.d. 1997).
Bowen Independent.
Briggs, Asa. *The Golden Age of Wireless* (London: Oxford University Press, 1965).
Broadcasting Business Year Book of Australia (Sydney: Australian Radio Publications, 1938).
Cameron, Eoin. *Rolling into the World: Memoirs of a Ratbag Child* (Perth: Fremantle Arts Centre Press, 2003).
Catholic Press.
Courier-Mail (Brisbane).
Clarke, Joan. *All on One Good Dancing Leg* (Sydney: Hale & Iremonger, 1994).
Corbett, Barbara. *No Ordinary Childhood: Barbara Corbett's Celebration of a Charmed Life in the 1920s* (St Lucia, QLD: University of Queensland Press, 1994).
Corder, R.E. 'Catching up with the wireless world', *Wireless Weekly*, 20 April 1928, p. 4.
Crocker, Patti. *Radio Days: A Personal View of Australia's Radio Heyday* (Brookvale, NSW: Simon & Schuster Australia, 1989).
Daily Examiner (Grafton).
Daily Telegraph (Sydney).
Dutton, Geoffrey. *Snow on the Saltbush: The Australian Literary Experience* (Ringwood, VIC: Viking Press, 1984).
Evans, Lindley. *'Hello, Mr. Melody Man': Lindley Evans Remembers* (London, Sydney and Melbourne: Angus & Robertson, 1983).
Evening News.
Examiner (Launceston).
Farmer & Co. Children's News Radio Birthday Club, Third Annual Swimming Party, Rose Bay Baths, 8 March 1930, http://photosau.com.au/WoollahraImages/scripts/ExtSearch.asp?SearchTerm=pf004609, accessed 11 June 2019.
'5AD Advertiser Broadcasting Network', Radio Heritage Foundation, https://www.radioheritage.net/Story210.asp, accessed 29 February 2020.
5DN 21st Anniversary, 1924–1945 (Adelaide: Hume Broadcasters, n.d. 1945).
Francis, Dennis. 'Memories of Mosman' (2013), http://mosmanmemories.net/story/269/dennis-francis-memories-of-mosman, accessed 11 June 2019.

Griffen-Foley, Bridget. *Changing Stations: The Story of Australian Commercial Radio* (Sydney: UNSW Press, 2009).
———. '"Let's Join In": Children and ABC radio', *Historical Journal of Film, Radio and Television*, 40(1), 2020, pp. 185–209, https://doi.org/10.1080/01439685.2019.1610267.
Goulburn Evening Penny Post.
Hallahan, P. 'The Evolution of Radio Broadcasting in Western Australia, 1924–1958', thesis (Teachers' College Claremont, WA, 1958).
Hatherley, Frank. 'The original Frank Hatherley' (2006), http://www.frankhatherley.com/the-original-frank-hatherley, accessed 21 June 2019.
How Do You Do (Brisbane: 4QG, 1926).
Huon Times.
Inglis, K.S. *This Is the ABC: The Australian Broadcasting Commission, 1932–1983* (Melbourne: Melbourne University Press, 1983).
Jenkins, Ida Elizabeth. *Good Rowing!* (Sydney: ABC, 1982).
Johnson, Lesley. 'The intimate voice of Australian radio', *Historical Journal of Film, Radio and Television*, 3(1) (March 1983a), pp. 43–50.
———. 'Images of radio: The construction of the radio audience by popular radio magazines', *Melbourne Working Papers* 4 (1983b), pp. 34–54.
———. *The Unseen Voice* (London: Routledge, 1988).
Johnson, Rob. *The Golden Age of the Argonauts* (Sydney: Hodder Headline, 1997).
Kent, Jacqueline. *Out of the Bakelite Box* (Sydney: ABC, 1983).
Lawrence Boemer, Marilyn. *The Children's Hour: Radio Programs for Children, 1929–1956* (Metuchen, N.J. and London: Scarecrow Press, 1989).
Lee, Nancy. *Being a Chum was Fun* (Melbourne: Listen & Learn Productions, 1979).
Lithgow Mercury.
Mercury (Hobart).
Messenger, Dally. 'Whitta, Clifford Nicholls', *Australian Dictionary of Biography* (*ADB*), National Centre of Biography (NCB), Australian National University (ANU), http://adb.anu.edu.au/biography/whitta-clifford-nicholls-12023/text21543, published first in 2002, accessed online 24 February 2020.
Murray Pioneer and Australian River Record.
National Archives of Australia (NAA)/NSW: C678/2, National Children's Session.
NAA: SP1762/1, 1058352, Ida Elizabeth Jenkins interview, 1968.
National Film and Sound Archive: 5DN Records, Kipling Boys' Club records.
Newcastle Morning Herald.
Newcastle Sun.
News (Adelaide).
North-Eastern Advertiser.
Northern Argus (Clare).
Northern Star (Lismore).

'Peter's Ice Cream', Only Melbourne, https://www.onlymelbourne.com.au/peters-ice-cream, accessed 21 June 2019.

Queensland Radio News.

'Radio 2WL The South Coast Station', Radio Heritage Foundation, https://www.radioheritage.net/Story222.asp, accessed 29 February 2020.

Radio Fun Book (Melbourne: Allan & Co., n.d.).

Radio Pictorial of Australia (RPA).

Register (Adelaide).

Richmond River Herald.

Robinson Whittle, Nancy. 'Hume, Stella Leonora', *ADB*, NCB, ANU, http://adb.anu.edu.au/biography/hume-stella-leonora-10571/text18775, published first in 1996, accessed 3 June 2019.

Semmler, Clement. *The ABC—Aunt Sally and Sacred Cow* (Melbourne: Melbourne University Press, 1981).

Southern Argus (Port Elliot).

Southern Cross (Adelaide).

Strawhan, Peter. 'Mills, Frederick John', *ADB*, NCB, ANU, http://adb.anu.edu.au/biography/mills-frederick-john-11131/text19823, published first in 2000, accessed 11 June 2019.

Sun (Sydney).

Taylor, Mark. *2017 Australian Radio, TV Stations, Newspapers & Theatres Australian Badge Guide* (2nd edition, 2017).

Telegraph (Brisbane).

Teleradio.

Thomas, Alan. *Broadcast and Be Damned: The ABC's First Two Decades* (Melbourne: Melbourne University Press, 1980).

Towler, D.J. *The First Sixty Years 1924–1984, 5DN 972* (Adelaide: 5DN, 1984).

Truth (Sydney).

Tweed Daily.

Uncle Ben. *Uncle Ben's Book-o'-Fun: For Boys and Girls* (Brisbane: Read Press, 1926 and 1928).

West Australian.

'Whitford Broadcasting Network 6PM Perth, 6AM Northam, 6KG Kalgoorlie, 6GE Geraldton', Radio Heritage Foundation, https://www.radioheritage.net/Story151.asp, accessed 29 February 2020.

Who's Who in Broadcasting in Western Australia (Perth: Patersons Printing Press, 1933 and 1936).

Wireless Weekly (WW).

CHAPTER 3

Club Loyalty

Abstract The spread of radio stations across Australia in the 1920s and 1930s was accompanied by the establishment of radio clubs with social and charitable functions, drawing in hundreds of thousands of listeners. This chapter examines the role and operations of these clubs, particularly those attached to commercial radio stations, which sought to capitalise on loyalty and goodwill. The chapter then considers the emergence of television clubs, especially for children and women, on commercial stations and the Australian Broadcasting Commission in cities and the regions since the late 1950s. It concludes with the demise of traditional radio clubs, with members and meetings, due to changing Australian patterns of work and leisure.

Keywords Radio clubs • Television clubs • Women • Children's Broadcasting • Australian Broadcasting Commission • Audiences

By the early 1930s, 4BH Brisbane's 'petite lady announcer' Dorothy Dawson had instituted a 'Lonely Listeners' Club'.[1] Perhaps more than any other commercial radio club, this 4BH undertaking pointed to the industry's capacity to provide—and be seen to provide—company and solace to isolated listeners. Radio clubs spread around Australia in the interwar years, with their role becoming even more significant during the Great Depression. By 1939 there were at least 117 clubs affiliated with Australia's commercial radio stations.[2] This chapter traces the industry's efforts to capitalise on goodwill and loyalty and, in the case of some commercial stations, to facilitate business sponsorship. The chapter moves on to consider commercial and Australian Broadcasting Commission (ABC) television, with new broadcast clubs emerging from the late 1950s, particularly in regional areas.

In 1925 Sydney's *Wireless Weekly* insisted that Australia's geography should help, rather than hinder, radio's development as 'those people separated by distance from centres of amusement and education must directly benefit'. It was not just radio periodicals like this which believed that the medium could, and would, prove to be 'a power for good'.[3] Radio, it was confidently thought by former Prime Minister W.M. Hughes, and Sir Ernest Fisk, managing director of Amalgamated Wireless Australasia Ltd (AWA), would draw the mother country and the dominions into the imperial family, the citizens of the city and the outback into the national family, and members of the household into a family circle.[4]

There were some clear synergies between the social and commercial endeavours of the two most public media of popular culture and communication in Australia during the interwar years. Film and radio interests established clubs for fans to enhance the industries' civic reputability, insinuate themselves in the lives of consumers, engender goodwill and facilitate tie-ins with businesses. From the late 1920s, American film interests set up clubs through local radio stations: the MGM Radio Movie Club was established in April 1928 through 2GB Sydney, 2UW Sydney opened the Fox Movietone Radio Club in 1930, and the Fox Hoyts Radio Club seems to have evolved into the 6ML Cheerio Club in Perth by 1932.[5] Radio historian Anne F. MacLennan has traced how Canadians, especially children, were actively recruited as club 'members' as well as listeners.[6]

One of Australian commercial radio's earliest and most successful clubs was the 2GB Happiness Club.[7] The founder was Mrs W.J. (Eunice) Stelzer, a music teacher whose women's session on 2GB drew letters from listeners confiding their worries and seeking advice. As the volume increased, Stelzer organised suburban branches to assist with replies. In September 1929 she announced her intention to form a club to gather together the branches. Two hundred and fifty women attended the meeting that spawned the 2GB Happiness Club.[8]

The Club's motto was 'Others First', its signature verse 'Pull Together'. Stelzer's brand of self-help, selflessness and sisterhood struck a chord with listeners during the early days of the Depression. The Club was non-political and non-sectarian, and cost nothing to join. Sixty-four branches, each opened by Stelzer on 2GB, were formed across Sydney and beyond.[9] Historian Catherine Fisher writes of radio clubs (particularly for women) as a Depression success story, providing support for the destitute, and companionship for the lonely. By conceptualising the role of radio as a social good, and through their charitable and philanthropic work, women deepened their political enfranchisement and their activities as citizens.[10]

Like the members of film clubs, Stelzer's ladies had enormous fun doing good. Afternoon teas, musicales and *conversaziones* were held at retail stores David Jones and Mark Foys. Monthly branch meetings usually commenced with the singing of 'Advance Australia Fair', and featured more music and dancing and, sometimes, appearances by 2GB personalities such as 'Uncle Frank' (Frank Grose). When one member was thrown a birthday party in 1930, she recorded simply in her branch's minute book: 'I'll never forget the Genuineness.'[11]

Proceeds from parties, concerts and community singing were donated to a children's home and other institutions. 2GB Happiness Club members (some 4000 by 1932) visited the sick, repaired shoes and collected and donated clothes for the needy. Its origins in the working-class Sydney suburb of Campsie, its spread to areas such as Wollongong and Woy Woy, and the range of its activities suggest that the Club was not directed at a purely middle-class audience, preferring instead to speak as if all women were one and the same. And at the centre of this community was 2GB.[12] Stelzer used her daily 2 pm broadcasts to make the Happiness Club central to members' lives.[13]

The Prime Minister's wife, Enid Lyons, opened the 5DN Happiness Club in 1933.[14] An executive explained to her that the Adelaide station (part of the Macquarie Network to which 2GB belonged) was placing 'the air' at the Club's disposal to bring happiness into the lives of the '*deserving* poor, suffering and friendless [emphasis added]'.[15] At least 20 listeners had named their children 'Eunice' after her, Stelzer boasted.[16] The activities of the two Happiness Clubs reaffirmed an impulse to use modern technology to help solve social problems, and a middle-class impulse for interventionist uplift.[17]

Meanwhile, in 1929 journalist Hattie Knight and physical education teacher Gwen Varley launched a Women's Association at the Australian Broadcasting Company. Its programs mixed domestic instruction with reports on sport and social activities such as golf and tennis competitions, and 'motor picnics', all coordinated by radio. Fullers Theatre provided members (around 500 by 1930) with a club room in Sydney, and there was a separate 6WF Women's Association in Perth, headed by announcer Dorothy Graham. The annual meeting in 1931 referred to 40 affiliated clubs, ranging across sport to needlecraft. The Association's broadcasts continued until November 1932, when the newly constituted Australian Broadcasting Commission (ABC) replaced them with more personality-based women's programs.[18]

The 6ML Cheerio Club, with announcer B.F. Saunders as secretary, was rather unusual in that it charged a modest annual membership fee (one shilling). The Club, which had its own nightly on-air session, attracted 1000 members in the first three weeks after its launch in 1932. It conducted hiking expeditions, fielded a cricket team, offered women craft lessons and hosted dances and bridge evenings.[19]

4BK Brisbane had the Association of Friends, headed by women's announcer 'Sally'. It was formed explicitly so that 'lady listeners who were suffering from reduced income or loneliness' could be provided with 'happiness and entertainment' at no cost to themselves. Some of the Association's gatherings, such as Christmas parties and a birthday party for Sally, were held at the homes of wealthy supporters, decorated in 4BK's colours of brown and gold.[20]

Feeling that the field was becoming a trifle crowded, 2GB's Jack Davey—one of Australian radio's most popular performers—formed the Miserable Club in 1934. His first news session facetiously reported on suicides, murders and funerals, and announced the launch of the Back to Long Bay Jail Week and a new serial, *How to Murder in Your Own Home*. *Wireless Weekly* reported on the versatile Davey's many roles in 1938:

> On Thursday, 'The Miserable Club' holds its doleful meeting, and its members are invited to weep nice salty tears over the declining death rate and the improving health of the nation, and other unsatisfactory matters.

'There's too much happiness about, anyway!,' Davey joked.[21]

But still the clubs came. 3UZ's women's announcer, 'Penelope' (Ida Coffey), introduced the Look Up and Laugh Club in 1937, named after the song that opened her program, and following on from a film starring Gracie Fields.[22] Another Melbourne commercial station, 3KZ, introduced a Friendship Circle for women that year, with a particular focus on helping youth. 'Uncle Vim' hosted events that included parties for children of the unemployed, picture nights, 'Personality Girl' competitions, and debutante balls.[23] The 3SH Women's Club in Swan Hill, led by 'Smiler' (Mrs Jack Broadbent), became the outstanding social and charitable club of the district, boasted the Macquarie Network. The Club staged a 'Microphone Ball', entered a float in the town's annual street parade and supported the local hospital.[24]

In rural Australia, radio clubs were at the heart of their local communities.[25] In outback Broken Hill, 2BH formed the Smilers' Club, largely for children and teenagers. It was headed by the host of the women's session and wife of the commercial station's manager, 'Aunty Ruby' (Dorothy Prider).[26] The 2WG Women's Club became a focal point for listeners in Wagga Wagga, where there was a club room, and the Riverina district of New South Wales. Aiming to 'foster a spirit of loyalty to our Queen and Country and of goodwill and service amongst members of the community',[27] the Club was the idea of Ida Annie Roberts ('Aunty Nan'), the wife of the station's founder, Eric Roberts. The Club held afternoon teas, film nights, card parties, balls and tennis tournaments. It distributed baby clothes, and raised funds for an ambulance, a maternity ward at the local hospital, and an old people's home.[28] Years later, Lindsay Knight would recall how he and his wife would come into town on Thursdays to shop '& first call was 2WG'.[29] The Club's twice daily on-air sessions primarily consisted of reading the letters of members, who were given radio names such as 'Boree Bell' and 'Dragonfly', and which helped to draw together women on the land. According to one estimate, Club compere and president Ada Webb ('Cobby') handled £200,000 between 1942 and 1954.[30]

By 1939, *Wireless Weekly* had a regular feature on 'What Women's Radio Clubs Are Doing'.[31] There were also clubs designed for listeners bound together by interest (such as the Fisherman's Club of 3XY Melbourne and the Gardening League of 7EX Launceston) and timeslot (the Night Owls' Club of 2CA Canberra and 3AW Melbourne, and the Breakfast Clubs of 3UL Warragul and 3YB Warrnambool). At 4BH Brisbane, The Nothing Under 60 Club emerged around 1940 when the popular afternoon announcer 'Frank H' (Frank Hatherley) decided he should do something more for his largely female audience. The station was already organising excursions for listeners, such as one to Southport with dedicated special trains, and Hatherley in charge of the 'Get Together Ladies' carriage. The new Club (open to those under as well as over 60, and men as well as women) invited members to come into 4BH's auditorium to watch the recording of his session. At Friday get-togethers, members who might have been considered to be beyond the age of entertaining others, were encouraged to present an item—a song, a recitation, an instrumental solo or a reminiscence—of general interest.[32]

Many Australian listener clubs were christened with upbeat names, as we saw in Chap. 2 with children's clubs including the 2GF Smile Club and 6ML's Junior Cheerio Club. Clubs were such a prominent feature of Australian radio that they began being listed in *Broadcasting Business Year Books*. There were at least 78 clubs by 1938, and 117 by 1939, including the Cheerio Club, the Friendship Circle, the Joy Club and the Look Up and Laugh Club. The *Year Books* also demonstrated how several stations elected to draw on notions of uplift and companionship even more than regional characteristics in their choice of slogans: 2HD Newcastle was 'The Voice of Friendship', 2MW Murwillumbah 'The Friendly Station', 4WK Warwick 'The Listener's Companion' and 6AM Northam 'The Happy Station'.[33]

The organisers of established clubs were sometimes persuaded to start them up elsewhere: Betty Errington, for instance, headed north from 3BO Bendigo to Cairns in 1939 to establish a women's club and host the women's and children's sessions from 4CA.[34] There was also cross-promotion and branding with newspapers in the same stable. 5AD's Margaret Warburton wrote and edited the Kangaroo Club children's pages for the Adelaide *Advertiser*.[35]

With commercial radio listeners viewed also as consumers, clubs facilitated tie-ins with local and national businesses. An executive with Western Stores, which advertised on 2GZ Orange, declared in 1940 that radio clubs were the 'most useful sessions of any. … Men's and women's apparel, domestic appliances, furniture, cosmetics, and foodstuffs can all be successfully sold by utilising the intimate appeal of these clubs.'[36] The 15,000 women members of 2GZ's Country Service Club dug out old aluminium, knitted socks, held 'button days', sent parcels to servicemen, equipped convalescent hospitals and purchased War Saving Certificates.[37] This kind of voluntary activity during World War II enabled the radio industry to demonstrate to citizens, and to government, its social utility.[38]

The Macquarie Network catalogues of 1941–1942 addressed the appeal of clubs associated with member and affiliated stations. 2GB Happiness Club's 18,310 members were said to constitute an audience of 'potential shoppers'. The combined membership of the 2GZ Country Service Club and the 2KA Radio Service Club in Katoomba, directed by Janet Archer ('the dearly loved friend, guide and counsellor of thousands of Country Women'), offered advertisers an audience of country housewives with tremendous merchandising possibilities. The Country Service Club of 2NZ Inverell was led by Nancye Lynn, who had the 'perfect voice to win friends and influence people'.[39]

The 1942 catalogue noted how central the 7LA Women's Association, founded by announcer Kathleen Grey a few years earlier, was to Tasmania women. In April 1940, 140 women gathered at a lounge in Launceston, when members of the Association entertained members from country branches, and visitors from Hobart's 7HO Women's Club. By 1942 there were more than 3000 members in 7LA's six service areas, enjoying social and sporting activities and dressmaking classes, supporting needy mothers and the local hospital, and aiding the war effort.[40]

The 1942 Report of the Joint Committee on Wireless Broadcasting (the 'Gibson Committee') found that around 40 stations had established women's clubs, totalling nearly 150,000 members. Almost 400,000 children belonged to children's clubs, some of which we encountered in Chap. 2. The parliamentary committee thought that listener clubs helped to 'guard morality on the air' and provided a valuable service to the Australian community.[41]

But there were to be challenges for radio clubs in the postwar era. Some, ironically, were in danger of outgrowing the stations that had seeded them. By the late 1940s there was a debate about whether the 2GB Happiness Club, with more than 20,000 members, should be called 'Mrs W.J. Stelzer's Happiness Club'.[42] '2GB' was dropped from the official title and the Club continued as a charitable endeavour, having raised £158,858 by 1950. Thirty-one units for aged and needy couples were constructed at Eurobodalla (Aboriginal for 'Home Between Two Waters') on the south coast of New South Wales.[43] In 1947 the 2WG Women's Club began to raise funds solely for a retirement village and nursing home complex in Wagga Wagga, culminating in the 1954 opening of the Haven on a plot of land bought by Eric and Nan Roberts.[44]

At 7LA, there was disquiet about the quality of the Women's Association radio sessions and the lack of a constitution, even though the Association had raised £30,000 for 73 organisations by 1950. There was less of on-air presence, and minutes from the late 1950s recorded less meetings, fundraising and 'Old Time Dance' attendance.[45]

The launch and spread of television across Australia, of course, posed new challenges for radio's endeavours. The interloper also established 'clubs', although they tended to be somewhat less about membership, social activities and charity. One of the first to emerge was a women's club at TCN9 in Sydney, which conducted its affairs during the *Thursday at One* afternoon program.[46] From its launch in 1959, NWS9 Adelaide produced *The Channel Niners*—with a sense of ownership and community implicit in the title—for children. Hosted by Kevin Crease and kindergarten teacher Denny Snowden, the program tried to give every child in the studio audience a chance to appear, however briefly, on-screen. It invited children to enter quizzes and art contests, and to bring their pets into the studio.[47]

On Monday, 3 December 1956, just its second day of operations, ATN7 in Sydney launched a morning program for children. The *Captain Fortune Show* starred actor Alan Herbert in a beard and naval uniform. His character spoke directly to kids, live and without a script. Education was combined with entertainment, with experts coming 'aboard' to talk to children about topics from road safety to the environment. Herbert visited children's hospitals and fêtes, and issued merit certificates to children who raised their own funds for good works. He also appeared at retail stores to sign up members of the Captain Fortune Club and meet little 'shipmates everywhere'. As the program gained in popularity, the television station's sister newspaper, the *Sun-Herald*, launched a comic strip and colouring competitions.[48]

Young Mike Bailey stopped going to the cinema in order to watch *Captain Fortune's Saturday Party* on neighbours' television sets. When his family took possession of their own set one Friday afternoon in 1960, Mike was bribed into going to bed with a promise of being allowed to watch television all the next day. *Captain Fortune* was the highlight. Later that year Mike went into the studio for the program. At the end of the show the audience presented Captain Fortune with a pile of comic books for the 'sick children', and heard the Captain deliver his famous catchcry, 'Ahoy there, Shipmates'.[49] Linked to the program was an invitation to join the TAA Junior Flyers' Club (presumably sponsored by Trans Australia Airlines), where children would write in to request their 'wings' (a badge). The Australian Broadcasting Control Board (ABCB) singled out *Captain Fortune* as 'the most positive attempt to bind children to its compere'.[50]

The word 'club' had multiple connotations. Young members of the Central Methodist Mission prepared for television in 1956 by buying a set for a church in inner-Sydney Darlinghurst. This was to enable members of the 'Television Club' to watch programs in a Christian environment, rather than in pubs.[51] Sydney's *TV Times* reported on Woolloomooloo being 'one big television club', with the inner-city working-class suburb believed to have a higher proportion of sets than most other parts of Sydney and Melbourne. Residents explained how the Television Club had 'shifts' in different homes, attracting housewives, schoolchildren and then all adults. Mrs J. Comer commented: 'We might not live in mansions, but I'll guarantee that the spirit of friendship is better here than any other big areas. And it's all been brought about by the club.'[52]

One of the most popular children's programs on early Australian television was *The Mickey Mouse Club*, first televised in the United States from 1955 to 1959. With television coming later to Australia than to North America, Australian media proprietors were keen to lock up an established hit.[53] Sir Frank Packer of TCN9 and Sir John Williams of HSV7 in Melbourne closed the deal in what one television writer described as one of 'the biggest scoops in Australian commercial television'. Repeats of *The Mickey Mouse Club* ran in Australia from 1958.[54] State banks came in as sponsors, with Barry Pitman hosting a Saving Bees' Club segment on *The Mickey Mouse Club* on Adelaide's ADS7.[55]

One afternoon a woman rang TCN9 to ask what time a bus was leaving with Channel Ninepins (fans of a children's show) to see star Mouseketeer Annette Funicello on a film set in Wagga Wagga. Station employees traced the rumour back to a 12-year-old girl, and were forced to keep making announcements that Funicello was not in Australia.[56] This episode may have prompted Walt Disney Productions or a local promoter to bring the cast to Australia to promote the show. Surprised by how the young entertainers had grown, 10,000 fans (who were still watching the first two seasons) nevertheless welcomed their idols with deafening enthusiasm in 1959. The frenzy as they disembarked at Sydney Airport onto a State Bank of Victoria float, accompanied by a car topped with a giant Mickey Mouse, surpassed anything the Mouseketeers had seen before—ironically, a year after their program had been dropped. They appeared in television specials and at events, including Melbourne's annual Moomba Festival, escorted by 70 local school children. A second Australian tour followed in 1960.[57] *The Mickey Mouse Club* included more than 200,000 Australian children.[58]

Meanwhile, the ABC was deliberating over what to screen for children after school. After watching experimental programs with the Argonauts Club, executives decided that Jason and his colleagues were too old to make the transition from radio. So in 1959 the broadcaster launched the *ABC Children's TV Club*, produced in Sydney and telerecorded for Melbourne, at 5 pm weekdays. Each day of the week featured a different theme. The series included some 'expert' presenters previously associated with the *Argonauts*, including artist Jeffrey Smart, on features better seen than heard, such as painting, photography and film.[59] In 1962 around 50 members of the NSW Association of University Women Graduates made a study of television programs for children. Their report, presented to the ABCB, the NSW Council for Film and Television, the ABC and commercial stations, praised the *ABC Children's TV Club* for balancing entertainment with enrichment, though many parents found 'their children do not share their enthusiasm for these sessions, especially with the lure of *Superman* and cartoons drawing them to the commercial channels'.[60] Indeed, the *TV Club* did not attract as many children as the Argonauts had done on radio, and was soon replaced by another program (Fig. 3.1).[61]

While the name of the Mickey Mouse endeavour was inherited, it is worth noting how many Australian television stations chose to use the word 'club' in their program titles, drawing on a sense of community, and

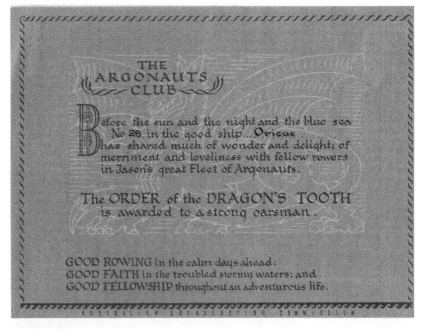

Fig. 3.1 The Argonauts Club 'Order of the Dragon's Tooth', certificate, c. 1965. (Copyright Linda Curry ('Oricus 28'))

echoing film and radio undertakings. And just as radio clubs had inspired a send-up, so too did television clubs. By 1959 the host of ATN7's *In Sydney Tonight* had formed the Keith Walshe Haters' Club. Some viewers went along for the ride, including a man from Paddington who wrote to Walshe declaring that the role of all 'mass media is to oscillate between a radical transcendentalism, frankly reduced to a solipsism of the living moment, and a materialism posited as a presupposition of conventional sanity', and signing his letter 'Venomously yours'.[62]

Clubs were a feature of regional television's spread. From its first weeks of transmission in 1962, Wollongong's WIN4 produced the weekday afternoon *Channel 4 Club* for children.[63] In Bendigo in central Victoria, BCV8 created *Cobbers' Teleclub*, an afternoon children's session hosted by John Crook and sponsored by Cohn Brothers, a local cordial manufacturer.[64] When Denzil Howson moved from Melbourne's GTV9 to become production manager of AMV4, on the border between New South Wales and Victoria, in 1964, he devised *Cohns Cobbers' Teleclub*. It was based on the *Tarax Show*, which Howson had created for GTV9. That show, sponsored by a soft drink company, produced membership badges, as well as fan cards for children. *Cohns Cobbers' Teleclub* was scheduled to launch AMV4 in Albury at 4.55 pm on Monday, 7 September. The first words to be heard by viewers were 'Anybody seen Olga-Mary?' as host Olga-Mary Whelan had been delayed getting to the studio. *Teleclub* ended up starting a minute late—not that the enthusiastic crowd of children who had assembled in the studio seemed to mind. After Whelan and colleague Ross Sellars finished their introductions and threw to *The Mickey Mouse Club*, there was cheering from the audience as a birthday cake and candles were wheeled in. Howson himself appeared as a variety of characters in *Teleclub*, including studio cleaner Barney Sludge, and his son Paul performed a weekly puppet sequence.[65]

Several stations conducted children's clubs more along the lines of radio clubs, with membership cards and competitions as well as live studio sessions. Within months of opening in Lismore in northern New South Wales in 1962, RTN8 reported its Juniors Club had 1861 members.[66] RTN8 also established a Junior Dance Club, with some members dancing in the studio on the associated program.[67] Ballarat had the BTV Channel 6 Juniors Club.[68]

These clubs were probably also designed to demonstrate a sense of responsibility to the ABCB—which wanted children to 'gradually acquire a sound standard of values, self-discipline, and an appreciation of adult responsibilities'[69]—and those concerned about the social impact of television. Run by 'Isabel' (Isabel Angel), RVN2's Channel 2 Children's Club in Wagga Wagga issued membership certificates encouraging homework before viewing, accepting parents' program selections and helping others. In Griffith, the Channel Niners' Club at MTN9, hosted by former schoolteacher Helen Hickey, reportedly amassed almost 2000 members within weeks of commencing in 1965, and 10,000 by 1970. In a sign of the close relationship between regional broadcasters and their audiences, the Club's 'Birthday Book' segment remained on-air until 2006.[70]

Broadcasters also continued to leverage the commercial potential of 'clubs'. When ATV0 launched in 1964, its bid to lure viewers away from the three established Melbourne television stations was made harder because older sets and antennas were not equipped to receive the frequency and needed to be re-tuned or replaced. The station announced the Channel 0 Viewers' Club, claimed to be the world's biggest television contest with £70,000 worth of prizes, in 1965. More than 650,000 individually numbered cards were distributed to households. Viewers were asked to fill in their details on the coupon and return it to ATV0. Then the station displayed randomly selected numbers on the screen each night. If the viewer identified the number as one on their card, they had 15 minutes to contact the station and answer some simple questions before claiming a prize.[71] ATV0 viewers could also watch *The Magic Circle Club*, a mixture of live pantomime and classic fairy tales. In 1966, the weekday series won the first Logie Award for Outstanding Contribution to Children's Television.[72]

Some viewers in Queensland's Wide Bay managed to pick up signals from Brisbane and Toowoomba before acquiring SEQ8, and then an ABC station, in 1965. Because of the competition from distant stations, SEQ8 worked hard to establish a local identity.[73] A fledgling local newsletter, *TV Review*, applauded the station's *Teleclub* for showcasing worthwhile endeavours in the district, including handicrafts and drama, and John Anderson's magic acts. In May 1966, the newsletter featured on its cover a photograph of 46 young Teleclub members enjoying a pool party at the home of a Wide Bay worthy. *TV Review* was perturbed when it detected a trend to include more recorded cartoons, rather than live content, in the program, noting that 'Mrs. Miller, Captain Fred, Dave Corbett, John Anderson, Miss Diana and fellow Teleclubbers' were exclusive to the station.[74] While *TV Review* went out of business with that issue, *Teleclub* was to continue on-air into the 1990s.[75]

On 26 July 1965, SAS10, which was later to join ATV0 as part of the Ten Network, launched in Adelaide. The debut program was *The Bobo Show*, starring Charles 'Hal' Turner as Bobo the Clown, who had first appeared on *The Channel Niners*. Bobo soon became a household name in South Australia, acquiring a newspaper column and radio shows. He was mobbed by crowds at public appearances, and his 'playmates' could join the Bobo Club, purchase Bobo dolls and drink Bobo cordial.[76]

More and more, the broadcast 'clubs' that appeared were actual programs, rather than associations with members and meetings. The old model of the radio club, particularly for adults, was fading. The 2WG Women's Club and its radio session declined in popularity and ceased in 1965. As 7LA's manager remarked of the Women's Association in 1966, 'the members are getting older & there are no young people joining the Assn. to take their place'. Women's increased involvement in paid work and changing patterns of leisure spelt the death knell for most radio clubs. As more farming families could afford cars, women could travel further and more easily. The 7LA club closed in the late 1970s, and it is doubtful whether many other radio clubs lasted much longer.[77]

GTW11—one of the last regional television stations to go to air (in 1977)—in Geraldton, Western Australia, had its own mascot, 'Doopa Dog'. By the late 1980s, GTW11 had been acquired by the Golden West Network, and Doopa was appearing on the network's *Saturday Club*. The young host, Lara Dalton, presented short stories and read jokes to Doopa sent in by children. In 1990, Doopa was relocated to Bunbury where he began presenting a 'Goodnight Girls and Boys' segment in addition to appearing on the *Saturday Club*.[78]

WIN4's Ace Club was one of the last commercial television children's clubs, with 12,000 members by 1981. The station regularly hosted a panel of 10–15-year olds at its Wollongong studio to discuss children's television. *Prime Saturday Club* was a two-hour Saturday-morning program aimed at 5–12-year olds with segments on science, sport, health and the arts. It was produced at the Prime Network's Canberra studio and on location, with hosts joined by 'Prime Possum', who had had an afternoon program since 1993. Production of *GWN Saturday Club* was also moved from Bunbury to Prime's Canberra studio in 2008. *Prime Saturday Club* was later recast as *Possum's Club*, and *GWN Saturday Club* (packaged around popular Disney cartoons) became *Doopa's Club*, both with Madelaine Collignon as host. Prime cancelled the shows in 2013, although the mascots continued to feature in goodnight segments and community promotions.[79]

Over five decades, radio clubs had been at the heart of their communities, metropolitan as well as regional, across Australia. While radio personalities strove for a warm and intimate tone, scores of stations had further reached out to listeners by establishing social and charitable clubs with a significant extracurricular dimension. Following the advent of television in 1956, new broadcast clubs had been created. The word 'club', with its connotations of community and intimacy, was frequently invoked, even though the broadcast offerings were varied. By the 1970s Australia's radio clubs had faded away, although clubs had continued to be associated with some television programs, especially for children. By the turn of the century, clubs associated with individual stations, particularly in the regions, were subsumed by the operations of commercial networks, as Australian television became less local and less live.[80] There continued to be 'clubs' on television, ranging from *The Saddle Club*, a live-action children's adventure series (2001–2009), to *The Book Club* (ABC, 2006–2017), but they no longer constituted popular social movements.

NOTES

1. 'Lonely listeners', *Teleradio*, n.d. In addition to this clipping, see *Telegraph*, 2 August 1933, p. 8 and 17 January 1934, p. 16.
2. *Broadcasting Business Year Book* (Australian Radio Publications: Sydney, 1939), p. 129.
3. *Wireless Weekly* (*WW*), 8 May 1925, p. 6, 18 September 1925, p. 6 and 2 October 1925, p. 29.
4. Mick Counihan, 'The formation of a broadcasting audience: Australian radio in the twenties', *Meanjin*, 41 (June 1982), p. 201; Bridget Griffen-Foley, 'Modernity, intimacy and early Australian commercial radio', in Joy Damousi and Desley Deacon (eds.), *Talking and Listening in the Age of Modernity: Essays on the History of Sound* (Canberra: ANU e-Press, 2007), p. 124.
5. Jill Julius Matthews, *Dance Hall and Picture Palace: Sydney's Romance with Modernity* (Currency Press: Sydney, 2005), pp. 134–35; *Who's Who in Broadcasting in Western Australia* (Perth: Patersons Printing Press, 1936), p. 14.
6. Anne F. MacLennan, 'Learning to listen: Developing the Canadian radio audience in the 1930s', *Journal of Radio & Audio Media*, 20(2) (2013), p. 322.

7. Some of the following discussion draws on Griffen-Foley 2007, pp. 123–32 and *Changing Stations: The Story of Australian Commercial Radio* (Sydney: UNSW Press, 2009), Chap. 4.
8. Rachel Grahame, 'Stelzer, Eunice Minnie', *Australian Dictionary of Biography*, National Centre of Biography, Australian National University, http://adb.anu.edu.au/biography/stelzer-eunice-minnie-11759/text21031, published first in 2002, accessed 25 June 2019; *WW*, 4 November 1927, p. 8, 18 September 1931, p. 8 and 16 March 1934, p. 8.
9. *WW*, 28 August 1931, p. 12 and 18 September 1931, p. 8.
10. Catherine Fisher, 'Sound Citizens: The Public Voices of Australian Women Broadcasters, 1923–1956', PhD thesis (Australian National University, 2018), pp. 85–86.
11. Matthews 2005, p. 137; *WW*, 28 August 1931, p. 12, 18 September 1931, p. 8.
12. *WW*, 5 August 1932, p. 8, 19 August 1932, p. 29 and 21 April 1933, p. 10; Lesley Johnson, *The Unseen Voice* (London: Routledge, 1988), p. 111.
13. Fisher 2018, pp. 87–88.
14. *News*, 4 April 1933, p. 8; *WW*, 21 April 1933, p. 10.
15. National Archives of Australia (NAA)/ACT: CP30/3, 51, letter from A. Longsford to E. Lyons, 'Friday' (March 1933).
16. *Australian Women's Weekly*, 27 June 1936, p. 47.
17. Bill Kirkpatrick, '"A blessed boon": Radio, disability, governmentality, and the discourse of the "shut-in," 1920–1930', *Critical Studies in Media Communication*, 29(3) (2012), p. 170.
18. Justine Lloyd, *Gender and Media in the Broadcast Age: Women's Radio Programming at the BBC, CBC, and ABC* (New York: Bloomsbury, 2020), pp. 35–36; Fisher 2018, p. 90. See also *Grenfell Record and Lachlan District Advertiser*, 31 October 1929, p. 3; *Evening News* (Sydney), 1 April 1930, p. 12; *Sydney Morning Herald* (*SMH*), 16 May 1931, p. 7.
19. *Sunday Times*, 26 June 1932, p. 1 and 3 July 1932, pp. 1 and 9; *West Australian*, 11 July 1932, p. 17; *Western Mail*, 14 July 1932, p. 10; *Daily News*, 5 November 1936, p. 4; *Who's Who in Broadcasting in Western Australia* (1936), p. 25.
20. *Teleradio*, 23 December 1933, p. 9 and 17 February 1934, p. 21.
21. *WW*, 18 May 1934, p. 8 and 20 May 1938, p. 42; *Daily Telegraph*, 5 April 1941, p. 7.
22. Ida Coffey, *Look Up and Laugh: 13 Years at the Mike* (Melbourne: National Press, 1945), p. 21.
23. *Record*, 6 November 1937, p. 2, 7 January 1939, p. 5, 18 March 1939, p. 2 and 24 June 1939, p. 1.

24. Swan Hill Regional Library: 3SH Women's Club constitution, 3 June 1939, and 50th birthday article.
25. Fisher 2018, pp. 264–69.
26. https://www.radioheritage.net/Story141.asp, accessed 29 February 2020.
27. Wagga Wagga City Library (WWCL): 2WG Collection, Constitution and Rules of 2WG Women's Club, p. 3.
28. *The Land*, 10 December 1937, p. 23; *Wagga Wagga Express*, 28 May 1938, p. 13, 4 June 1938, p. 3 and 11 June 1938, p. 2; *Radio Pictorial of Australia*, 1 July 1938, p. 34; Fisher 2018, pp. 89, 270–71. See also WWCL: 2WG Collection.
29. WWCL: 2WG Collection, letter from Lindsay Knight, n.d. (c. 1988).
30. Fisher 2018, pp. 271–72.
31. For example, *WW*, 18 November 1939, p. 15.
32. *Telegraph*, 9 October 1939, p. 12; *Teleradio*, 10 February 1940, pp. 46–47 and 22 June 1940, p. 22.
33. *Broadcasting Business Year Book* (1938), pp. 163, 166; (1939), pp. 100, 129; (1940), p. 95. See also David Ricquish, 'Koalas, Kangaroos & Kiwis— The Australian Radio Listener Clubs', https://www.radioheritage.net/Story79.asp, accessed 29 February 2020.
34. *Cairns Post*, 7 October 1941, p. 7 and 4 August 2006, p. 19.
35. https://www.austlit.edu.au/austlit/page/A58280, accessed 26 June 2019; *Advertiser* (Adelaide), 2 December 1939, p. 9.
36. *Broadcasting Business* (*BB*), 9 May 1940, pp. 16–17.
37. NAA/ACT: SP112/1, 31/12/2, notes of conference, 14 August 1940, pp. 10–11.
38. Griffen-Foley 2007, pp. 133–34.
39. State Library of Tasmania Launceston Reference Library (SLTLRL): 7LA Women's Association Records, Macquarie Network Catalogues, 1941–42.
40. SLTLRL: 7LA Women's Association Records, Macquarie Network Catalogue (1942), p. 87. See also *Mercury* (Hobart), 17 April 1940, p. 10 and 26 February 1944, p. 14; *Examiner* (Launceston), 27 February 1943, p. 6, 22 June 1944, p. 6 and 10 March 1945, p. 6.
41. *Report of the Joint Committee on Wireless Broadcasting* (Canberra: AGPS, 1942), p. 53.
42. EHCOR: 2GB Happiness Club Visitors' Book 1938–1996, 26 October 1940; Group Leaders Committee and General Meetings minute book, pp. 35, 52, 76.
43. NAA/ACT: A463, 1958/2199, letter from L.M. Rowland to R.G. Menzies, 15 May 1957. See also Grahame 2002.
44. Fisher 2018, p. 274.
45. SLTLRL: 7LA Women's Association Records.
46. *TV News*, 26 July 1958, p. 23.

47. *TV Week* (Adelaide), 16 December 1959, pp. 12–14; http://www.awesomeadelaide.com/tag/nws-9/, accessed 1 January 2020.
48. Madeleine Hastie, 'Free-to-air: A History of Sydney's Commercial Television Programming, 1956–2012', PhD thesis (Macquarie University, 2014), p. 275; *SMH*, 2 September 1957, p. 4; *Sun-Herald*, 22 December 1957, p. 35 and 28 June 1959, p. 53.
49. http://www.captainfortune.com/bailey.html, accessed 10 January 2020.
50. Hastie 2014, pp. 275–76; captainfortune.com/, accessed 10 January 2020; Nan Musgrove, 'Television parade', *Australian Women's Weekly*, 17 July 1957, p. 45.
51. *SMH*, 14 July 1956, p. 6.
52. *TV Times*, 3 July 1959, pp. 28–29.
53. http://www.originalmmc.com/show3.html (accessed 1 January 2020).
54. John Query, 'They all run in Packer's colors', *TV News-Times*, 15 November 1958, p. 11.
55. *TV Week* (Adelaide), 16 December 1959, pp. 14–15.
56. *TV Week* (Sydney), 11 April 1959, pp. 16–17.
57. *TV Week* (Sydney), 18 April 1959, pp. 8–11; Tara Oldfield, 'The Mickey Mouse Club Mouseketeers' (2018), https://prov.vic.gov.au/about-us/our-blog/mickey-mouse-club-mouseketeers, accessed 30 December 2019.
58. Brian Davies, *Those Fabulous TV Years* (North Ryde, NSW: Cassell Australia, 1981), p. 174.
59. K.S. Inglis, *This Is the ABC: The Australian Broadcasting Commission, 1932–1983* (Melbourne: Melbourne University Press, 1983), p. 210; *SMH*, 16 February 1959, p. 17; Tammy Burnstock, 'Curator's notes', https://aso.gov.au/titles/tv/abc-childrens-tv-club/notes/, accessed 1 January 2020.
60. Hastie 2014, pp. 273–74; *New South Wales Association of University Women Graduates 43rd Annual Report* (Sydney: NSW Association of University Women Graduates, 1962), p. 7.
61. Inglis 1983, p. 210.
62. *TV Times*, 26 June 1959, p. 54.
63. https://documents.uow.edu.au/content/groups/public/@web/@lib/documents/doc/uow256678.pdf, accessed 1 January 2020. See also, for example, *SMH*, 31 January 1966, p. 11.
64. Andrew Bayley, 'BCV: Television Centre of Victoria' (2011), https://televisionau.com/2011/12/bcv-television-centre-of-victoria.html, accessed 2 January 2020.
65. Michael Thurlow, 'Switched On: A History of Regional Commercial Television in Australia', PhD thesis (Macquarie University, 2020), p. 200; Mark Taylor, *2017 Australian Radio, TV Stations, Newspapers & Theatres Australian Badge Guide* (2nd edition, 2017), pp. 68–69; Andrew Bayley,

'Prime7 Albury turns 50' (2014), https://televisionau.com/2014/09/prime7-albury-turns-50.html, accessed 2 January 2020; Barry Skinner, 'A Master of All Trades' (2005), http://tdgq.com.au/dha/tributes/skinnerb.html, accessed 2 January 2020.
66. Thurlow 2020, p. 135.
67. Gary Cribb, 8 February 2018, https://www.facebook.com/pg/GaryHSavins/photos/?tab=album&album_id=434437846761533, accessed 1 January 2020.
68. Mark Taylor, *2017 Australian Radio, TV Stations, Newspapers & Theatres Australian Badge Guide* (2nd edition, 2017), pp. 56–57.
69. *Australian Broadcasting Control Board 10th Annual Report* (Canberra: AGPS, 1957–58), p. 9.
70. Thurlow 2020, pp. 197–200.
71. Andrew Bayley, 'ATV0: The Channel 0 Viewers' Club' (2014), https://televisionau.com/2014/07/atv0-the-channel-0-viewers-club.html, accessed 1 January 2020.
72. Thurlow 2020, p. 111; Albert Moran and Chris Keating, *Historical Dictionary of Australian Radio and Television* (Lanham, Maryland, Scarecrow Press, 2007), p. 243; https://www.woorillacaught.com/tv-shows/the-magic-circle-club/, accessed 3 January 2020.
73. Andrew Bayley, 'Seven Queensland turns 50' (2015), https://televisionau.com/2015/04/seven-queensland-turns-50.html, accessed 10 January 2020.
74. *TV Review*, January–May 1966.
75. Thurlow 2020, pp. 311–12. For the 1991 launch of *Teleclub*, see https://www.facebook.com/watch/?v=690780484353212, accessed 3 January 2020.
76. https://www.nfsa.gov.au/collection/curated/bobo-clown, accessed 3 January 2020; Bob Byrne, 'Bobo the Clown' (2014), https://www.adelaideremememberwhen.com.au/bobo-the-clown/, accessed 3 January 2020.
77. Fisher 2018, pp. 274–75; Griffen-Foley 2009, pp. 141–42. See also SLTLRR: 7LA Women's Association Records.
78. Thurlow 2020, p. 448; Lara Dalton, 30 December 2016, https://www.facebook.com/laraforgeraldton/posts/ok-geraldtonheres-a-flash-back-friday-straight-from-the-vaultwho-remembers-the-g/732901536875663/, accessed 12 January 2020; see also comments on Dalton's post. Footage of Doopa Dog can be seen on the WAtvPresentation YouTube channel.
79. Thurlow 2020, pp. 384–85, 476, 514–15, 573.
80. See Thurlow 2020.

BIBLIOGRAPHY

Advertiser (Adelaide).
Australian Broadcasting Control Board 10th Annual Report (Canberra: AGPS, 1957–1958).
Australian Women's Weekly.
'NWS9', *Awesome Adelaide*, http://www.awesomeadelaide.com/tag/nws-9/, accessed 1 January 2020.
Bayley, Andrew. 'BCV: Television Centre of Victoria' (2011), https://televisionau.com/2011/12/bcv-television-centre-of-victoria.html, accessed 2 January 2020.
———. 'ATV0: The Channel 0 Viewers' Club' (2014a), https://televisionau.com/2014/07/atv0-the-channel-0-viewers-club.html, accessed 1 January 2020.
———. 'Prime7 Albury turns 50' (2014b), https://televisionau.com/2014/09/prime7-albury-turns-50.html, accessed 2 January 2020.
———. 'Seven Queensland turns 50' (2015), https://televisionau.com/2015/04/seven-queensland-turns-50.html, accessed 10 January 2020.
'Bobo the Clown', National Film and Sound Archive (NFSA), https://www.nfsa.gov.au/collection/curated/bobo-clown, accessed 3 January 2020.
Broadcasting Business (BB).
Broadcasting Business Year Book (Sydney: Australian Radio Publications, 1938, 1939 and 1940).
Burnstock, Tammy. 'Curator's notes', https://aso.gov.au/titles/tv/abc-childrens-tv-club/notes/, accessed 1 January 2020.
Byrne, Bob. 'Bobo the Clown' (2014), https://www.adelaiderememberwhen.com.au/bobo-the-clown/, accessed 3 January 2020.
Cairns Post.
Campion, Margaret. *3AW is Melbourne: 75 Years of Radio* (Collingwood, VIC: Prime Advertising Marketing Publishing, 2007).
Coffey, Ida. *Look Up and Laugh: 13 Years at the Mike* (Melbourne: National Press, 1945).
Counihan, Mick. 'The formation of a broadcasting audience: Australian radio in the twenties', *Meanjin*, 41 (June 1982), pp. 196–209.
Cribb, Gary. Facebook, 8 February 2018, https://www.facebook.com/pg/GaryHSavins/photos/?tab=album&album_id=434437846761533, accessed 1 January 2020.
Daily News (Perth).
Daily Telegraph (Sydney).
Dalton, Lara. Facebook, 30 December 2016, https://www.facebook.com/lara-forgeraldton/posts/ok-geraldtonheres-a-flash-back-friday-straight-from-the-vaultwho-remembers-the-g/732901536875663/, accessed 12 January 2020.

Davies, Brian. *Those Fabulous TV Years* (North Ryde, NSW: Cassell Australia, 1981).
Captain Fortune, http://www.captainfortune.com, accessed 10 January 2020.
Evening News (Sydney).
Examiner (Launceston).
Grahame, Rachel. 'Stelzer, Eunice Minnie', *Australian Dictionary of Biography*, National Centre of Biography, Australian National University, http://adb.anu.edu.au/biography/stelzer-eunice-minnie-11759/text21031, published first in 2002, accessed 25 June 2019.
Grenfell Record and Lachlan District Advertiser.
Griffen-Foley, Bridget. 'Modernity, intimacy and early Australian commercial radio', in Joy Damousi and Desley Deacon (eds.), *Talking and Listening in the Age of Modernity: Essays on the History of Sound* (Canberra: ANU e-Press, 2007), pp. 123–32.
———. *Changing Stations: The Story of Australian Commercial Radio* (Sydney: UNSW Press, 2009).
Fisher, Catherine. 'Sound Citizens: The Public Voices of Australian Women Broadcasters, 1923–1956', PhD thesis (Australian National University, 2018).
Hastie, Madeleine. 'Free-to-air: A History of Sydney's Commercial Television Programming, 1956–2012', PhD thesis (Macquarie University, 2014).
Inglis, K.S. *This Is the ABC: The Australian Broadcasting Commission, 1932–1983* (Melbourne: Melbourne University Press, 1983).
Johnson, Lesley. *The Unseen Voice* (London: Routledge, 1988).
Kirkpatrick, Bill. '"A blessed boon": Radio, disability, governmentality, and the discourse of the "shut-in," 1920–1930', *Critical Studies in Media Communication*, 29(3) (2012), pp. 165–84, https://doi.org/10.1080/15295036.2011.631554.
MacLennan, Anne F. 'Learning to listen: Developing the Canadian radio audience in the 1930s', *Journal of Radio & Audio Media*, 20(2) (2013), pp. 311–26, https://doi.org/10.1080/19376529.2013.825534.
'Magic Circle Club', *Woorilla Caught*, https://www.woorillacaught.com/tv-shows/the-magic-circle-club, accessed 3 January 2020.
Matthews, Jill Julius. *Dance Hall and Picture Palace: Sydney's Romance with Modernity* (Currency Press: Sydney, 2005).
The Land (Sydney).
Lloyd, Justine. *Gender and Media in the Broadcast Age: Women's Radio Programming at the BBC, CBC, and ABC* (New York: Bloomsbury, 2020).
Mercury (Hobart).
Moran, Albert and Keating, Chris. *Historical Dictionary of Australian Radio and Television* (Lanham, MD: Scarecrow Press, 2007).
Musgrove, Nan. 'Television parade', *Australian Women's Weekly*, 17 July 1957, p. 45.

National Archives of Australia (NAA)/ACT: A463, 1958/2199. Mrs W.J. Stelzer—Civil Honour.
———. CP30/3, 51. Personal Correspondence of Mrs Enid Lyons, 1933.
———. SP112/1, 31/12/2. Conference between D. of I. and the Australian Federation of Commercial Broadcasting Stations, 14 August 1940.
News (Adelaide).
Oldfield, Tara. 'The Mickey Mouse Club Mouseketeers' (2018), https://prov.vic.gov.au/about-us/our-blog/mickey-mouse-club-mouseketeers, accessed 30 December 2019.
Original Mickey Mouse Show, http://www.originalmmc.com/show3.html (accessed 1 January 2020).
Query, John. 'They all run in Packer's colors', *TV News-Times*, 15 November 1958, pp. 10–12.
Radio Pictorial of Australia.
Record (Emerald Hill).
Report of the Joint Committee on Wireless Broadcasting (Canberra: AGPS, 1942).
Ricquish, David. 'Koalas, Kangaroos & Kiwis—The Australian Radio Listener Clubs', Radio Heritage Foundation, https://www.radioheritage.net/Story79.asp, accessed 29 February 2020.
'SEQ TV/Sunshine Television Memories', Facebook, https://www.facebook.com/watch/?v=690780484353212, accessed 3 January 2020.
Skinner, Barry. 'A Master of All Trades' (2005), http://tdgq.com.au/dha/tributes/skinnerb.html, accessed 2 January 2020.
State Library of Tasmania Launceston Reference Library (SLTLRL): 7LA Women's Association Records.
Sun-Herald (Sydney).
Sunday Times (Perth).
Swan Hill Regional Library: 3SH Women's Club.
Sydney Morning Herald (*SMH*).
Taylor, Mark. *2017 Australian Radio, TV Stations, Newspapers & Theatres Australian Badge Guide* (2nd edition, 2017).
Telegraph (Brisbane).
Teleradio.
Thurlow, Michael. 'Switched On: A History of Regional Commercial Television in Australia', PhD thesis (Macquarie University, 2020).
TV News.
TV Review.
TV Times.
TV Week (Adelaide, Sydney).
University of Wollongong Archives, https://documents.uow.edu.au/content/groups/public/@web/@lib/documents/doc/uow256678.pdf, accessed 1 January 2020.

Wagga Wagga City Library (WWCL): 2WG Collection.
Wagga Wagga Express.
West Australian.
Western Mail.
Who's Who in Broadcasting in Western Australia (Perth: Patersons Printing Press, 1936).
Wireless Weekly (*WW*).

CHAPTER 4

The Fan Mail Trail

Abstract This chapter intercepts the fan mail received by Australian broadcasters between the 1920s and the 2000s. It considers who wrote to the Australian Broadcasting Commission and commercial broadcasters, and why; how letters were solicited handled, and responded to; how stations and producers used fan mail to help understand their audiences before the adoption of ratings surveys; the expectations of advertising agencies and commercial broadcasters concerning fan mail; and the ways audiences marked the ending of iconic programs such as *Blue Hills* and *Mother and Son*. We delve into the papers of some of Australia's most popular radio and television personalities, including music broadcaster Bernard Heinze, writer Gwen Meredith, actress Ruth Cracknell and the satirical sports broadcasters 'Roy and H.G.'

Keywords Audiences • Sports media • Fan mail • Australian Broadcasting Commission • Radio • Television

'Thousands of letters are received annually by each station', wrote 2UW humourist Jack Win in a long article on 'The Broadcasting Mail Bag' for *Wireless Weekly* in 1928.[1] The letters from listeners from every social grade, trade and profession that poured in were variously 'sad, amusing, quaint, businesslike, critical', reported Win. More correspondence was received from country than city stations, the Sydney commercial broadcaster wrote, hinting at the social importance of radio in more isolated communities. Win grouped letter-writers into categories: those who enjoyed only the highest class of music and talks; those (especially the young) who demanded more jazz and popular songs; those who wrote in with requests for information from speakers; and children and their mothers who listened in to bedtime stories.

Win was charmed by letters from 'tiny tots' that were written on ruled paper and sometimes got through unstamped. He reported that many of the listeners to children's sessions were adults, with one writing in about an 87-year-old relative who tried to use the loudspeaker as a telephone to talk to a station's Aunts and Uncles. Win was moved by the 'genuine pathos' of a letter from a mother whose little girl had died singing a piece which a radio orchestra had played one evening, and another from a middle-aged invalid whose musical aspirations had been revived by hearing Faust for the first time in two decades. His commentary was consistent with American media scholar Bill Kirkpatrick's analysis of how the industry used the discourse of the 'shut-in'—isolated, disabled, elderly and typically feminised—to justify radio's noble social purpose.[2] Win also learned from 2FC that one of its recent special 'Empire Broadcasts', in which the Sydney A-class (later Australian Broadcasting Commission) station had joined with Amalgamated Wireless Australasia Ltd (AWA) in a relay of performances from Sydney, England and North America, had attracted 1000 admiring letters. Win wrote that one unnamed station had a 'mad' file, with ridiculous requests for an urgent SOS to help locate a lost parrot, and another from a 'lonesome' young woman who wanted her name and address broadcast so a 'lot of folks' would write to her.[3]

This chapter intercepts and interrogates some of the fan mail received by Australian broadcasters—ABC and commercial—since the 1920s. Radio fan mail was an international phenomenon. As one American commentator remarked, programs made 'thousands of people feel free to sit down and write a friendly and personal letter to a large corporation'. Advertising man Howard Dickinson marvelled in 1929 at the arrival 'personal, intimate, and cordial' letters. Radio was 'humanising' business and restoring the 'personal touch' of earlier days.[4]

There was 'big "fan" mail' at 4BC Brisbane, reported *Truth* in 1932. The morning session for women of Ruth Rutherford, an accomplished craftswoman and singer, was extended by the commercial station in response to the volume of mail and queries she received for helpful hints.[5] Meanwhile, the fan mail of 'Uncle George' (George Saunders), 'the "daddy" of Australian radio uncles' who was now heard on 2GB, peaked at 1102 letters in one day.[6]

Years later, Hobart bookseller W.E. Fuller would claim to have written with solicitor Marcus Gibson the first radio serial in Australia. *The Adventures of Harry and Grace Smith* ran for about two years before the hugely popular American serial *One Man's Family* began being adapted for Australian radio in 1935. Such was their fan mail, Fuller and Gibson asked listeners for suggestions on how to end the serial, receiving 'astonishing' plotlines in response.[7] Promotion for *One Man's Family*, in turn, often showed 'the family' in their living rooms listening in to the Barbour family. But the program was heard in Australia for only two years before Carlton Morse declined to supply any further scripts, prompting 5000 letters of complaint from dismayed Australian listeners.[8]

By 1934 3AR and 3LO in Melbourne were reportedly receiving a fan mail of 36,500 letters a year, part of the 190,000 letters received annually by the ABC. The ABC let it be known that it welcomed programming suggestions, with four 'girls' just in Melbourne to sort the mail. The ABC spent £1600 in stamps on replying to every letter received across the country. Program critics were 'legion', reported Western Australia's *Kalgoorlie Miner*, although letters were by now 'mostly constructive' and provided 'ample proof' of the consolation radio provided for the 'human heart'.[9]

2CH made available to W.A. McNair, a director and research manager of the Australian office of American advertising agency J. Walter Thompson, 3952 letters it received from November 1934 to June 1935. Half were in response to a competition for the best joke. 2GB also provided him with 1652 letters from children in 1933 in response to an offer of a book of 'Red Indian' tribal lore. McNair used the correspondence to assist him with determining the suburban (and rural) locations of the two commercial stations' audiences.[10]

McNair remarked on how Australian stations would advertise the fact that a certain session brought in 10,000 letters, thus 'proving' that the station had a large and responsive audience. Or they would boast that they received mail from New Zealand, New Guinea and California, thus inferring a wide coverage. But, as he noted, mail received by stations and advertisers was a poor indication of the size of a station's audience. A substantial prize would attract more entries than for a small prize, just as an easy competition would attract more entries than a challenging competition.[11] McNair might have added the very fact that stations held competitions for listener entries was in good part a plea for demonstrable 'fan mail'.

A correspondent to Brisbane's *Sunday Mail* in 1935 suggested that a 'scientific' ballot paper, distributed by the ABC to every licence holder, would provide an answer to the question 'what does the listener want?' As the *Sunday Mail*'s L. Fitz-Henry noted, something similar had been conducted by the *Courier-Mail* in partnership with 4BK the previous year. Popular concert items had topped that ballot, with birthday calls coming in last. The votes had been accompanied by observations about issues ranging from the 'highbrow' to women's voices, and condemnations of crooning, thrillers and advertising. 'Nothing will do more to improve radio generally than an intelligent contact between the listener and the broadcasting station', Fitz-Henry maintained: 'Fan-mail is the only direct contact.'[12]

Wireless Weekly devoted another full page to the phenomenon in 1936: 'some radio announcers exist on fan mail, some exist for fan mail, and some exist despite fan mail'. Isabelle Grace reported that some enthusiasts enclosed a photograph with their first letter. Some letters took serial form. Some correspondents reported on the meanderings of husbands and the misdoings of offspring. 'Letters, and letters alone', were the test of the announcers' popularity, contended the journalist: 'no mail, no proof for manager and advertiser, no job'. Sorting the mail was no easy job for stations, for amidst pages of adulation could be requests for a sample of this or that, or an entry to a competition. 'Uncle Si' (Si Meredith) told Grace he had received 1400 letters in response to the last serial he had read on 2CH, as well as a handmade silk scarf. John Dunne at Sydney's Catholic station 2SM seems to have been irritated by fan mail, although he did concede that if a letter concerned a particular session, it was usually forwarded to the advertiser (Fig. 4.1).[13]

In an article on the radio announcer's mail bag, 2UW's 'Uncle Jack' (J.M. Prentice) wrote about receiving innumerable queries, all of which he tried to answer, as well as compliments and requests. By 1936 he had presided over the funeral of one listener and been in touch with another for more than a decade. But he was enraged by anonymous letters, particularly those that were sent to station managements 'complaining or objecting to some announcer upon whom their wrath has fallen'.[14]

In a 1937 article about the fan mail received by 2GB, the *Australian Women's Weekly* reported that singers seemed to get the most letters. Young Julie Russell liked hearing about what listeners thought and felt as

Fig. 4.1 'Favourites of the air get fan mail', *Wireless Weekly*, 10 July 1936. (Copyright Silicon Chip Publishing)

she missed the audience reaction after stage performances. Dorothy Vautier, host of the 2GB women's session, received 'businesslike' queries and entries to competitions, although they were interspersed with opinions about her voice and her interviews. Most of their mail, 2GB's female announcers and performers said, came from women. Entertainer Jack Davey received letters asking for advice on how to get into radio, or forwarding him a 'good joke' to put over the air.[15]

Hilda Morse, host of the 2UW women's session, was sent letters from 'all over the place': serious letters, letters of appreciation, and 'screamingly funny letters'. *Radio Pictorial of Australia* photographed a messenger carrying a suitcase to the GPO to collect Morse's mail, which he was said to do two or three times a day. Along with letters came gifts of underwear, honey, vegetables and lollies. The morning broadcaster worked until 7 pm each night reading and answering the correspondence, with 2UW bringing in a typist to help. One elderly listener compiled an album of every poem Morse had read aloud. The broadcaster looked out for ideas and suggestions from 'Old Faithfuls', as well as new correspondents.[16] Thousands of entries to a competition centred on *Katy and John*—a session written by and starring Morse—appeared each week. Some postal workers wondered if 'Mr and Mrs John Peel' were real people.[17]

Even so, the volume of fan mail received by each station seems to have declined as the number of stations and personalities increased (and, perhaps, as people became used to the novelty of radio). In February 1937 the ABC in Melbourne received 7300 letters about its programs (78 per cent of them favourable), about half of what it had received three years earlier. Even so, this was still quite substantial and exceeded what the BBC reportedly received: about 1000 letters a month (compared with 1000 a week several years earlier).[18]

In 1938 the ABC's NSW manager, Basil W. Kirke, invited journalists to his office to discuss the broadcaster's plans for the following year. Some of the questions involved fan mail, which Kirke reported had declined. He dismissed many of the letters that had been received in the ABC's early years as from 'neurotic women': 'They all wrote the same thing—that they had fallen in love with an announcer's voice'.[19]

Kirke was echoing overseas assessments of radio fan mail in the 1930s, as well as some of Jack Win's earlier Australian account. When a sample of fan mail was brought to popular American philosopher Will Durant, he concluded that it was mostly written by the very young and the very old, the sick and the lonely, hero worshipers—and a 'few from the average man or woman'. Psychology Professor Cyril Burt, consulting for the BBC, announced that 'an excessive proportion of the writers were obviously neurotic'. Overviewing some of this work in 1950, sociologist Elihu Katz contended that fan mail was valuable if only because it expressed sentiments which were shared, although somewhat less volubly and by people who did not write. He also restated that much of what was lumped together as 'fan mail' was solicited, although the focus of these letters on given topics still made them valuable to radio and other researchers.[20]

Commercial broadcasters interviewed by the *Newcastle Sun* in response to the Kirke interview were more positive. 2GB's manager, D.R. Armstrong, continued to encourage fan mail 'as a personal contact between the announcer and the listener'. Si Meredith reported that he received 200–300 letters per week, and his birthday loot included five birthday cakes, six ties, 300 cigarettes and 'one set of milanese underwear in pale blue'.[21] 'If it's Mail you want—Use 2CH' screamed an advertisement in the industry periodical *Commercial Broadcasting*. It advised that mail received by the station—from middle-class families, industrial areas and financial districts—had tripled between 1939 and 1940. Showing three young women dutifully reading and acknowledging piles of letters, the ad offered advertisers details of the 'mail-response' to regular features.[22] It seems that commercial stations created entire programs (as well as competitions) involving cash prizes in a deliberate effort to attract 'fan mail' that could then be shown to advertisers.[23]

In interviews about her new 2GB program in 1937, Goodie Reeve reported that her fan mail was almost invariably from women. Women wrote reams to her once they felt they got to know her, they encouraged her, they rebutted criticisms of her—and they bought the goods she advertised. Reeve now launched *For Men Only* on Saturday afternoons, a time when men were typically out or listening to horse-racing. She invited men to write in with their views and their 'grouches' about their womenfolk, using nom-de-plumes. After an uncertain start, Reeve was inundated by men, and many wives wrote back in 'violent self-defence'. But lest she alienate her devoted women listeners, Reeves expressed her appreciation of 'Still a Lover', who wrote in to express his frustration that some correspondents 'don't seem to realise that women are the most precious things in the world, and that it is up to men to take care of them'.[24] Ten young bachelors, who despatched ridiculous letters when *For Men Only* was launched, began to take it seriously. 'Well-Wisher' confessed that they felt 'cheap' about pulling Reeve's leg, declaring that she could now be sure of their support for her 'session of mutual help'. *Radio Pictorial of Australia* photographed Reeve sorting her mail (including confessions of theft and attempts at suicide) with her devoted dog by her side.[25]

In the late 1930s Norman Myer asked 3KZ's star announcer, Norman Banks, to create a program that would help the Myer department store to sell furniture on credit. Banks came up with the idea of a weekly program of popular classics, and appealed to listeners who enjoyed that kind of music to write in. Staff at the commercial station were overwhelmed by the 'sensational' response. After Banks took a dozen folders of mail into Myer's office there emerged *Myer Musicale*, one of the longest-running programs on Melbourne radio.[26]

Following the launch of a weekly discussion program, *The Voice of Youth*, by a young schoolteacher, George Ivan Smith, on the ABC's national network in 1939, Sydney's *Daily Telegraph* reported that his fan mail would 'fill some Hollywood starts with envy'. Letters were (in an echo of McNair) said to come from as far afield as Darwin and the

Kimberleys, with thousands requesting the designs of toys Smith talked about building on-air.[27] When the prominent country-and-western singer Tex Morton began a musical tour for the ABC that year, his contract included a weekly allowance of £5 to respond to fan mail and send out signed photographs.[28] 'Jock the Backyard Naturalist' (zoologist Dr A.J. Marshall) from the ABC's Argonauts Club, which we discussed in Chap. 2, received surely the most unusual fan mail, with parcels of specimens such as teeth and bones to be identified. His successor, 'Tom the Naturalist' (Alan Colefax), was even sent a living snake.[29]

After becoming writer and producer of the Australian version of the popular *Lux Radio Theatre* on the Macquarie Network, Harry Dearth was reported to receive the most widespread fan mail in Australia, including around 20 letters per week proposing plays for production.[30] A fan of *Australia's Amateur Hour* wrote to tell host Dick Fair that he and his fellow workers at a remote cattle station dressed up each Thursday night to listen to it together on the AWA network, and held animated discussions about it with others in the district the next day.[31] Meanwhile, the 'fearless' '2GB News Reviewer' (Eric Baume) claimed to be disappointed that there was too much 'friendly' fan mail mixed in with the 'hostile' letters he attracted.[32]

In a report on 'progress in radio fan-mail analysis' in 1939, Jeanette Sayre of the Princeton Radio Research Project studied the mail received in response to the previous season of the public discussion program *America's Town Meeting of the Air*. Noting that the majority of the mail consisted of requests for transcripts, Sayre still attempted to show how certain audience characteristics (like gender and social status) for programs might be inferred from fan mail, and how this mail might further knowledge of what different programs meant to different people.[33]

Some actual listener and viewer letters survive in the papers of individual broadcasters and stations. As Charlene Simmons has pointed out in a consideration of interwar American fan mail, surviving letters record something of the thoughts of actual listeners at or near the time of listening.[34]

In 1939 Dame Enid Lyons, widow of Prime Minister J.A. Lyons, began a series of Sunday-evening broadcasts on the Macquarie Network. With 11 children, Lyons was, unsurprisingly, viewed as a maternal figure and a kind of mother to the nation. Listeners—not all of them women—praised her 'sweet voice' and 'intensely human and deeply moving' form of address. But 2GB's general manager, H.G. Horner, was disquieted early in the 18-month series when Lyons directly acknowledged the letter of a listener, whose address she had lost, on-air. He wanted her to avoid a practice of reading individual letters that was 'sometimes indulged in by Women Announcers' during the day, and in so doing help entrench her evening talks as serious and important. As Catherine Fisher has shown, Lyons' broadcasts straddled expectations of the feminine and the intimate, and a new public space in which women could speak about a range of issues and claim a voice as citizens in mid-twentieth-century Australia. Letters to Lyons also again highlighted the social role of radio: 'now I am old my greatest pleasure comes from Radio', wrote M. Sayer; 'I have a very lonely life, therefore my radio friends become very real to me', began Miss Elsie Hankins, another Sydney listener.[35]

As music adviser to the ABC, Professor Bernard Heinze introduced and conducted children's concerts that educated decades of boys and girls. His manuscript collection bulges with letters from children, parents and teachers, each of which he read and responded to, as well as accepting proposals for inclusion in future concerts. Heinze was grateful to Joan Butler of Adelaide for her 'charming and appreciative letter', urging her to listen to contemporary as well as classical music on the school gramophone. He replied good-naturedly to a teacher, also from Adelaide, who confessed her girls were 'too shy to write to a Professor!' In 1942 he was struck by a report from a 14-year-old girl from Bendigo, telling her father that 'although I have received many letters from young people who fill my youthful audiences, I have never been given an indirect appreciation such as your Barbara sent to you', and forwarded it to the ABC's chairman, W.J. Cleary.[36] He replied to a Brisbane mother: 'I believe that in these concerts we have an opportunity of making and forming cultured minds. ... It is letters such as yours that encourage me to go on believing.'[37]

The ABC presented *Country Hour*, launched on the national network in 1945, as an answer to its 'many country friends'. Listeners, said the *ABC Weekly* in 1946, had given the program their 'emphatic approval', as it set aside a dedicated page 'based upon the best and most accurate form of listener research there is—letters from satisfied listeners'.[38] Commercial stations such as 2LM Lismore, with its *Request Hour*, were also able to present aspects of programs, such as songs, as responses to suggestions from fan mail.[39]

Possibly inspired by the popularity of Heinze's orchestral broadcasts, Hector Crawford Productions made for 3DB and affiliated stations *Opera for the People* from 1946 to 1948, when the company ran out of operas suitable for translation.[40] The half-hour distillations on Sunday nights gave rise to letters such as this from one Adelaide listener: 'The simple dramatic presentation of the story is giving me a truer appreciation of opera than I have ever had before'.[41]

Listeners wrote to broadcasters for a range of reasons, concluded a 1949 study of mail sent to the New York Philharmonic Symphony Orchestra broadcast on CBS. These included the desire to make a comment about something related to a program, to express an emotional identification with a performer or show or to register a vote of approval or criticism. Fan mail was a way in which listeners could 'participate more fully in the experience of "listening"'.[42] But the phenomenon imposed a practical burden on broadcasters. The time taken up by reading and replying to fan mail was raised by an announcer at Brisbane's 4KQ in 1950 during negotiations for a new industrial award.[43]

As we saw with *One Man's Family*, correspondents also expressed grief on the end of long-running shows. In 1953 *Fred and Maggie Everybody*, which had depicted the lives of a middle-class couple in a gently comic style, and had been heard on dozens of commercial stations since 1932, was discontinued.[44] Letters from devoted listeners were addressed to co-stars Edward Howell and his wife Therese Desmond—and also simply to 'Fred and Maggie'. One Sydney fan wrote of how he and his wife, as well as his parents, started their weekends by listening to the 'Everybodies' on Friday nights:

> Twenty-one years may be a long time for a radio programme to run, but it's not too long. In that period you've become part of a lot of people's lives, you've provided some humour, some tears and many happy hours for a lot of world-weary people. We don't want to feel it's all over. We want to share with Fred and Maggie again all the ups and downs of modern living, because in doing that we learn how to laugh at some of our own problems.[45]

Author and *Sun* radio writer J.H. Adams was intrigued by listeners who didn't write fan mail, or even notes to say they were 'not amused'. In a 1954 column on the breakfast radio endeavours of Sydney commercial stations, he speculated about how many listeners opted to vent their irritation by 'flick[ing] the dial around' rather than writing to a station (or participating in a ratings survey).[46] Western Australian broadcaster Catherine King reportedly once remarked that 'if <u>one</u> letter in praise was received the ABC counted it as ten—knowing how farmers wives, daughters, mothers were appreciative but "slow to put pen to paper".[47] This seems to have been a conservative estimate, with overseas researchers speculating that one fan letter was received for every 500–4000 listeners.[48]

Michelle Arrow has studied some of the letters received by the ABC and writer Gwen Meredith over the decades *The Lawsons* (1944–1949) and *Blue Hills* (1949–1976) were broadcast across Australia. They help to reveal the ways in which people absorbed the serials into the routine of their daily lives, and the personal identification listeners made with the middle-class characters in their rural setting.[49] Megan Blair has also argued that the responses of city listeners to *The Lawsons* show how the serial helped to bridge an urban-rural divide in Australia, and reversed the usual expectation of radio entertainment flowing from city to country.[50]

An early, detailed appreciation of *The Lawsons* came from Edward D. Breillat of northern New South Wales, who was concerned that 'most people are prone to take much for granted, or are stinting in praise and lavish in criticism'.[51] As Blair observes, it is telling that even letters professing to dislike *The Lawsons* indicated some knowledge of its characters and storylines.[52] Suggestions for alternative plot twists were common, with one university employee even suggesting a tie-in with the BBC's long-running serial, *The Archers*.[53] *Blue Hills* also provided a place for discussion for 'mildly controversial' social issues, including the assimilation of Aborigines.[54]

When the *Country Women's Session* moved into *Blue Hills*' slot on one day of the week in 1953, host Lorna Byrne received many 'insulting' letters.[55] When the actress who played Hilda, Nellie Lamport, died in 1969, Meredith sent off the character to Tasmania for an extended visit rather than distress listeners by 'killing her off'.[56] 'Probably you receive hundreds and hundreds of fan letters', Mrs Laurie East from suburban Melbourne wrote self-consciously in 1973:

> I've never written a fan letter in my life ... tonight I would [just] like to tell you how much I value the pleasure you bring. 'Blue Hills' is a lovely clean story of decent people in this world today.[57]

When Meredith decided to wind up *Blue Hills* four years later, there was widespread grief. Amongst several boxes of letters from listeners in Meredith's own papers are three plumb folders of 'Correspondence relating to "drawing Blue Hills to a close"'.[58] One listener documented the momentousness of the event: 'On the day when men landed on the moon, a hush came into many homes, as we viewed, per TV, that historic event. Today, another hush fell upon us, as we listened to the final episode of Blue Hills.'[59]

Fan mail could still help to guide programming decisions. The reaction to the 1955 *Guest of Honour* broadcast by F.C. Green, the veteran Clerk of the House of Representatives, was such that the ABC scheduled two more Sunday talks by him.[60] The ABC also ensured that the voluminous fan mail received by the Le Garde Twins, Australia's singing cowboys, was answered and filed during and after the national tour it sponsored, and that fans were sent Christmas cards.[61]

As television began being rolled out in Australia from 1956, viewers debated its merits. Susan Bye has considered the 'duel-by-pen' between fans of Melbourne entertainers Bert Newton (host of HSV7's *The Late Show*) and Graham Kennedy (host of GTV9's *In Melbourne Tonight*) in the late 1950s, focusing on letters to broadcasting periodicals. Bye sees the writing of letters as partly a political act, with viewers forming loose collectives in which they sought to make a difference to what they were watching. She cites the example of the response to GTV9's 1960 decision to slot Panda Lisner back into her nightly barrel spot on *IMT* following her honeymoon. Some listeners bombarded the station with letters and phone calls demanding that Lisner's young fill-in, Elizabeth Scott, be retained. According to *TV Week*, GTV9 executives reconsidered their earlier verdict, deciding they 'had a duty to viewers' and handing Scott two weekly appearances.[62]

'The TV Wedding of 1960', with Kennedy as best man and fans clad in raincoats outside the church, had been televised live. He had to change his silent telephone number every few months because fans and journalists paid money to get hold of it.[63] The State Library of Victoria holds a scrapbook carefully compiled by school-girl Carol Emery, with newspaper clippings of Lisner and Kennedy on the cover and a handwritten index to the clippings, as well as a 'Graham Kennedy Fan Club' card.[64]

From the very beginning, the Australian television industry produced fan cards (photographs signed by personalities designed to boost their profiles) that could be handed out to studio audiences or sent to fans. Amongst the archives of Melbourne's ABC station ABV2 is an early set of fan cards picturing 18 personalities including reporter Gerald Lyons and newsreader Jocelyn Terry.[65] (ABC television stations also soon found themselves receiving letters asking them to settle bets.)[66] Some fan cards—for programs including *The Sullivans* (1976–1983) and *Neighbours* (1985–), as well as personalities—would later make their way onto eBay.

Australian viewers also responded to overseas developments. During a 1959 contract dispute between actor Clint Walker and Warner Bros., fans of *Cheyenne* bombarded TCN9 with petitions, letters and telephone calls pleading for a better deal for the hit Western's star. Letters threatened to boycott the Sydney station if it ever showed an episode with a new lead, Ty Hardin.[67] But an article in *TV Week* suggested that not all viewers realised that some shows were imported. Teenage girls were reported to be writing to stations requesting dates not just with Australian television personalities, but with Americans including Walker and Raymond Burr (star of *Perry Mason*).[68] When American singer Johnnie Ray visited Australia in 1966 and appeared on TCN9's *Tonight* show with Don Lane, television correspondent Nan Musgrove reported on the sacks of fan mail that were carted up to his hotel suite.[69] In a study of mail received by the ABC in 1965, psychologist Alicia Lee found that some teenagers seemed to regard the broadcaster 'as part of the adult world which disapproves of them', and expressed some surprise that it should seek to please them with radio programs like *Pop Opera*.[70]

Australia's 'youngest TV personality', two-year-old Tony Crease, who appeared with his father Kevin on the NWS9 children's program *The Channel Niners*, also received fan mail.[71] So too did 'Florrie Johnson', a cat that hopped up on to the desk during a Saturday-afternoon sports program on QTQ9 soon after the Brisbane station's launch in 1959. The intrusion proved so popular with viewers that QTQ9 gave her a grand name and featured her as a kind of mascot.[72] An even more enduring identity was *Skippy*, the bush kangaroo star of Australia's most successful television export. She received fan mail from all over the world, particularly after she gave birth to a joey in 1972. Woodrow the bloodhound was a kind of mascot for *Simon Townsend's Wonder World* (1979–1987), a children's program on the Ten Network, receiving up to 400 letters a day.[73] Brisbane's BTQ7 was one commercial television station that reproduced fan mail in advertisements as evidence of its popularity.[74]

When George Donikian began reading the news on SBS television, part of Australia's new multicultural network, in 1980, he was flooded by fan mail. Such was the interest in the handsome young newsreader that he began being stopped for autographs, and (in echoes of Kennedy's experience) he received so many phone calls at home he had to change to a silent listing.[75] Even so, another television personality though Australian fans were somewhat more restrained than their overseas counterparts. Val Lehman, star of Ten's *Prisoner*, found that Americans were somewhat 'less inhibited' than Australians in their letters, and was struck by fans picketing a station in New York when it took the drama serial off-air.[76]

In a 1982 article about children's engagement with television, an ABC spokesman reported that children generally responded more when asked to do something, rather than when they were exhorted to simply write in for 'handouts'.[77] When Canberra station 2CN encouraged young listeners to write to Father Christmas via the ABC, some 1000 letters came in a week. Santa replied to each one, and read out some on-air.[78] Some broadcasters' fan mail related to their specific roles. Capital Television's weather presenter Mike Larkin received endless comments about forecasts, along with requests, such as for good windy conditions for a sailing club in three months' time. (But, in something of an echo of Lehman, Larkin also remarked on his surprise when visiting the United States to discover how 'famous' weather presenters were there.)[79]

Ruth Cracknell attracted a substantial mail in response to her role as Maggie Beare in the ABC sitcom *Mother and Son* (1984–1994). ABC colleague Phillip Adams was moved to write his own 'fan letter' in 1985, complementing Cracknell on her 'complex, contradictory and painfully, tragically funny' turn as an older woman with memory loss tormenting her stay-at-home son. When the unlikely hit was criticised by talkback host John Laws, a Queensland nurse sat down to write to a 'complete stranger' to tell Cracknell she found her depiction 'true to life'.[80] Another viewer rang the ABC and spent 20 minutes telling the Head of Publicity why she didn't like the program, criticising it for making a mockery of the aged. When the ABC manager ventured to suggest that perhaps she shouldn't watch *Mother and Son*, the woman retorted 'But I have to watch it, my mother loves it'.[81]

A Sydney woman analysed Maggie as 'a loving and supportive person at the same time as she is devious and manipulative', and 'threatened with loneliness and abandonment'. A viewer from southern Queensland wrote of the importance of Australian entertainment on 'the Box' due to geographical isolation and financial constraints. Children requested photographs, recounted their favourite scenes, told Cracknell about themselves, and begged for replies. One girl wrote simply: 'I think you are excellent on Mother and Son but I couldn't stand to have a mother like you.' (She also attached a certificate she had made 'awarding' the actress a Logie.)[82] A scene showing Maggie dropping oranges from her shopping bag into a freshly dug grave was a particular favourite, even inspiring an independent artist to design a hoodie for sale online.[83]

The satirical program *This Sporting Life* (1986–2008) presented by 'Roy Slaven' (John Doyle) and 'H.G. Nelson' (Greig Pickhaver) on the ABC's youth radio channel (then network), Triple J, attracted a huge fan mail. Pickhaver's papers contain letters from politicians, lawyers, accountants, scientists, waitresses, teachers, students, suburban football players, aspiring broadcasters, academics (a couple working on theses about the program), and at least one pathologist and one marriage celebrant.[84] They documented how they listened: on the lounge, at work, on the train, on ships and in pubs and prisons.

Correspondents wrote in with reports on their local football teams, and named their own teams (for Australian Rules in 'Heaven and Hell', and Rugby League with 'political enigmas'). They christened Roy and H.G. with names such as 'Consorts of Footy Commentary'. Their letters displayed a humorous and intimate knowledge of the pair's lexicon, and poked fun at the sometimes risible phraseology used by sporting commentators. They enclosed snippets from local newspapers, requested outside broadcasts from local grounds, and suggested absurd new sports (like long-distance golf). They penned sample scripts and sent in artwork, from cartoons to calendars, as well as slapstick entries to competitions. They bought the book *Pants Off: This Sporting Life* (1989) and associated merchandise. There were hundreds of requests for birthday greetings and wedding messages, some of which were met by Roy and H.G. ('you had our guests in hysterics').

'A mere fan' who listened to the show with his mates 'for a bit of music, to learn new words, to have a laugh and to get the footy updates', was perturbed by the two-hour time delay from Sydney and asked for the program to be relayed live to Perth. Letters recounted playing with technology, by for example taping the first part of a commentary, then playing it back with the television on mute to avoid the 'ramblings of "Big Dazza"' (Darryl Eastlake) on Channel 9. Another correspondent, from Sydney, penned an unflattering 'ode' to 'The Ubiquitous Kenny' (Nine Network sports anchor Ken Sutcliffe). One Melbourne fan ('The Dobber') informed the pair their act was being 'sabotaged' by a commercial FM station, with a character called 'Mick' who seemed to be based on HG Nelson.[85] The letters inspired by *This Sporting Life* and the associated radio and television endeavours of Roy and H.G. contain numerous reflections on other aspects of Australian broadcasting, and sports media, during this period.

The mail shows listeners following the pair to television. One fan wrote of the ABC's *Club Buggery* (1995–1997) being the highlight of his week: 'I have long since forgone the pleasures of a Saturday night out to ensure possession of the prime armchair come 9.30.' But at least one listener thought Roy and H.G. were selling out, declaring that '*T.S.L.* was a bastion of Australia, pure Aussie grit, often obscure, often exciting and always genuine' and regretting that they seemed to be succumbing to the commercial pressures of television and 'mass produced idiot humour'. Other audience members proposed whole new programs, such as a spoof equine drama with television game show host Ian Turpie (a good-natured target of, and then participant in, the levity): 'As "Blue Hills" did it for the ABC in the past, "Turps About the Horse" will do it for Aunty [the ABC] again!'

There seems to have been little criticism, and along the lines of this in a Valentine's Day card: 'I find you two absolutely lewd, crude, & unrefined, disgusting at times, and <u>absolutely gorgeous</u>'. One Queensland correspondent cut through the blokeyness of the endeavour, asking the pair to extend their banter to cover women's Rugby League. When another listener, who had 'feigned headaches and funerals' to not miss an episode, thought *Club Buggery* wasn't coming back, 'well the bottom dropped out of my life'. An electricity blackout would lead to requests for repeats. There were laments about no longer being able to listen or watch when fans found themselves 'marooned' on the Great Barrier Reef, or overseas. Some fathers were pressed into recording and mailing episodes to their expatriate sons.

In 2006, 21-year-old Stuart McMillen started a Wikipedia entry on an 'Australian cultural institution': Roy and H.G.'s annual call of three 'State of Origin' Rugby League matches. 'They were my favourite three nights of the year. ... I would turn on the Channel 9 TV coverage of the football game, and mute the audio', McKinnon later recalled. He found the pair's call, in the language of club football dressing sheds, the perfect antidote to the 'self-important, overblown' and corporatised commentary of Nine's experts.[86]

Following the fan mail trail has the capacity to expand and enhance our understanding of radio and television history, more probably in a qualitative than a quantitative sense. Searching out and recovering the writings— whether unsolicited or solicited—of active consumers of Australian broadcasting (and industry responses to this writing) can shed light on why people listened or watched; what they consumed (given the fragmentary and piecemeal archival record of actual broadcast production); what people valued in programs and performers; how they responded to and used media technologies; and how they negotiated social, cultural and political issues.

Notes

1. Jack Win, 'The broadcasting mail bag', *Wireless Weekly* (*WW*), 27 January 1928, pp. 5–6.
2. Bill Kirkpatrick, '"A blessed boon": Radio, disability, governmentality, and the discourse of the "shut-in," 1920–1930', *Critical Studies in Media Communication*, 29(3) (2012), pp. 165–84.
3. Win 1928, p. 5.
4. Roland Marchand, *Advertising the American Dream: Making Way for Modernity, 1920–1940* (Berkeley: University of California Press, 1985), p. 93.
5. *Daily Standard*, 21 November 1931, p. 7; *Truth*, 8 May 1932, p. 21.
6. *WW*, 24 November 1933, p. 8.
7. *Mercury*, 24 October 1950, p. 14.
8. Lesley Johnson, *The Unseen Voice* (London: Routledge, 1988), pp. 96–97; Bridget Griffen-Foley, *Changing Stations: The Story of Australian Commercial Radio* (Sydney: UNSW Press, 2009), p. 213.
9. *Kalgoorlie Miner*, 4 January 1934, p. 3.
10. W.A. McNair, *Radio Advertising in Australia* (Sydney: Angus & Robertson, 1937) pp. 279–83.
11. McNair 1937, pp. 259–60.
12. *Courier-Mail*, 28 August 1934, p. 12; L. Fitz-Henry, 'Letters from radio listeners help the broadcaster', *Sunday Mail*, 24 February 1935, p. 9. See also the 'programme plebiscite' in *WW*, 21 March 1940, p. 4.
13. Isabelle Grace, 'Favorites of the air get fan mail', *WW*, 10 July 1936, p. 13.
14. J.M. Prentice, 'The radio announcer's mail bag', *Radio Pictorial of Australia* (*RPA*), 1 December 1935, pp. 15, 36.
15. *Australian Women's Weekly* (*AWW*), 24 July 1937, p. 36.
16. *RPA*, 1 June 1937, pp. 5, 21.
17. *WW*, 3 April 1936, p. 26 and 31 May 1939, p. 7; *ABC Weekly*, 2 August 1947, p. 9.
18. *RPA*, 1 January 1937, p. 47; *Kyogle Examiner*, 26 February 1937, p. 2.
19. *Labor Daily*, 4 November 1938, p. 2; *Daily Telegraph*, 4 November 1938, p. 5.
20. See Elihu Katz, 'The happiness game: A content analysis of radio fan mail', *International Journal of Communication*, vol. 6, no. 1, 2012, pp. 1297–45.
21. *Newcastle Sun*, 5 November 1938, p. 7.

22. *Commercial Broadcasting*, 11 April 1940, p. 2.
23. See, for example, photographs of 2GB children's host Jim Max with letters to his competitions, *RPA*, 1 November 1941, p. 37.
24. Goodie Reeve, 'Men write to her', *WW*, 5 March 1937, pp. 4–5.
25. *RPA*, 1 October 1937, pp. 6–7, 46, 48; *WW*, 10 March 1939, p. 4.
26. State Library of Victoria: PA02/07, Norman Banks Records, Box 13, 'Salesmanship'.
27. *Daily Telegraph*, 8 May 1939, p. 10; K.S. Inglis, *This Is the ABC: The Australian Broadcasting Commission, 1932–1983* (Melbourne: Melbourne University Press, 1983), p. 61.
28. *WW*, 4 November 1939, p. 7. Other country music performers also proved popular. Fan mail in response to Gordon Kirkpatrick's appearances on 2KM Kempsey persuaded him to adopt the name 'Slim Dusty'; see Slim Dusty and Joy McKean, *Slim Dusty* (Sydney: Pan Macmillan, 2003 edn), pp. 21–34.
29. *WW*, 27 September 1941, p. 23; *Pittsworth Sentinel*, 4 June 1948, p. 1.
30. *Merredin Mercury and Central Districts Index*, 11 September 1941, p. 2.
31. *RPA*, 1 March 1945, p. 9.
32. *RPA*, 1 July 1938, p. 48.
33. Jeannette Sayre, 'Progress in radio fan-mail analysis', *Public Opinion Quarterly*, 3(2) (April 1939), pp. 272–78.
34. Charlene Simmons, 'Dear radio broadcaster: Fan mail as a form of perceived interactivity', *Journal of Broadcasting & Electronic Media*, 53(3) (2009), pp. 444–59.
35. Catharine Fisher, 'Broadcasting the woman citizen: Dame Enid Lyons' Macquarie Network talks', *Lilith: A Feminist History Journal*, 23 (2017), pp. 34–46; National Library of Australia (NLA): MS 4852, Dame Enid Lyons Papers, Box 8, File: Correspondence re broadcasts.
36. See State Library of Victoria: MS9824Y Bernard Heinze Records, Folder: Children's Concerts—Letters of Appreciation, 1941–1942. See also Inglis 1983, p. 10; *Sydney Morning Herald*, 10 June 1941, p. 10.
37. Heinze Records, Folder: Prof. Heinze—Children's Concerts—Appreciation, 1943–1944, letter from Heinze to Mrs Phyllis E. Price, 17 May 1943.
38. *ABC Weekly*, 25 May 1946, p. 2.
39. *Kyogle Examiner*, 24 September 1946, p. 2.
40. Albert Moran and Chris Keating, *Historical Dictionary of Australian Radio and Television* (Lanham, Maryland: Scarecrow Press, 2007), p. 285.
41. *Barrier Miner*, 14 July 1947, p. 4.
42. L. Bogart in Simmons 2009, p. 449.
43. *Brisbane Telegraph*, 27 April 1950, p. 3.

44. Michelle Arrow, 'Howell, Edward Welsford (Teddy)', *Australian Dictionary of Biography*, National Centre of Biography, Australian National University, http://adb.anu.edu.au/biography/howell-edward-welsford-teddy-12660/text22815, published in 2007, accessed 16 August 2019.
45. State Library of NSW (SLNSW): MLMSS 7081, Edward Howell Papers, Box 1, Folder: Correspondence 1949–1983, letter from E.V. Copeman to Howell, 2 October 1953.
46. J.H. Adams, 'Radio Roundup', *Sun* (Sydney), 20 July 1954, p. 19.
47. NLA: MS 6789, Gwen Meredith Papers, Box 10, Folder C, letter from Marjorie Caw to Meredith, 1 September 1976.
48. Sayre 1939, p. 272.
49. Michelle Arrow, '"Good entertainment & good family life": Listener readings and responses to Gwen Meredith's *The Lawsons* and *Blue Hills*', *Journal of Australian Studies*, 22(58) (1998), pp. 38–47.
50. Megan Blair, 'Listening in to The Lawsons: Radio crosses the urban-rural divide', in Graeme Davison and Marc Brodie (eds.). *Struggle Country: The Rural Ideal in Twentieth Century Australia* (Clayton Vic, Monash University ePress, 2005), pp. 0.71–0.719.
51. NLA: MS 6789, Gwen Meredith Papers, Box 10, Folder C, letter from Breillat to Meredith, 31 August 1946.
52. Blair 2005, p. 0.713.
53. NLA: MS 6789, Meredith Papers, Box 8, Folder E, letter from Maisie Fock to Meredith, 31 May 1972; Box 10, Folder B, letter from Harry Torr to Meredith, 30 September 1953.
54. Arrow 1998, p. 43; see also Arrow, '"The most sickening piece of snobbery I have ever heard": Race, radio listening, and the "Aboriginal question" in *Blue Hills*', *Australian Historical Studies*, 38(130) (2007), pp. 244–60.
55. Catherine Fisher, 'Sound Citizens: The Public Voices of Australian Women Broadcasters, 1923–1956', PhD thesis (Australian National University, 2018), pp. 282–84.
56. Blair 2005, p. 0.714.
57. NLA: MS 6789, Meredith Papers, Box 8, Folder B, letter from Mrs Laurie East to Meredith, 19 September 1973.
58. NLA: MS 6789, Meredith Papers, Box 12, Folders B–D.
59. Arrow 1998, p. 45.
60. *Canberra Times*, 20 October 1955, p. 7.
61. *Farmer and Settler*, 4 February 1955, p. 14; *ABC Weekly*, 3 December 1958, p. 8.
62. Susan Bye, 'Debating the barrel girl: The rise and fall of Panda Lisner', *Media International Australia*, 131 (May 2009), pp. 117–26.

63. Graeme Blundell, *King: The Life and Comedy of Graham Kennedy* (Sydney: Pan Macmillan, 2003), pp. 166, 210.
64. Carol Emery, 'Graham Kennedy and Panda', scrapbook held by State Library of Victoria.
65. National Film and Sound Archive: 741067, ABV2 Set of 18 Fan Cards, c. 1956.
66. *TV Week* (Sydney), 11 April 1959, pp. 16–17.
67. *AWW*, 8 April 1959, p. 58.
68. *TV Week* (Sydney), 11 April 1959, pp. 16–17.
69. Nan Musgrove, 'Fans still cry over Johnnnie Ray', *AWW*, 23 February 1966, p. 19.
70. NAA/NSW: C1175, 6, Alicia Lee, 'The Writing Public: A Study of Audience Correspondence' (1966), p. 24.
71. *TV Week* (Adelaide), 17 February 1960, pp. 16–17.
72. *AWW*, 4 May 1960, p. 71.
73. *Canberra Times*, 16 December 1972, p. 15 and 12 April 1986, p. 8.
74. *Broadcasting and Television Year Book* (Sydney: Greater Publications, 1968), p. 176.
75. Julie McGlone, 'George pays price of fame', *AWW*, 14 January 1981, p. 20.
76. Clay Adams, 'Val cuts through the times', *AWW*, 24 June 1981, p. 140.
77. Deidre Macpherson, 'How to thumb your nose at purists', *SMH* (The Guide), 23 August 1982, p. 2.
78. Rohan Greenland, 'Radio', *Canberra Times*, 10 December 1984, p. 25.
79. *Canberra Times*, 17 December 1990, p. 21.
80. NLA: MS 9848, Ruth Cracknell Papers, Box 2, Folders 9–15; Box 3, Folders 16–17.
81. Geoffrey Atherden, *Mother and Son: Five Award-winning Scripts from the ABC TV Series* (Sydney: ABC Books, 2001 edn), pp. 6–7.
82. NLA: MS 9848, Ruth Cracknell Papers, Box 2, Folders 9–15; Box 3, Folders 16–17.
83. https://www.teepublic.com/en-au/hoodie/2683097-mother-and-son-roadside-oranges, accessed 10 March 2020.
84. SLNSW: MLMSS 7035, Greig Pickhaver Further Papers, 1988–1995, Box 3; MLMSS 7094, Greig Pickhaver Further Papers and Video Recordings, 1991–1997, Boxes 6–7; MLMSS 7632, Greig Pickhaver Further Papers, 1996–1999, Boxes 3–4.
85. The breakfast program appears to have been presented by the 'D-Generation' on Eon-FM (not FOX-FM as stated in the letter).
86. Stuart McMillen, 'Roy and H.G.'s State of Origin commentary' (2014), http://www.stuartmcmillen.com/blog/roy-hg-state-of-origin-commentary/, accessed 10 March 2020.

Bibliography

ABC Weekly.
Adams, Clay. 'Val cuts through the times', *Australian Women's Weekly*, 24 June 1981, p. 140.
Adams, J.H. 'Radio Roundup', *Sun* (Sydney), 20 July 1954, p. 19.
Arrow, Michelle. '"Good entertainment & good family life": Listener readings and responses to Gwen Meredith's *The Lawsons* and *Blue Hills*', *Journal of Australian Studies*, 22(58) (1998), pp. 38–47.
———. 'Howell, Edward Welsford (Teddy)', *Australian Dictionary of Biography*, National Centre of Biography, Australian National University, http://adb.anu.edu.au/biography/howell-edward-welsford-teddy-12660/text22815, published in 2007a, accessed 16 August 2019.
———. '"The most sickening piece of snobbery I have ever heard": Race, radio listening, and the "Aboriginal question" in *Blue Hills*', *Australian Historical Studies*, 38(130) (2007b), pp. 244–60.
Atherden, Geoffrey. *Mother and Son: Five Award-winning Scripts from the ABC TV Series* (Sydney: ABC Books, 2001 edn), pp. 6–7.
Australian Women's Weekly (AWW).
Barrier Miner.
Blair, Megan. 'Listening in to The Lawsons: Radio crosses the urban-rural divide', in Graeme Davison and Marc Brodie (eds.). *Struggle Country: The Rural Ideal in Twentieth Century Australia* (Clayton Vic, Monash University ePress, 2005), pp. 0.71–0.719.
Brisbane Telegraph.
Broadcasting and Television Year Book (Sydney: Greater Publications, 1968).
Bye, Susan. 'Debating the barrel girl: The rise and fall of Panda Lisner', *Media International Australia*, 131 (May 2009), pp. 117–26.
Canberra Times.
Commercial Broadcasting.
Courier-Mail (Brisbane).
Cumberland Argus and Fruitgrowers Advocate.
Daily Standard (Brisbane).
Daily Telegraph (Sydney).
Dusty, Slim and McKean, Joy. *Slim Dusty* (Sydney: Pan Macmillan, 2003 edn).
Emery, Carol. 'Graham Kennedy and Panda', scrapbook held by State Library of Victoria.
Farmer and Settler.
Fisher, Catharine. 'Broadcasting the woman citizen: Dame Enid Lyons' Macquarie Network talks', *Lilith: A Feminist History Journal*, 23 (2017), pp. 34–46.
———. 'Sound Citizens: The Public Voices of Australian Women Broadcasters, 1923–1956', PhD thesis (Australian National University, 2018).

Fitz-Henry, L. 'Letters from radio listeners help the broadcaster', *Sunday Mail* (Brisbane), 24 February 1935, p. 9.
Grace, Isabelle. 'Favorites of the air get fan mail', *WW*, 10 July 1936, p. 13.
Greenland, Rohan. 'Radio', *Canberra Times*, 10 December 1984, p. 25.
Griffen-Foley, Bridget. *Changing Stations: The Story of Australian Commercial Radio* (Sydney: UNSW Press, 2009).
Inglis, K.S. *This Is the ABC: The Australian Broadcasting Commission, 1932–1983* (Melbourne: Melbourne University Press, 1983).
Johnson, Lesley. *The Unseen Voice* (London: Routledge, 1988).
Kalgoorlie Miner.
Katz, Elihu. 'The happiness game: A content analysis of radio fan mail', *International Journal of Communication*, 6(1) (2012), pp. 1297–445.
Kirkpatrick, Bill. '"A blessed boon": Radio, disability, governmentality, and the discourse of the "shut-in," 1920–1930', *Critical Studies in Media Communication*, 29(3) (2012), pp. 165–84, https://doi.org/10.1080/15295036.2011.631554.
Kyogle Examiner.
Macpherson, Deidre. 'How to thumb your nose at purists', *SMH* (The Guide), 23 August 1982, p. 2.
Marchand, Roland. *Advertising the American Dream: Making Way for Modernity, 1920–1940* (Berkeley: University of California Press, 1985), p. 93.
McGlone, Julie. 'George pays price of fame', *AWW*, 14 January 1981, p. 20.
McMillen, Stuart. 'Roy and H.G.'s State of Origin commentary' (2014), http://www.stuartmcmillen.com/blog/roy-hg-state-of-origin-commentary/, accessed 10 March 2020.
McNair, W.A. *Radio Advertising in Australia* (Sydney: Angus & Robertson, 1937).
Mercury (Hobart).
Merredin Mercury and Central Districts Index.
Moran, Albert and Keating, Chris. *Historical Dictionary of Australian Radio and Television* (Lanham, Maryland: Scarecrow Press, 2007).
Musgrove, Nan. 'Fans still cry over Johnnnie Ray', *AWW*, 23 February 1966, p. 19.
National Archives of Australia/NSW: C1175, 6, The Writing Public 1966 (Box 1).
National Film and Sound Archive: 741067, ABV2 Set of 18 Fan Cards, c. 1956.
National Library of Australia (NLA). MS 4852, Dame Enid Lyons Papers.
———. MS 6789, Gwen Meredith Papers.
———. MS 9848, Ruth Cracknell Papers.
Newcastle Sun.
Pittsworth Sentinel.
Prentice, J.M. 'The radio announcer's mail bag', *Radio Pictorial of Australia*, 1 December 1935, pp. 15, 36.
Radio Pictorial of Australia (RPA).
Reeve, Goodie. 'Men write to her', *Wireless Weekly*, 5 March 1937, pp. 4–5.

Sayre, Jeannette. 'Progress in radio fan-mail analysis', *Public Opinion Quarterly*, 3(2) (April 1939), pp. 272–78.
Senate Official Hansard, No. 29, 1945, pp. 4123–45.
Simmons, Charlene. 'Dear radio broadcaster: Fan mail as a form of perceived interactivity', *Journal of Broadcasting & Electronic Media*, 53(3) (2009), pp. 444–59.
Sun (Sydney).
State Library of NSW (SLNSW). MLMSS 7081, Edward Howell Papers.
———. MLMSS 7035, Greig Pickhaver Further Papers.
———. MLMSS 7094, Greig Pickhaver Further Papers and Video Recordings.
———. MLMSS 7632, Greig Pickhaver Further Papers.
State Library of Victoria. MS9824Y, Bernard Heinze Records.
———. PA02/07, Norman Banks Records.
Sunday Mail (Brisbane).
Truth (Brisbane).
TV Week (Adelaide).
TV Week (Sydney).
Weekly Times (Melbourne).
Win, Jack. 'The broadcasting mail bag', *Wireless Weekly*, 27 January 1928, pp. 5–6.
Wireless Weekly (*WW*).

CHAPTER 5

Outrage and Complaint

Abstract Just as Australian broadcasters attracted fan mail, so too did they attract letters of complaint. This chapter surveys some of the letters and telephone calls of complaint received by radio stations and personalities, broadcasting periodicals, the Australian Broadcasting Commission and the Postmaster-General's Department. It then delves into the complaints files of the Australian Broadcasting Control Board, which was responsible for most aspects of broadcasting regulation between 1949 and 1977. The chapter considers what sorts of listeners and viewers were motivated to complain; the relative preoccupations of complainants; and how the regulator, and radio and television stations themselves, viewed, handled and responded to complaints.

Keywords Complaints • Radio • Television • Australian Broadcasting Commission • Broadcasting regulation • Audiences

Who Complains?, asked Australian Broadcasting Tribunal researchers Kate Aisbett, Kathryn Paterson and Milica Loncar in 1992.[1] Just as Australian broadcasters attracted fan mail, so too did they complaints. Listeners and viewers wrote to (and sometimes telephoned) stations and personalities, the Australian Broadcasting Commission (ABC) and broadcasting periodicals. Many complaints went to regulators, beginning with the

Postmaster-General's (PMG) Department and then the Australian Broadcasting Control Board (ABCB). This chapter examines broadcasting complaints since the late 1920s, with a particular focus on little-explored ABCB files between 1949 and 1977. The chapter considers what sorts of listeners and viewers were motivated to complain; the relative preoccupations of complainants (including advertising, violence and sex); and how the Board, and broadcasters themselves, viewed, handled and responded to complaints.

A radio conference in 1924 agreed that Australia should have a dual system, with A-class stations funded by licence fees, and B-class stations to operate privately. Industry periodicals enabled critics to vent their dissatisfaction with programs, as well as to highlight their favourites. In its first issue for 1927, Sydney's *Wireless Weekly* published two pages by a 'Man with a Grouch', whose irritants included radio Uncles ('a riot of unoriginality') and women's session presenters who described what their fashionable sisters were wearing.[2]

As radio became more of a broadcast medium, periodicals gradually focused less on technical aspects (including poor reception) and more on content.[3] 'Safety Valve', launched by *Wireless Weekly* in 1927, was one of the earliest columns to run readers' letters. The editor anticipated that the column would build on suggestions that came in privately from readers about what they wanted from the magazine. However, the letters of 'commendation and condemnation' that were now solicited also allowed listeners, as well as readers, to comment on programs and stations.[4] Listeners debated issues, such as whether religious broadcasts were helpful for people prevented from going to church by sickness or family obligations, or whether more variety should be provided for most people's only day of leisure.[5] Topics were suggested by readers, or triggered by editorials. Debates could continue over weeks or months, and were sometimes revisited. In 1931, there was much discussion again about religious broadcasting, with complaints about unfamiliar hymns and tedious sermons (Fig. 5.1).[6]

B-class stations initially appeared as largely a residual category in planning, but in 1930 the PMG's Department issued new regulations governing their operations, including advertising. In 1931, departmental secretary H.P. Brown noted that stations run by newspaper, manufacturing, political and religious interests were 'thriving'. Advertising on what were to become known as 'commercial' stations was to emerge as a frequent target of attack. Many listeners were simply irritated by the volume,

5 OUTRAGE AND COMPLAINT   77

Fig. 5.1   *Wireless Weekly*, 26 December 1930. (Copyright Silicon Chip Publishing)

with correspondents to periodicals suggesting that no more than four ads should be broadcast per hour. One Sydney listener contended that 2GB only put on records to give 'the announcer a breather between advertisements'.[7]

Letters like this contradicted the buoyant 1933 appraisal of a contributor to *Rydge's*: 'Broadcasting can be made to create ... intimate goodwill in a friendly and unobtrusive way without causing offence, and rather bringing about a feeling of gratitude and pleasing obligation.'[8] Radio was also already thought of as an intrusion into the private domain; two years after her own family acquired a receiver in suburban Sydney, middle-aged writer Miles Franklin was complaining about a neighbour's radio keeping her awake.[9]

Australian listeners engaged in a fierce cultural debate about the comparative merits of the two broadcasting sectors.[10] Some listeners were

Fig. 5.2 *Wireless Weekly*, 9 December 1932. (Copyright William Edwin Pidgeon/Copyright Agency, 2019)

convinced that A-class stations (consolidated into the ABC in 1932) were superior to their commercial cousins. Some argued that while public broadcasting offered high-quality music and improving talks, commercial stations divided programs into 'jerky, quarter-hour sugar-coated tablets for the conveyance of commercial propaganda'. A correspondent sniffily asserted that it would be 'unfair to expect factory-hands, laborers, navvies, etc., to understand and enjoy music and speech that are natural to men of professional status' (Fig. 5.2).[11]

Producing Australian drama for radio was expensive, and required new skills from playwrights and producers (and even listeners, who were sometimes urged to turn down the lights in their homes to listen to plays). Thrillers, readily enabling the exploitation of sound effects, became commonplace.[12] Listeners to *The Crime Game* on 4BH complained about interruptions necessitated by the Brisbane commercial station's coverage of the Ashes: 'We can pick up our papers on Saturday morning and for the small sum of twopence read all about the cricket thrills … but we cannot for even a thousand twopences again the thrills of the radio thriller.'[13]

But the sensational content of thrillers also concerned government, legal and religious figures. While the ABC imposed restrictions on coarse expression and representations of sex and insanity, commercial stations, in their bid for listeners, were less censorious.[14] In 1934 the PMG's Department compiled a file of newspaper editorials and letters to the editor, and excerpts from a New South Wales parliamentary debate, about thrillers. A Labor member of parliament, R.J. Heffron, was concerned about the effect of screams and murders on the minds of young people, especially before they went to bed. *Tarzan of the Apes* was the subject of some discussion, with the toothpaste sponsor Pepsodent asking listeners to write in if the program should continue. Melbourne commercial station 3KZ advised the Department that 12,000 letters were received over ten days, and the response to Sydney's 2GB was similar. (This was due in part to the promise of a Tarzan game being sent in return; as we saw in Chap. 4, what was sometimes presented as 'fan mail' came in response to solicitations.) PMG inspectors who listened to *Tarzan* thought it harmless entertainment, and in a minute paper Brown wrote about the responsibility of parents to monitor what their children were listening to.[15]

Listeners disturbed by radio content did not always distinguish between the broadcasting sectors. In October Ern H. Moroney from suburban Sydney 'humbly' wrote to ABC chairman W.J. Cleary about blood-curdling murders on commercial stations: 'I have 2 children, both under 11 and they go mad to listen to these stories and it causes quite a lot of unhappiness in my home when the wireless is switched off.' Moroney obviously confused the 'Australian Broadcasting Commission' with an industry body or regulator. Cleary forwarded the letter to the PMG's Department, which replied to Moroney saying that comments on thrillers demonstrated that it was impossible to always please everyone, and to point out that Sydney listeners had a choice of eight stations.[16]

Commercial stations sometimes exercised self-censorship, which in turn could lead to protests by telephone and mail. In 1935 listeners complained to the PMG about 6ML Perth's refusal to broadcast a talk by Judge Rutherford, the forthright American head of the Jehovah's Witnesses. As the Department advised the complainants (whom they presumed to be members of the 'sect'), the handling of broadcasts of a controversial nature was up to individual stations, not the PMG.[17]

World War II brought an increase in the proportion of radio time occupied by news. The ABC's 7 pm bulletin quickly became an institution.

When the new Department of Information (DoI) assumed responsibility for it in June 1940, many listeners complained that bulletins were stale and propagandist. They were quickly returned to the ABC.[18] As news punctured the day, some leading citizens complained to the Director-General of Information, Sir Keith Murdoch, about repetition and about worrying workers. Murdoch's response to retailer (and inaugural ABC chairman) Charles Lloyd Jones was to loftily ask whether it would be fair to 'restrict the number of emissions because some listeners cannot keep away from the microphone, and, in effect, do not impose any self-discipline'.[19]

There was also a debate about German and Italian classical music. As early as November 1939, T. Lee from Sydney was complaining to the DoI that playing German music amounted to an admission that 'the Enemy' excelled. In June 1940 the Department banned foreign-language broadcasting due to the military situation, leading to some confusion about whether this extended to music. Mrs M. Larsen rang 2KO Newcastle to complain about the broadcast of German opera and folk songs. Dissatisfied with the response ('all I got for my trouble was that I must be very patriotic'), she wrote to the Department asserting that 'the language ... can not be tolerated at the present time'. W. Macmahon Ball, the DOI's director of short-wave broadcasting and a prominent intellectual, was enraged, instructing the Department to write back saying that Beethoven, Mozart and Bach had no connection with Nazism: 'They are part of the common culture of Western civilisation which we are fighting to preserve.'[20]

Meanwhile, in 1940 the Good Film League was renamed the Good Film and Radio Vigilance League of New South Wales.[21] Affiliated with the Women's Christian Temperance Union, it had a particular interest in children's sessions, and in 1941 launched a 'campaign' for radio purity.[22] A Parliamentary Joint Committee on Wireless Broadcasting (the 'Gibson Committee') inquired into radio in 1941–1942. It heard evidence that some broadcasters had been lax in selecting program material, notwithstanding periodic warnings from the PMG. The Federation of Australian Radio Broadcasters (FARB) tried to highlight the self-regulation exercised by commercial stations: the proscription of 'obscene and off-colour jokes ... oaths, sacrilegious expressions, and anything of doubtful propriety' and, in children's programs, 'remarks derogatory to good morals'.[23]

Commercial broadcasters trod a fine line, appreciating the need for what advertising executive George Patterson labelled 'tricks', but fearing greater broadcasting regulation and perhaps sanctions, from fines and boycotts of sponsors' products to the suspension of performers and the cancellation of licences.[24] Comedy scripts were usually carefully vetted by station employees like Sam See, armed with a red pencil, at Sydney's 2UE.[25] The Colgate-Palmolive Radio Production Unit learned that while scripts may have seemed fine in rehearsal, an inflection during a live broadcast could make a joke 'blue'.[26]

In early 1942 J.M. Michel, from a pastoral station in Western Australia, complained of overhearing a woman crying (presumably in a drama or thriller) on a radio on the other side of the wall. The set seems to have been listened to by his son, but instead of asking the boy to turn it down, Michel wrote to 'Mr the Postmaster General' imploring him to stop that 'cursed woman':

> if I knew her name and address I would send her a packet of Cyanide or Strychnine or a rope to hang herself or a knife to cut her neck ... if the Japs come bombing in Australia I hope they get that woman alone and no one else.

The PMG's Senior Radio Inspector for Perth, E.L. Greig, wrote to ask for details of the station and specifics of the broadcasts, but seems not to have heard back.[27]

This was a crucial year in broadcast complaint handling. The Gibson Committee recommended that legislation governing the ABC, and existing regulations for the commercial sector, be combined into one act.[28] It also recommended that the minister should have powers to punish those who selected or passed objectionable items for broadcast.[29] Labor PMG Senator W.P. Ashley informed H.S. Harvey, who had complained about a Jack Davey sketch on 2GB in May, while the broadcasting bill was being debated, that ABC and commercial stations were offering the 'fullest cooperation' with a measure that would result in 'fewer causes for complaint'.[30] Section 91 of the *Australian Broadcasting Act*, which became law on 12 June, stipulated that stations were not to broadcast any matter that was blasphemous, indecent or obscene. Under section 92, persons who broadcast or passed objectionable items could be suspended or banned from broadcasting.[31]

Following the passing of the new Act, the Department sent a circular to all stations requesting adequate precautions to avoid the transmission of objectionable items.[32] Correspondence following on from Harvey's complaint revealed that the Department regarded 2GB as one of the three 'worst offending' stations. With all parties trying to navigate the new terrain, the Chief Inspector of Wireless, J.M. Martin, called on 2GB's general manager. H.G. Horner was somewhat alarmed by the developing situation, assuring Martin that he was in discussions with Patterson and the Colgate-Palmolive Unit to ensure there would be no recurrence. Horner did however gingerly suggest that comments by 'our lady friends' from the Vigilance League, as well as a disgruntled actor, had helped to keep 2GB in the 'unpleasant limelight'.[33]

3DB was almost certainly the second of the stations that troubled the Department. (It is not entirely clear which was the third culprit.) '[E]ven a bullock driver would have blushed at the unadulterated filth' on 3DB's *George Wallace Show*, Mrs Jane Keon complained to the PMG. Although an official concluded that the material was no more crude than 'in the usual manner of a comedian of the vaudeville stage', the station attracted other complaints. In August Martin referred 2KY, 3DB and 3KZ scripts to the Deputy Crown Solicitor, who advised that a court would be unlikely to regard them as indecent or obscene.[34] While this early test of the Act suggested that sections 91 and 92 could require a high burden of proof, the legislation put broadcasters on notice. They would also have been mindful of the hostile attitude towards the media held by Labor's Arthur Calwell, who chaired the Parliamentary Standing Committee on Broadcasting (PSCB) created under the Act.[35]

Broadcasters and the PMG continued to receive complaints about a range of matters. The NSW Council of Churches warned that radio could help break down 'Christian civilisation' with broadcasts of sporting results, and advertisements for dances, on Sundays.[36] In late 1942 the Gibson Committee's first occasional report, about education, led to some attention to 'incorrect English' and 'parodies of Australian speech and character'. When the PMG's Department sought input from state education departments, *Dad and Dave*, based on Steele Rudd's comic stories about a Queensland farming family, was singled out for exaggerating 'the mistakes in speech of the most ignorant people one could imagine'. Horner defended the series, arguing that speaking in dialect had been a feature of comedy since the time of Shakespeare. He was backed up by 3DB's David Worrall: 'It would be absurd to put Oxford English into a rustic character like Dad.' Letters about poor pronunciation from people such as stockbrokers further hinted at a class divide amongst Australian listeners.[37]

In July 1945 Brisbane's *Courier-Mail* described the 'fan mail' received by the PMG, Senator Donald Cameron, as both 'abusive and congratulatory'. The report was inspired by the minister's decision to suspend for three months four artists attached to the Colgate-Palmolive Unit following a broadcast which he deemed 'objectionable' on the grounds of vulgar humour. Cameron quoted listeners who agreed that the air needed 'cleaning up', as well as condemnations of his 'dictatorial intolerance'.[38]

Surviving minutes (1945–1955) of the Good Film and Radio Vigilance League document members being rostered on to listen to programs in Sydney. They listened mainly to commercial stations, which worried them more than the ABC. On encountering instances of too many murders, too much drinking or suggestive lyrics, the League would despatch letters of protest, and sometimes try to meet with sponsors of offending sessions. But it also wrote to stations praising wholesome sessions, such as a 2GB program on the Book of Genesis. Broadcasters, in turn, endeavoured to maintain good relations with the League, with 2UW inviting members to tour the AWA Tower, Sydney's tallest building.[39]

As we shall see in Chap. 6, the *Australian Broadcasting Act* of 1948 established the ABCB to ensure the provision of radio (and future television) services in accordance with plans approved by the minister.[40] The Board began compiling files of 'Complaints and Criticisms' on issues (including advertising, audience participation and objectionable items), genres (including news and talk) and, where it seemed warranted, on individual radio and then also television stations and programs.[41]

In the lead-up to the 1949 election, the Board was confronted by the controversial question of the Liberal Party's dramatisations of political matter. Its clumsy order concerning the allocation of time to political interests was rescinded when it became apparent that it would not pass through the Senate. This complex episode brought the limitations of the ABCB's powers into sharp focus. The Board survived by ensuring it did not offend the government of the day or powerful interests, and discreetly avoiding any confrontation with the ABC over its programs.[42] Allegations of bias, or a lack of balance, by broadcasting stations, particularly the ABC, are beyond the scope of this chapter.

From its second annual report, the ABCB included 'Broadcasting of Objectionable Items' as a heading.[43] The 1950–1951 report credited the vigilance of broadcasters in excluding material to which offence might be taken, and revealed that monitors at Post Office observation centres in each capital city devoted 7000 hours to listening to observe the quality of services and detect any breaches of the Act.[44] Future reports did not include this detail, and it seems likely that the hours declined due to resourcing pressures.

By 1951–1952 the ABCB was preoccupied with ensuring that broadcasters provided an 'adequate and comprehensive' service. It was irritated by too many sporting sessions on at the same time, and too many quiz and 'giveaway' programs.[45] Competitions could also cause consternation for listeners and contestants. In 1946 Sydney labour station 2KY had run a 'jumbled word' competition, with J.T. Kennedy winning a 'Victory Home', sponsored by Moncrete builders, worth £2500. The prize was an odd one as it had already been built, and Kennedy initially did not have land to move the house to. Then he complained to the Board that he had had to pay rent for two years before his family could move into the house. 2KY's general manager explained that part of the delay had been due to labour shortages, and dismissed Kennedy as 'quite unreasonable'.[46]

Calwell and fellow Labor Minister E.J. Ward began compiling a dossier of complaints about competitions. One was from Frank E. Gilbert of Port Melbourne, who had responded to the 'high pressure advertising campaigns conducted by that happy-blatherman Bob Dyer' by submitting 60 entries (with the right answer) to a radio competition but failed to win a prize. 'So now you know why I emulate Johnny Ray and CRY', he told Ward. In 1952 Hilda Weekes, from rural New South Wales, wrote to the ABCB about a competition on the *Atlantic Show* that had offered a house as the prize. Widowed, ill and on a pension, Mrs Weekes had spent months working 'mathematically', long into the night, towards the solution; then the prize was awarded for a concocted word not in the dictionary. Now on 'the verge of a complete breakdown', she implored the regulator to:

> please prevent such 'Things' from falling on us from the Sky. A clean sweep, please! We have far too much to contend with—without it coming into our homes from above us! ... I suggest that you make a clean sweep of such deceptions from God's Fresh Air. Let us breathe pure Air.

The competition's intricacies cannot be known today, but the Commonwealth Broadcasting Network (headed by 2UW) vigorously rejected the 'libellous' claim that the winner had already 'been picked out'.[47] What Weekes' correspondence—there were further letters—does demonstrate is how much hope some listeners invested in competitions, and how radio was perceived as penetrating the atmosphere, the domestic sphere and even the mind.

A few months after Weekes' complaints, B.M. Cavanagh sent a poem to 'Mr. Radio Licenses Dept.' The first stanza declared that he had 'refused your set' and 'hence any consent to your ideas'. The untitled poem went on to object to 'killings' (presumably in thrillers) and the power of broadcasting to 'affect people's minds (Psychic Power)'. E.L. Greig, now Superintendent of Wireless in Perth, wrote back inviting him to provide details if he was complaining 'regarding some broadcast programmes'. Cavanagh replied with another poem. When forwarding the correspondence to the ABCB, poor Greig remarked that although Cavanagh's letters were 'enigmatical ... I have formed the impression that the writer does not appreciate programmes depicting killing and crimes'. The Board's Director of Program Services, Adrian Jose, who relied on reports from PMG officers, and then the Board's own Senior Program Officers, across Australia proposed no further action: 'Mr. Cavanagh's complaint is not stated with sufficient lucidity. ... It seems unlikely that any useful purpose will be served in attempting to give specific replies to letters of this type.'[48]

By now the ABCB was also concerned about 'quips of a suggestive nature' slipping into competition banter,[49] culminating in a meeting with FARB in 1953. Fearing 'drastic actions', FARB begged commercial stations to exercise more discretion. Bob Dyer's *Cop the Lot*, which allowed listeners and the studio audience to submit jokes, was of particular concern. The number of competitions seems to have declined as a result.[50] Nineteen-year-old Graham Kennedy, who broadcast with Clifford Nicholls Whitta ('Nicky') on 3UZ, where they tilted at Melbourne's sacred cows, was also a target of the 'clean it up' order.[51]

As we have seen throughout this book, the Australian radio industry worked hard to engage, and be seen to engage, listeners. Sometimes, however, its efforts backfired. In 1954 Adelaide invalid pensioner Hannah M. Murphy wrote to the Country Party PMG, H.L. Anthony, about being 'debarred' from community singing on 5KA. Although she did not have a strong voice, she objected to being 'singled out for such a stigma'. Struggling with her bills, and having no friends to help her, the 56-year-old seems to have hoped for a little financial assistance from radio 'sing songs' or quiz shows. 5KA's general manager, Eric Pearce, replied that Miss Murphy was well known to the commercial station: she sang off-key, seemed unable to control her emotions and sometimes screamed. The assistant manager had gently tried to remove Murphy, talked to her over tea and given her a movie ticket. Jose sent a sympathetic reply to Pearce, marked 'personal', in which he said 5KA's actions seemed both necessary and kind, and volunteered to smooth things over with the PMG.[52]

Amongst the complaints received by the ABCB concerning perennial issues such as advertising were letters about more local issues. One Board file contains a maze of correspondence about the attacks of 2CA broadcaster Rex Morrisby on a Canberra furniture company, showing the impact (feared or real) that one prominent announcer could have on a business in a city such as Canberra, or an even smaller town.[53] The proprietorial feeling some country listeners had for their stations was evident in 1952, when 5RM in Renmark, north-east of Adelaide, which had been receiving some content from 5DN, entered into a relay arrangement with 5KA.[54] Eric Pearce received a local deputation protesting at the changes. In 5RM's annual report in November 1953, he wrote of how the station had concentrated on community service, saying he had received a 'most complimentary' letter from the man who had organised the original deputation.[55]

New portable technology enabled the recording and transmission of the voices of eyewitnesses and others who were in the news. Actuality broadcasts were particularly embraced by commercial stations in a quest to be first with dramatic news stories.[56] These types of broadcasts led to some listener disquiet, and the scrutiny of ABCB officers. A broadcast on 3UZ's *Newsbeat* one Sunday in 1957 resulted in at least one telephone call and three letters complaining about the groans of a dying man being included in the 'on the spot' description of a car accident. The ABCB quickly brought the unfortunate incident to the attention of station manager Lewis Bennett, who wrote back conveying his personal apology, and advising that he had disciplined those involved in producing the program. An ABCB memo noted that people of 'mature judgement' should exercise 'meticulous care' to avoid programs like *Newsbeat* becoming sensationalist.[57]

Commercial stations' forays into dramatising news as they sought to counter the new medium of television could also get them into trouble with the courts—something also beyond the scope of this chapter. Following claims of distress, the Board requested special care in the dramatisation of events in living memory, and in depictions of mental illness. FARB had a dedicated committee to decide which musical recordings were suitable for broadcast, with the ABCB alert to the possibility of suggestive pop lyrics.[58]

The *Broadcasting and Television Act* of 1956 excised the more specific program functions of the ABCB, leaving it with the central function of ensuring 'adequate and comprehensive' commercial radio and television programs. ABC programs were also removed from the Board's supervision.[59] The ABCB, the Country Party PMG Sir Charles W. Davidson informed parliament, 'took the view that while responsibility for the selection of programmes to be seen and heard in each home must to some extent lie with the viewer', it was reasonable for viewers to expect that programs would be in the best interests of the community. Television Program Standards required programs to accord with 'ordinary good taste and commonsense'; respect for the law, social institutions and the individual opinions of the public; and regard children's 'special needs'. An Advisory Committee on Children's Television Programs, consisting of people with expertise in education and child welfare, was also established.[60]

Section 18 of the Act provided that a licensee should not televise blasphemous, indecent or obscene material. The ABCB's 1957–1958 annual report reported on instances of vulgar and suggestive material, observing that the 'less desirable meaning' of some words and actions, particularly in variety shows, had not been missed by the audience. The Board drew the attention of television stations to the dangers of insufficient rehearsal and, as with radio, live banter. A year later, the ABCB observed that the critics of television programs who wrote to it and the PMG seemed to be both 'more articulate' and harsher than critics of radio programs.[61]

In 1959 *TV Week* featured a story on the Board's capacity to put 'a TV station off the air', accompanied by a photo of a program monitor watching a set, with a stopwatch, reel-to-reel recorder and movie camera to assist with playing back programs. Monitors were said to ask themselves 'Now, would I like my wife, mother or children to see this?'[62] Commenting on a McNair Survey of the Melbourne television audience in 1963, the ABCB's annual report emphasised the high 'proportion of viewers who have not yet reached an age of mature judgment'.[63] In 1965 the Board distributed a pamphlet to schools on 'Helping Children to Use Television Wisely!', recommending parental control, planned viewing, and 'a balanced diet' of children's club programs, comedies, travelogues, and hobby and activity sessions.[64]

Year after year, the Board expressed concern about unscripted banter on television. Detecting a tendency for performers to play 'to the few people in the studio audience and to forget that the real audience is the family circle', the ABCB in 1962–1963 raised with television station managements several 'crude, vulgar, or suggestive' incidents.[65] While the Board tried to forestall grounds for audience complaints, there is also evidence of some viewer dissatisfaction with tasteless programs. Graham Kennedy, who had moved to GTV9 to present *In Melbourne Tonight* (*IMT*), had become a huge star. However, his variety show drew censure: 'Lots of people obviously thought I was a sinner because I kept getting Bibles through the post.'[66]

When viewers complained about 'excessive' advertising, the Board explained that nothing could be done unless stations exceeded the prescribed limit of 1½ minutes in every 15 minutes of programming. When viewers complained about the intrusion of advertisements in feature films, ABCB secretary Joseph O'Kelly pointed out that commercial stations had no other revenue. R.W. Curtis of suburban Melbourne thought that 'quite unsuitable advertising ruins the mood created by a fine film', while acknowledging that ads could be muted (presumably manually, as remote control units were expensive and uncommon until the 1980s).[67] It was evident that some viewers confused the two broadcasting sectors, demanding to know why they paid licence fees (for the ABC) 'just to see advertisements all the time'. Other complaints related to the types of products advertised, such as toilet paper and deodorants,[68] and 'women's foundation garments'.[69]

Meanwhile, complaints surfaced about the type and variety of commercial radio programming. Some listeners resented the rise of Top 40 pushing some stations more into music. In 1959 L.E. Davis, a Sydney invalid pensioner, rang the ABCB to object to 'hysterical' disc jockeys. In parliament two years later, Labor's Alan Bird sought to draw the PMG's attention to too much rock 'n roll for adolescents, at the expense of the broader community.[70] By now the Board itself had adopted the somewhat dismissive term 'transient music (hits)'. Its hopes that stations might replace some of these programs with more drama were unrealistic. Radio serials had begun declining in popularity in the 1950s, and then writers, performers and audiences moved to television, where nightly drama became entrenched.[71]

2UW abruptly removed all its serials from air in May 1964, and those other metropolitan commercial stations that had not already done so followed suit.[72] In a meeting with FARB in July, ABCB chairman R.G. Osborne raised 'real public concern'. Due to missives to the Board, questions in parliament and letters to the editor, it had 'reluctantly felt compelled to appear to defend the commercial radio industry'.[73] Miss R. Hurrell, from the Eyre Peninsula in South Australia, spoke for others living in areas still without television when she lamented the decline of radio drama.[74]

A drop in children's programs also disappointed the ABCB. 'Very few [stations] seem to be interested in helping the 10–15 year olds to do anything but twist', said Osborne in an address to FARB's 1963 convention.[75] In religious programming, the amount of free time on commercial radio was decreasing, while the amount of time sponsored by religious (especially American) organisations expanded.[76] When 3XY's program manager, Dick Heming, discontinued religious programs, one woman's letter of complaint, signed 'Yours in Christianity', concluded: 'I have prayed to the Lord that you be struck dead.'[77]

On 26 January 1963, Norm Delaney sat down to write a letter to the 'Australian (?) Broadcasting Control Board' that he finished three days later. 'It has been said that the A.B.C. is misrun by a team of Englishmen' was his opening gambit. He objected to inclusions in a program of 'Australian' music at 7 am on Australia Day and described it as tokenism, claiming that the scheduling was '99% foreign as usual'. He thought commercial radio and television even worse: '100% Non-Australian' and too Americanised, 'aided and abetted by the "No Control" Board'. He concluded by asking the regulator to direct stations to ensure that around half of drama and music was Australian. Jose noted on one memo that there were other, more 'subtle' ways of displaying one's 'Australian-ness'. Internal memos suggest that Delaney was something of a serial complainant, and that the ABC also had 'quite a substantial file' of correspondence from 'this same gentleman'.[78]

In its 1963–1964 annual report, the ABCB acknowledged changing 'social standards and conventions in entertainment', while reminding stations that television had a 'largely uncontrolled entry into the home'.[79] In 1964 the Board's Program Services Division began compiling a monthly table of radio and television complaints.[80] Some were from individual listeners and viewers, or organisations such as churches and the United Associations of Women. Some were drawn from the reports that Senior Program Officers submitted to Jose. The rest came from politicians—usually the PMG but sometimes local members—who received deputations or letters from constituents, or who put parliamentary questions 'on notice' for ABCB advice.

The tables included complaints about *The Mavis Bramston Show* (1964–1968), a weekly satirical comedy revue on the Seven Network. The column summarising how to reply to correspondents confirmed that the Board was gradually becoming mindful of changing social mores. It assured early complainants about bad language ('bloody') by Gordon Chater and impersonations of the Queen that its officers were closely watching *Mavis Bramston*:

> it seems fair to say that the station has been making a determined and not unsuccessful attempt to present a different type of Australian television programme of reasonably high quality … it must be remembered that this is essentially adult material.

The ABCB had been informed by Seven that of 200 letters in response to the first episode, only four were critical, and that the sound was cut off when it appeared that undesirable words might be used. In its 1964–1965 annual report, the Board acknowledged that the emergence of 'satire and sophisticated humour', 'encouraged by a generally favourable reception from viewers and responsible critics', had not been foreseen when the Television Program Standards were determined. But when Melbourne viewers complained about a skit's 'homosexual theme', the ABCB advised them that it would discourage any such imputations and pass on their complaints to Seven. When Arthur Calwell, a devout Catholic and now leader of the Opposition, criticised the program, the Board advised that it had stepped up its monitoring of *Mavis Bramston* and was in regular communication with the producers, but did not exercise direct censorship.[81]

The tables included complaints about the televising of words like 'breasts', 'menstruation' and 'intercourse', and current affairs programs showing prostitutes. There were complaints about poor grammar and speech; advertisements for adult films during children's viewing; programs running over time; and sport displacing regular programs. By 1966 it was clear that there were more complaints about television than radio, and that *Mavis Bramston* (which scored its own column in the ABCB's tables) was a particular target of community concern.

Psychologist Alicia Lee wrote a report entitled 'The Writing Public' for the ABC's Audience Research section based on 701 letters to ABC management, and 563 letters to five announcers, between October and December 1965.[82] A substantial proportion of the first category related to a reorganisation of programs, particularly in radio, in 1965,[83] with several protests at the axing of favourite programs. Letters to management were more inclined to object to content on moral grounds, and to be 'less amiable' than those to announcers. 'In general, of course, when people have a complaint about a person, they find it easier to tell someone else rather than tell him to his face', reasoned Lee, observing that letters to announcers generally lacked 'the abusiveness, the intemperance, the sheer bad manners' of letters to management. Lee was troubled by petitions with multiple signatories, wondering if they might form part of a 'new populist movement' against television that attempted to treat human issues seriously and could be accused of 'moral subversion'.

The ABC did receive complaints about violence in newsreels from Vietnam, with general manager Talbot Duckmanton replying that although the ABC sometimes cut out 'gruesome' scenes, it had to carefully assess each case individually. The first episode of *You Can't See Round Corners*, a drama series set during the Vietnam War, in 1967 prompted a flurry of complaints about an attempted seduction. This resulted in the ABCB instructing Seven to delete the scene if the episode were repeated, and the network agreeing to schedule the series after 8.30 pm.[84] Alerted to complaints about the antics of, and violence in, *World Champion Wrestling*, TCN9's chief executive Bruce Gyngell agreed to talk to the producer, while noting that 'far from receiving complaints, there was much evidence to show that viewers enjoy the program'.[85]

Macquarie Network managing director S.R.I. Clark returned from an American tour in 1964 bubbling with enthusiasm for 'conversation' radio, along with the potential for more audience participation through talkback.[86] The ABCB's concerns about unscripted material on radio narrowed to discussions of 'topical issues' which offended listeners, and soon spread to television current affairs. The Board also worried about callers not being 'qualified' to speak on social and moral issues,[87] and 'unseen telephone caller[s] whose bona fides have little chance of being properly assessed'.[88]

In 1967 listeners' voices were finally allowed to go to air with a seven-second delay. The ABCB's program officers hoped that talkback would be suitably 'serious', while Liberal PMG Alan Hulme hoped that telephone conversations would be used to probe important matters and provide a 'community service'.[89] Board replies to complaints about talkback typically noted that 'provocative remarks' were deliberately made by hosts to stimulate listener interest and discussion.[90] Reviewing the first two years of the format, the ABCB was pleased to note that there had been very few complaints about remarks by callers themselves.[91]

After the outspoken journalist Claudia Wright joined 3AW in the early 1970s, her conservative stablemate, veteran broadcaster Norman Banks, initially refused to engage in slanging matches with her. But when letters and telephone calls poured in accusing him of cowardice, Banks began to counter-attack. (It is not clear whether he succeeded in showing up the 'tempestuous woman' as 'a common person without any sense of good taste'.)[92]

One Melbourne listener's telegram to Osborne in 1968, asking that stations be required to play classical music on a roster between midnight and 6 am, was not well-received. The ABCB table's 'action' column recorded that 'Mr. Bush had complained previously and is well known as a self appointed guardian of the public', and that receipt of his telegram should merely be acknowledged. When the man then wrote to Calwell, the politician was told that Bush had written at least ten letters to the Board about the matter, and was also 'an inveterate sender of telegrams to "VIP's"'. It advised Calwell not to reply.[93]

Under chairman Myles Wright, the ABCB was more publicly active through advisory committees and research.[94] Annual reports from 1970–1971 onwards included more detail about complaints received in response to 'broadcasting' (as it still anachronistically referred to radio) and television, as well as investigations of potentially 'objectionable matter'. It advised that that one in four viewer complaints concerned sex, crime or violence, and about one in eight related to language and vulgarity.[95]

A singular source of ABCB concern was Graham Kennedy, who after signing off as host of *IMT* returned to commercial radio in 1970 on 3XY.[96] Adrian Jose asked officers in Brisbane to be on alert when Kennedy's program started being heard on 4BK: 'It would be well for you to monitor the early editions of this programme because of Kennedy's well-known propensity towards advertising embellishment and close-to-the-bone comments.' The broadcaster was known for hilarious ad-libbing during advertisements, and by now he also seems to have been challenging advertising time limits. A three-page list of dubious remarks accompanying Jose's memo concluded by highlighting Kennedy's jibes at 'Broadcast Control'.[97]

Meanwhile, two other contentious television shows had emerged. Launched by the Ten Network in 1972, *Number 96* featured nudity and sex, set in a Sydney block of flats. After the first three nights, the Board directed TEN10 to excise objectionable scenes before recordings went to other stations. The ABCB then also invoked section 101 (enabling the censorship of objectionable matter) of the *Broadcasting and Television Act* to allow it to view each episode before transmission, relaxing the requirement after 30 episodes.[98] Not surprisingly, the Board had by now started a special file on complaints about, and potential breaches by, *Number 96*.[99] The locally produced show seems to have had more fans than critics, with its ratings encouraging ATV0 to commission its own racy soap opera. Set in a fictional Melbourne television station, *The Box* launched in 1974 and was soon second in the ratings to *Number 96*. It scored its own ABCB file and had some sex scenes censored.[100]

In 1971, the Board had advised that 15 per cent of complaints were from viewers disturbed about the overall standard of the medium.[101] One such complaint went to Senator Douglas McClelland, who held the new post of Minister for the Media in the Whitlam Labor government, in 1973. Describing herself as living alone, 'existing on a widows' pension, in a country village, without public transport, twenty-three miles from the nearest city [Orange]', Irene Alexander wrote of the CBN8 schedule:

> We are given an indigestible diet of cheap half-hour comedies, films made before 1945, tenth rate hour long repeat shows about 10 years old, a surfeit of Hector Crawford sausages and '[Number] 96' (but, of course!).[102]

By now Graham Kennedy was doing battle with the ABCB over his choice of words on GTV9's *The Graham Kennedy Show*. In 1973 he challenged Myles Wright to an on-air debate, and claimed that an excerpt of a David Williamson play shown on the ABC's *This Day Tonight* included words 'which I considered far worse than words I would ever use'.[103] A showdown came when Kennedy's program moved to colour. Having become somewhat obsessed by broadcasting politics, he opened on 3 March 1975 with the words 'Good evening, Myles Wright', and then unfolded what an *Age* critic described as a 'carnal catalogue'. During a hairspray advertisement, Kennedy imitated the sound of a crow ('faark'), which was interpreted as 'fuck'. The episode sparked hundreds of telephone calls from viewers, many of them Catholics, protesting against sexual innuendo and a sketch involving a priest and a nun.[104]

The ABCB directed that the ad be deleted from future telecasts, and asked Kennedy to 'show cause' why it should not ban him from television or take other action against him under section 119 (relating to offensive broadcasts) of the *Broadcasting and Television Act*. As Kennedy sought legal advice, and further baited Wright,[105] viewers' letters poured in. A bulging file of correspondence about the episode survived a later fire at the ABCB's headquarters in Melbourne,[106] which does not seem to have been accessed by Graeme Blundell in his otherwise fine biography of Kennedy.

Many letters demanded a 'clean-up' of *The Graham Kennedy Show*. A Melbourne viewer explained that she had been nominated by her family of 'six University graduates' to protest at the program displacing the British period drama *Upstairs, Downstairs*: 'we are neither narrow-minded nor bigoted'. Ivan Bodenko of North Melbourne recounted how he and another 'New Australian' friend had fallen upon Kennedy and as their knowledge of English improved, the performer's 'filth' became more and more apparent. One Sydney viewer wrote of how 'dirty talk and filthy references' left parents embarrassed when watching television with teenagers and 'mixed company', and expressed gratitude for 'a Board with the power and right to keep the quality of T.V. and Radio programmes on a level acceptable to everybody'. A viewer from Surfers Paradise paid for a telegram demanding the regulator 'DISPLAY SOME BACKBONE' and 'GET THAT SEWER RAT KENNEDY OFF RADIO AND TELEVISION'.

But there was another substantial element to the singed file of 'Complaints and Criticism', captured in a later qualification by the National Archives of Australia: '[and letters of support]'. Sydney viewer T. Becker seems to have spoken for many:

> as the voices of those people who are always dissatisfied about one thing or another are usually the loudest. ... I would like to use this opportunity, being so far a mute member of the public, for pointing out that the more intelligent and the less bigoted ought to have some rights, too, in choosing, amongst many things, the form and quality of their entertainment.

Several correspondents expressed dismay at proposed action against Kennedy, saying they thought in 'this day and age people were more liberal minded'. A Melbourne viewer declared that he was 'beginning to believe what Graham Kennedy says in that you're a bunch of 90 year old men so out of touch with things that you're pathetic'.

On 18 March the full ABCB met and unanimously voted to restrict Kennedy to pre-recorded appearances, approved by responsible station employees. Twelve days later, he resigned when GTV9 executives deleted a scathing attack on Doug McClelland, before the show went to air. In May Kennedy wrote to the ABCB seeking a lifting of the order and undertaking to abide by the Board's standard in future live performances. With the order revoked, Kennedy returned to radio—and was soon attracting more controversy.[107]

The events of 1975 constituted probably the most public episode in the ABCB's history. While it would be an exaggeration to say the handling of the 'crow call' spelled the death knell for the Board, it is hard not to conclude that the regulator was struggling to keep up with changing community standards. And the media and political landscape were changing too, with the formation of the Department of the Media and the ground laid for the emergence of a community radio sector. In 1976 the Fraser Coalition government abolished the ABCB and established the Australian Broadcasting Tribunal (ABT) in Sydney. It revised program standards after public input, and published an unprecedented range of research and reports.[108]

One of these was *Who Complains?*, following on from 3374 complaints received by the ABT about commercial radio and television. Sixty-two of these complaints were also about ABC radio, suggesting a continuing public confusion about regulatory jurisdiction. The authors' survey found that around nine per cent of the general population had lodged a complaint about television, compared with just three per cent about radio. People with strong religious beliefs were more likely to complain. The issue of most concern was violence, with 'too many ads', 'sex scenes', 'bad language' and 'nudity' the other preoccupations. The survey indicted a low level of community awareness of the ABT's complaints handling function, and a belief that broadcasting stations were the most appropriate recipient of complaints. In focus groups, people who were asked why they did not complain expressed concern about bureaucratic red tape, and doubt their complaints would have any real impact.[109]

This chapter has explored some of the complaints from Australian listeners and viewers between the 1920s and the 1970s. It has concentrated on some of the hundreds of ABCB complaint files, meaning that the focus has been more on commercial broadcasters than the ABC. In teasing out how the Board handled complaints, the Board emerges as a kind of audience in itself, with its own expectations for disciplined broadcast consumption and suitable content. Captured within the clinically archived files of the regulator are the voices of Australians over more than a generation—lonely, sad, angry, indignant and sometimes funny. Reading more of these files, delving into the records of the ABCB's successors, and working to locate and access surviving complaints files from individual stations, networks and the ABC, has the potential to illuminate what Australians listened to and watched, and why, and how Australians negotiated questions of culture, power and value over a century.

NOTES

1. Kate Aisbett, Kathryn Paterson and Milica Loncar, *Who Complains?* (Sydney: Australian Broadcasting Tribunal, 1992).
2. *Wireless Weekly* (*WW*), 7 January 1927, pp. 7, 47.
3. Bridget Griffen-Foley, *Changing Stations: The Story of Australian Commercial Radio* (Sydney: UNSW Press, 2009), p. 15.
4. *WW*, 21 January 1927, p. 10.
5. *WW*, 26 August 1927, p. 6.
6. *WW*, 27 February–29 May 1931; Griffen-Foley 2009, p. 174.
7. Griffen-Foley 2009, pp. 14, 18.
8. D. Graham-Dowland, 'The fourth great dimension of advertising: The air as a media', *Rydge's*, 1 December 1933, pp. 1116–17.
9. Jill Roe, *Stella Miles Franklin: A Biography* (Sydney: HarperCollins, 2008), p. 309.
10. For a consideration of cultural hierarchies in the American context, see Michele Hilmes, *Radio Voices: American Broadcasting, 1922–1952* (Minneapolis: University of Minnesota Press, 1997), pp. 184–86.
11. Bridget Griffen-Foley, 'The birth of a hybrid: The shaping of the Australian radio industry', *Radio Journal*, 2(3) 2004, p. 163; *WW*, 1 June 1934, p. 21, 31 August 1934, p. 19 and 11 October 1936, p. 19.
12. Griffen-Foley 2009, pp. 206–7.
13. *Teleradio*, 30 June 1934, p. 22.
14. K.S. Inglis, *This Is the ABC: The Australian Broadcasting Commission, 1932–1983* (Melbourne: Melbourne University Press, 1983), p. 29; Griffen-Foley 2009, p. 207.
15. National Archives of Australia (NAA)/Vic: MP404/1, 1942/5789.
16. NAA/Vic: MP404/1, 1942/5789, letters from Moroney to Cleary, 10 October 1934; J. Malone to Moroney, 2 November 1934.
17. NAA/WA: K301, WB6/1/4, correspondence, 24 June–16 August 1935.
18. Inglis 1983, pp. 82–83.

19. NAA/ACT, SP112/1, 31/2/3, letter from Murdoch to Jones, 31 July 1940.
20. Griffen-Foley 2009, p. 255; NAA/ACT: SP112/1, 31/2/5.
21. *The Methodist*, 31 August 1940, p. 5.
22. *WW*, 1 March 1941, p. 5 and 26 April 1941, p. 3.
23. Griffen-Foley 2009, p. 230.
24. George Patterson, *Life Has Been Wonderful* (Sydney: Ure Smith, 1956), p. 158; Griffen-Foley 2009, p. 231. The League had referred to US boycotts of radio advertisers in a letter to the *Sydney Morning Herald*, 2 August 1941, p. 8.
25. National Library of Australia (NLA): MS 8021, Gordon Leed and Dick Heming, 'From 78s to Satellites: The Journey of Two Men through the Radio Broadcasting Industry', p. 22.
26. Griffen-Foley 2009, p. 230.
27. NAA/WA: K301, WB6/1/4, letters from Michel to PMG, 8 January 1942; Greig to Michel, 14 January 1942.
28. Mark Armstrong, *Broadcasting Law and Policy in Australia* (Sydney: Butterworths, 1982), p. 37.
29. NAA/Vic: MP404/1, 1945/10453, letter from D. Cameron to G. Kirkpatrick, 24 August 1945.
30. NAA/Vic: MP404/1, 1944/3914, letter from Ashley to Harvey, 29 May 1942.
31. *Australian Broadcasting Act* 1942, sections 91–92, https://www.legislation.gov.au/Details/C1942A00033, accessed 19 February 2020.
32. Griffen-Foley 2009, p. 231.
33. NAA/Vic: MP404/1, 1944/3914.
34. NAA/Vic: MP404/1, 42/13455, correspondence, 23 June–24 September 1942.
35. For more detail on the PSCB, see Chap. 6.
36. NAA/Vic: MP404/1, 1942/10013.
37. NAA/Vic: MP404/1, 44/6008.
38. *Courier-Mail*, 18 July 1945, p. 3 and 19 July 1945, p. 3.
39. State Library of New South Wales (SLNSW): MLMSS 3641, Women's Christian Temperance Union of NSW Records, Good Film & Radio Vigilance League of NSW minutes, 1945–1955.
40. See also Armstrong 1982, p. 38.
41. These files are in the Victorian office of the National Archives of Australia.
42. Armstrong 1982, pp. 38–39; Griffen-Foley 2009, pp. 47–48.
43. *Australian Broadcasting Control Board (ABCB) 2nd Annual Report* (Canberra: Commonwealth of Australia, 1949–1950), p. 26.
44. *ABCB 3rd Annual Report* (1950–1951), p. 19.

45. Griffen-Foley 2009, pp. 48–49, 309; NAA/Vic: MP1170/3, BC/6/1 PART 1, letter from J. O'Kelly to M.D. Carlson, 16 November 1953.
46. George Hart, 'Radio roundup', *Sun*, 4 September 1946, p. 6; NAA/Vic: MP1170/3, BC/6/2 PART 1, correspondence mid-1949.
47. NAA/Vic: MP1170/3, BC/6/2 PART 1, correspondence, 1951–1952.
48. NAA/WA: K301, WB6/1/4, correspondence, 11 December 1952–19 January 1953.
49. *ABCB 4th Annual Report* (1951–1952), p. 25.
50. *ABCB 5th Annual Report* (1952–1953), p. 27; NAA/Vic: MP1170/3, BC/6/2 PART 1, correspondence, 5 August–12 October 1953.
51. Graeme Blundell, *King: The Life and Comedy of Graham Kennedy* (Sydney: Pan Macmillan, 2003), p. 48.
52. NAA/Vic: MP1170/3, BC/6/1 PART 1, correspondence, January 1954.
53. NAA/Vic: MP1170/3, BC/6/1 PART 1, correspondence, 6 January 1952–11 May 1953.
54. *Advertiser*, 7 November 1952, p. 6.
55. NAA/Vic: MP1897/2, 5RM/8, River Murray Broadcasters Ltd—Report to the Board of Directors re 5RM, 2 November 1953.
56. Griffen-Foley 2009, pp. 336–37.
57. NAA/Vic: MP1170/3, BC/6/5 PART 1, ABCB agendum 1957/195.
58. *ABCB 8th Annual Report* (1955–1956), pp. 28–29; *ABCB 12th Annual Report* (1959–1960), p. 25; *13th Annual Report* (1960–1961), p. 27; *14th Annual Report* (1961–1962), pp. 25–26.
59. Armstrong 1982, pp. 39–40.
60. *ABCB 8th Annual Report* (1955–1956), pp. 42–43, 61–69; *ABCB 9th Annual Report* (1956–1957), p. 41.
61. *ABCB 10th Annual Report* (1957–1958), p. 44; *11th Annual Report* (1958–1959), p. 48.
62. *TV Week* (Adelaide), 25 November 1959, pp. 13–14.
63. *ABCB 15th Annual Report* (1962–1963), p. 55.
64. *TV Week* (Sydney), 2 January 1965, pp. 38–39; *ABCB 17th Annual Report* (1964–1965), p. 64.
65. *ABCB 15th Annual Report* (1962–1963), pp. 64–65.
66. Blundell 2003, p. 212.
67. NAA/Vic: MP1170/4, TC/5/3 PART 1, letters from Curtis to ABCB, 27 June 1961 and O'Kelly, 1 August 1961. See also Mary Bellis, 'The television remote control: A brief history', 2019, https://www.thoughtco.com/history-of-the-television-remote-control-1992384, accessed 5 March 2020.
68. NAA/Vic: MP1170/4, TC/5/3 PART 1, correspondence, 14 December 1961–16 October 1964.
69. *ABCB 19th Annual Report* (1966–1967), p. 101.

70. NAA/Vic: MP1170/3, BC/6/1 PART 1, ABCB memo, 17 June 1959; telegram, 20 April 1961.
71. Griffen-Foley 2009, pp. 236, 270.
72. Griffen-Foley 2009, p. 236.
73. NAA/Vic: B4069, VB/2/2 PART 1, notes of meeting, 16 July 1964.
74. NAA/WA: K308, WP/1/19 PART 1, ABCB Agendum, 6 July 1965.
75. NAA/Vic: MP1170/3, BA/9/1 PART 2, address by Osborne, 14 October 1963.
76. Griffen-Foley 2009, p. 190.
77. NLA: MS 8021, Leed Papers, 'From 78s to Satellites', p. 157.
78. NAA/Vic: MP1170/3, BC/6/5 PART 1, letter from Delaney to ABCB, 26–29 January 1963; ABCB memos, 31 January and 11 October 1963.
79. *ABCB 16th Annual Report* (1963–1964), p. 71.
80. NAA/Vic: MP1170/3, BC/6/1 PART 2, ABCB agendum 1964/93. The following discussion is based on the 1964–1968 tables in this file.
81. *ABCB 17th Annual Report* (1964–1965), p. 60. The ABCB also compiled individual files of complaints about *The Mavis Bramston Show*: MP1170/4, TC/5/3 PARTS 1–4.
82. NAA/NSW: C1175, 6, Alicia Lee, 'The Writing Public: A Study of Audience Correspondence' (1966).
83. See Inglis 1983, pp. 256–58.
84. *ABCB 19th Annual Report* (1966–1967), p. 102; NAA/Vic: MP1170/3, BC/6/1 PART 2.
85. NAA/Vic: MP1170/3, BP/10/4.
86. Griffen-Foley 2009, pp. 348–49.
87. *ABCB 16th Annual Report* (1963–1964), pp. 71–72; *ABCB 17th Annual Report* (1964–1965), p. 32; *18th Annual Report* (1965–1966), p. 29; *19th Annual Report* (1966–1967), p. 49.
88. Griffen-Foley 2009, pp. 347–48.
89. Griffen-Foley 2009, pp. 349–52.
90. NAA/Vic: MP1170/3, BC/6/1 PART 2.
91. *ABCB 21st Annual Report* (1968–1969), pp. 65–66.
92. State Library of Victoria: PA02/07, Norman Banks Records, Box 13, 'Claudia Wright'.
93. NAA/Vic: MP1170/3, BP/10/4, 1968–1969.
94. Mark Armstrong, 'Australian Broadcasting Control Board', in Bridget Griffen-Foley (ed.) *A Companion to the Australian Media* (North Melbourne: Australian Scholarly Publishing, 2014), p. 42.
95. *ABCB 23rd Annual Report* (1970–1971), p. 136.
96. Blundell 2003, pp. 274–78.
97. NAA/Vic: B2153, 4BK/20 PART 1, memo from Jose, 2 November 1970.

98. *ABCB 24th Annual Report* (1971–1972), pp. 117–18. See also Armstrong 1982, p. 57.
99. *ABCB 25th Annual Report* (1972–1973), p. 132; NAA/NSW: C546, NV/5/12 PART 1.
100. Albert Moran and Chris Keating, *Historical Dictionary of Australian Radio and Television* (Lanham, Maryland: Scarecrow Press, 2007), p. 67; *ABCB 26th Annual Report* (1973–1974), p. 137.
101. *ABCB 23rd Annual Report* (1970–1971), p. 136.
102. Michael Thurlow, 'Switched On: A History of Regional Commercial Television in Australia', PhD thesis (Macquarie University, 2020), p. 226.
103. Blundell 2003, pp. 289–90; *ABCB 25th Annual Report* (1972–1973), p. 136; NAA/Vic: MP1897/3, TP/2/57 PART 1.
104. Blundell 2003, pp. 312–14.
105. Blundell 2003, pp. 314–17; Armstrong 1982, p. 59; *ABCB 27th Annual Report* (1975–1976), pp. 122–23.
106. The following discussion is based on NAA/Vic: MP1897/3, TC5/11 PART 1.
107. Blundell 2003, pp. 317–21; Armstrong 1982, p. 61; *ABCB 27th Annual Report* (1975–1976), p. 123.
108. Armstrong, 'Australian Broadcasting Control Board' and 'Australian Broadcasting Tribunal', in Bridget Griffen-Foley (ed.) *A Companion to the Australian Media* (North Melbourne: Australian Scholarly Publishing, 2014) pp. 41–42, 46–47.
109. Aisbett et al. 1992.

Bibliography

Advertiser (Adelaide).
Aisbett, Kate, Kathryn Paterson and Milica Loncar. *Who Complains?* (Sydney: Australian Broadcasting Tribunal, 1992).
Armstrong, Mark. *Broadcasting Law and Policy in Australia* (Sydney: Butterworths, 1982).
———. 'Australian Broadcasting Control Board', in Bridget Griffen-Foley (ed.) *A Companion to the Australian Media* (North Melbourne: Australian Scholarly Publishing, 2014a), pp. 41–42.
———. 'Australian Broadcasting Tribunal', in Bridget Griffen-Foley (ed.) *A Companion to the Australian Media* (North Melbourne: Australian Scholarly Publishing, 2014b), pp. 46–47.
Australian Broadcasting Act. 1942, https://www.legislation.gov.au/Details/C1942A00033, accessed 19 February 2020.

Australian Broadcasting Control Board (ABCB). *2nd Annual Report* (Canberra: Commonwealth of Australia, 1949–1950).
———. *3rd Annual Report* (1950–1951).
———. *4th Annual Report* (1951–1952).
———. *5th Annual Report* (1952–1953).
———. *8th Annual Report* (1955–1956).
———. *9th Annual Report* (1956–1957).
———. *10th Annual Report* (1957–1958).
———. *11th Annual Report* (1958–1959).
———. *12th Annual Report* (1959–1960).
———. *13th Annual Report* (1960–1961).
———. *14th Annual Report* (1961–1962).
———. *15th Annual Report* (1962–1963).
———. *16th Annual Report* (1963–1964).
———. *17th Annual Report* (1964–1965).
———. *18th Annual Report* (1965–1966).
———. *19th Annual Report* (1966–1967).
———. *21st Annual Report* (1968–1969).
———. *23rd Annual Report* (1970–1971).
———. *24th Annual Report* (1971–1972).
———. *25th Annual Report* (1972–1973).
———. *26th Annual Report* (1973–1974).
———. *27th Annual Report* (1975–1976).
Bellis, Mary. 'The television remote control: A brief history', 2019, https://www.thoughtco.com/history-of-the-television-remote-control-1992384, accessed 5 March 2020.
Blundell, Graeme. *King: The Life and Comedy of Graham Kennedy* (Sydney: Pan Macmillan, 2003).
Courier-Mail (Brisbane).
Graham-Dowland, D. 'The fourth great dimension of advertising: The air as a media', *Rydge's*, 1 December 1933, pp. 1116–17.
Griffen-Foley, Bridget. 'The birth of a hybrid: The shaping of the Australian radio industry', *Radio Journal*, 2(3) 2004, pp. 153–69.
———. *Changing Stations: The Story of Australian Commercial Radio* (Sydney: UNSW Press, 2009).
Hart, George. 'Radio roundup', *Sun* (Sydney), 4 September 1946, p. 6.
Hilmes, Michele. *Radio Voices: American Broadcasting, 1922–1952* (Minneapolis: University of Minnesota Press, 1997).
Inglis, K.S. *This Is the ABC: The Australian Broadcasting Commission, 1932–1983* (Melbourne: Melbourne University Press, 1983).
The Methodist.

Moran, Albert and Keating, Chris. *Historical Dictionary of Australian Radio and Television* (Lanham, Maryland: Scarecrow Press, 2007).
National Archives of Australia (NAA)/ACT. A11663, PA69. State Publicity Censor, Melbourne, Broadcasting in Foreign Languages.
———. SP112/1, 31/2/3. Department of Information, News Broadcasts, Complaints.
———. SP112/1, 31/2/5. Department of Information, Complaint re German music.
NAA/NSW. C546, NV/5/12 PART 1. Australian Broadcasting Authority, Number 96, Complaints and Possible Breaches of Standards.
———. C1175, 6. Australian Broadcasting Commission, Report on Programme Statistics, 1950.
NAA/Vic. B2153, 4BK/20 PART 1, ABCB, 4BK, Complaints and Criticisms.
———. B4069, VB/2/2 PART 1. ABCB, Board Rulings – FACB.
———. MP404/1, 1942/5789. Postmaster-General's Department (PMG), Radio Broadcasting Complaints ("Thrillers").
———. MP404/1, 1942/10013. PMG, Radio Broadcasting Complaints Regarding Sunday Broadcasting of Sports.
———. MP404/1, 1944/3914. PMG, Radio Broadcasting Complaints, 2GB.
———. MP404/1, 1945/10453. PMG, Radio Broadcasting Complaints, Section 91 and 92.
———. MP1170/3, BA/9/1 PART 2. ABCB, Federation of Australian Commercial Broadcasters, General.
———. MP1170/3, BC/6/1 PART 1. ABCB, Complaints and Criticisms, General.
———. MP1170/3, BC/6/1 PART 2. ABCB, Complaints and Criticisms, General.
———. MP1170/3, BC/6/2 PART 1. ABCB, Complaints – Audience Participation.
———. MP1170/3, BC/6/5 PART 1. ABCB, Complaints and Criticisms – Broadcast Talks, News, etc.
———. MP1170/3, BP/10/4. ABCB, Programmes – Monthly Reports on Criticisms.
———. MP1897/2, 5RM/8. River Murray Broadcasters Ltd.
———. MP1897/3, TC5/11 PART 1. ABCB, Television, Complaints and Criticisms, Graham Kennedy Show.
———. MP1897/3, TP/2/57 PART 1. ABCB, Programs, Graham Kennedy Show.
NAA/WA: K301, WB6/1/4. PMG (Perth), Complaints From Radio Listeners.
———. K308, WP/1/19 PART 1. PMG (Perth), Programmes, Complaints From Viewers and Listeners.
National Library of Australia: MS 8021, Gordon Leed Papers.
Patterson, George. Life Has Been Wonderful (Sydney: Ure Smith, 1956).
Roe, Jill. *Stella Miles Franklin: A Biography* (Sydney: HarperCollins, 2008).

State Library of New South Wales: MLMSS 3641, Women's Christian Temperance Union of NSW Records.
State Library of Victoria: PA02/07, Norman Banks Records.
Teleradio.
Thurlow, Michael. 'Switched On: A History of Regional Commercial Television in Australia', PhD thesis (Macquarie University, 2020).
TV Week (Adelaide, Sydney).
Wireless Weekly (*WW*).

CHAPTER 6

Viewing Television by Committee

Abstract This chapter explores, for the first time, the operations and management of the Australian Broadcasting Commission (ABC) Television Viewers' Committees between 1959 and 1965. It traces the role of the public service broadcaster's original radio Advisory Committees before investigating the establishment and composition of, and the negotiations around, its state-based Television Viewers' Committees. In examining the Committees' rise and fall, the chapter touches on the special role of Western Australia in the ABC's federal imaginings.

Keywords Australian Broadcasting Commission • Television viewing • Audiences • Ratings • Western Australia

This chapter is about the operations of Australian Broadcasting Commission (ABC) Television Viewers' Committees, established in Australian capital cities from 1959, and disbanded between 1963 and 1965. It sets their emergence against the background of Advisory Committees since the early years of the ABC. The chapter looks at why the Viewers' Committees were established; how they were constituted to represent the 'man [sic] on the street'; some of what members liked, disliked and debated; how the ABC responded to their discussions; and how seriously ABC officials took their views. Based on hitherto unused records in the National Archives of

© The Author(s) 2020
B. Griffen-Foley, *Australian Radio Listeners and Television Viewers*, Palgrave Studies in the History of the Media, https://doi.org/10.1007/978-3-030-54637-3_6

Australia, it concludes by examining the Viewers' Committees decline in the context of audience research and measurement within the ABC.

Advisory Committees were part of the ABC from the very beginning. However, they have received little attention, not even appearing in the index to Ken Inglis' history of the ABC.[1] State School Broadcast Advisory Committees were launched in Victoria, New South Wales and South Australia between 1931 and 1933. A federal Committee, consisting of all state directors of education, followed in 1934.[2] That this was one of the national broadcaster's earliest federal Advisory Committees is understandable given that education was run by the states.[3] A Talks Advisory Committee was also established in 1934. Alan Thomas alludes to the 'many other programme advisory committees scattered throughout the country' by the 1940s.[4] Their somewhat ad hoc emergence was designed to harness external expertise related to specialist program areas.

In his study of the early ABC, Thomas suggests the idea of a formal mechanism for consulting with audiences came from individual state managers. A Western Australian (WA) Advisory Committee was formed in 1935, with ABC chairman W.J. Cleary emphasising that it was to be purely advisory (not 'executive') and unpaid. It emerged in response to concerns about distance from ABC head office in Sydney, where program policy and content were controlled.[5]

Thirteen members were recruited, including Colonel A.C.N. Olden from the RSL, and three University of Western Australia professors.[6] Cleary played an active role in considering possibilities put forward by state manager Basil W. Kirke. Two members were female, with Cleary having declined the suggestion of Miss Sheila McClemens, a young barrister, wanting someone 'more mature', and asking for nominations in addition to Dr Roberta Jull, the first woman to establish a medical practice in Perth. Miss Gladys E. Pendred, principal of the Free Kindergarten College of Western Australia, was appointed, Kirke describing her as 'a very cultured person, a forceful speaker and a woman of unusual intelligence'.[7]

At the first meeting, on 28 May 1936, Dr J.S. Battye, state librarian and incoming University Chancellor, was elected chair. It soon became apparent that this high-level Advisory Committee wanted more agency than the Commission was willing to offer. Cleary had decided that meetings should be quarterly, but former Premier and outgoing Chancellor Sir Walter James thought they should be monthly. Members also proposed forming specialist programming groups. The Commission asserted itself, ensuring that the next meeting was not until August. The Committee was informed that ABC general manager Charles Moses thought that it should not offer detailed criticism of past programs, but rather 'constructive suggestions' for the future.[8] No sub-committees were formed. Cleary and Moses attended a Committee meeting in June 1937, while visiting Western Australia, with the chairman noting that it had been formed because of Perth's 'comparative radio isolation'.[9]

Later that year, Moses issued a clumsy directive stating that members of Advisory Committees were not to be heard on-air themselves. Enraged, Battye had to be reassured that the decision had not been aimed at existing members and that the ABC appreciated that the WA Committee included some of the state's best speakers. Citizens of the mining town of Kalgoorlie also wanted their own Advisory Committee. (Even though the Committee had 'Western Australia' in the title, it was very much a Perth affair.) WA manager Conrad Charlton did not support the idea, for it was clear that the ABC was struggling to deal with the Advisory Committees that had already emerged; he even hoped that their 'unwieldy' size might be halved.[10]

By this time, a South Australian (SA) Advisory Committee had been established. The Commission grasped the symbolic significance of these initiatives at least, announcing the Committee's formation in October 1937 when meeting in Adelaide. As in Western Australia, membership was hardly grassroots. Members were chosen as individuals, rather than as representatives of organisations. Under SA manager L.R. Thomas, the 16 members appointed included three politicians, assorted academics, charity worker Lady (Constance) Bonython, and the president of the National Council of Women and a founder of the School of the Air, Adelaide Miethke. Adelaide's *News* was soon reporting on 'much speculation' about whether the Committee had any right to consider whether the programs aired and the artists employed were the 'best'.[11]

In 1941 the WA Committee questioned whether it should continue, with Professor Walter Murdoch noting it had not done any 'great work'. South Australia was thought to be even less successful. At the next meeting, when he was visiting Perth, T.W. Bearup (acting for Moses, who had enlisted) reported that the 'Commission felt it was an excellent idea to have these Committees in the far distant States' to put a local point of view, and it was hoped that members 'could be helped to see exactly what the Commission was driving at in many of its undertakings'. Bearup may have been slightly more favourably disposed to Advisory Committees than Moses, although it is telling that he mistakenly claimed that there were

Committees in all states other than New South Wales and Victoria. In a memo for the Commission's next meeting, he conceded that most discussions of program matters involved personal preferences, and could have been taken up with the state manager. He thought that the Committee might be more valuable as an 'influential body of citizens in this State by endeavouring to protect broadcasting from short-sighted [political] onslaughts'.[12]

It was not long before an opportunity for the ABC's WA Advisory Committee to prove its usefulness surfaced. Recommendations of the Joint Committee on Wireless Broadcasting (the 'Gibson Committee') were embodied in the *Australian Broadcasting Act* of 1942. It legislated for not just a Parliamentary Standing Committee on Broadcasting (PSCB), but six State Broadcasting Advisory Committees to help advise the Minister.[13] The Curtin Labor government worried the Commission, especially when it was returned to office at the August 1943 election, and the irascible Arthur Calwell, who chaired the PSCB, became Minister for Information. The first year of the Act yielded two ministerial interventions noted in the ABC's annual report.[14]

In overtures to both Calwell and the Postmaster-General (PMG), W.P. Ashley, Cleary attempted to play off the ABC's own WA and SA Advisory Committees against the fledgling State Broadcasting Advisory Committees, and demonstrate both community consultation and independence. In August 1943 Cleary reported to Battye, now an ally, that preliminary meetings of the State Broadcasting Advisory Committees indicated that some members proposed to 'embark on a wide and detailed journey of exploration' of issues that could 'only have time-wasting and embarrassing results'. The ABC now moved to establish its own NSW, Victorian, Queensland and Tasmanian Advisory Committees.[15]

At the same time as the ABC realised the public relations value of Advisory Committees, it became more interested in collecting information about listening habits and preferences. The broadcaster allocated £15,000 for the establishment of a Listener Research section similar to that of the BBC's recently formed division in late 1943, and soon after began subscribing to two sets of audience surveys.[16]

The ABC's Advisory Committees still represented something of a challenge to manage. In 1944–45 there were debates in Perth, and in Sydney, about whether they should be expanded in size, and be more representative (of youth, education, sport, music, unions and so on). It was also decided that people should be appointed for one year, with the possibility of renewal, to enable Committees to be refreshed.[17]

Meanwhile, State Broadcasting Advisory Committees withered on the vine as the PMG's Department deprived them of support and of opportunities to express a view. The *Australian Broadcasting Act* of 1948 under which the Australian Broadcasting Control Board (ABCB) was established converted the ministerial committees into committees to advise the Board on programs. Then the *Broadcasting and Television Act* of 1956 abolished these committees altogether.[18]

Television reached Australia later that year, with one ABC and two commercial stations opening in both Sydney and Melbourne. At the same time, the ABCB's Program Services Division was recruiting staff to analyse audience measurement surveys, and university and ABC research. The ABC rightly concluded that the Board was primarily interested in analysing research already done in Australia (or overseas), although the Board was willing to consider undertaking some limited (and ideally collaborative) research into specific issues. An ABC manager who visited the University of Melbourne's Audio-Visual Aids Department reported that although it was 'lavishly' equipped to research television audience reactions, the director Newman Rosenthal was 'considered to have only the sketchiest notions on research matters'. ABC Controller of Programs Dr Keith Barry concluded in mid-1957 that the broadcaster should collaborate with the ABCB's research efforts as far as possible to avoid any duplication of effort (Fig. 6.1).[19]

That New Year's Eve, A.N. Finlay wrote to program directors about the report on the 'general problem of [small] TV audiences', based on surveys by George Anderson and Lintas, that he had been asked to prepare for the Commission's next meeting. 'Huck' Finlay, formerly a champion footballer and athlete, had risen from sporting editor at the ABC to become assistant general manager. While noting that viewers seemed to move between stations more than they did with radio, Finlay was understandably concerned that viewers might stay away from the ABC if they found its programs unattractive.[20] Throughout 1958, there were discussions within the ABC about poor reception, the impact of ABC stations closing down between 6 and 7 pm, the extent to which the ABC should cater for minority audiences, a lack of high-profile 'personalities', and other funding constraints.[21]

This was the background to the first ABC Television Viewers' Committee. What seems to have been the initiative of Finlay, who became

Fig. 6.1 *Australian Women's Weekly*, 19 September 1956. (Courtesy of Stan Hunt estate)

chair, was explained in a memo from Moses. A pencilled note at the top recorded that it was 'similar to NSW Advisory Ctte'. But while the Sydney Viewers' Committee was also honorary and advisory, there were some key differences from the older state committees. The ABC asked government departments, banks and other private companies for nominations of keen television viewers. While this suggests the pool skewed towards white-collar workers, the 30 people chosen, aged from 20 to 55, were somewhat more 'representative of "the man in the street"', as Moses put it, than the members of the state Advisory Committees, who were generally prominent in public life. The Viewers' Committee was explicitly a Sydney rather than a state-based one, as television did not start spreading to regional areas until 1961. Meetings were envisaged as monthly, not quarterly. Moses hoped that in addition to providing comments and suggestions about ABC programs, members might be educated—through studio tours, meetings with artists and periodic attendance by program heads—about some of the challenges involved in making television.[22]

The first meeting was held at the ABC's Gore Hill studios at 8 pm on Monday, 16 June 1959. From 17 August, Finlay recorded detailed summaries—there were never formal minutes—'for reference and follow-up'. Discussions at this meeting ranged across plays, 'old foreign films' and *Men at the Top* (with criticism of interviewer Michael Baume's 'tendency to monopolise' the series). The quality of fill-in presenters, the best times to schedule documentaries and talk programs like *The Critics*, and the possibility of filming live theatre were considered. 'Unfortunately' few Committee members had seen *Woman's World*. This may suggest that the composition (which isn't recorded) of the Committee was largely male, or it may reflect Inglis' point that the afternoon program's audience was tiny, with no strong faith in it from the male originators or the female presenters. In a memo attaching his meeting notes, Finlay urged colleagues to follow up on all matters raised 'as advice from such people is extremely valuable'.[23]

Around this time, members were asked to complete a viewing habits questionnaire. Forty-seven per cent watched television every evening, while only seven per cent watched during the day. News, talk and interviews were the most popular types of live ABC programs. In 'film' (prerecorded) programs, situation comedies were the most popular on the ABC, and crime and mystery programs on commercial stations TCN9 and ATN7. *The Phil Silvers Show* (a CBS sitcom) was the most watched on the ABC, while *Perry Mason* was the most watched commercial program.[24]

Moses and ABC chairman Sir Richard Boyer seem to have been ex-officio members of the Committee, but never to have attended. At the September meeting, Barry asked members what they would like included in *The Handyman*. They were particularly keen on including demonstrations of car and tool maintenance, and Finlay assured them that these suggestions would be investigated and implemented wherever possible. It was agreed *The Phil Silvers Show* was 'outstanding'. *Six O'Clock Rock*, a music program that had started on Saturday evenings, was discussed at some length. It was generally agreed that the ABC should cater to teenagers, although some thought the American accent was too strongly emphasised. Assistant Controller of Programs Clement Semmler explained that *Six O'Clock Rock* was based around the American idiom, and Finlay advised that it was a 'considerable improvement' on programs he had seen in the United States. One member reported that several acquaintances had only been introduced to 'Channel 2' through the program, and most concurred it was superior to commercial counterparts. Commercial light entertainment programs—the local *Teen Time* and *Bobby Limb Show*, and the American import *I Love Lucy*—were also considered.[25]

In his memo attaching September meeting notes, Finlay restated the importance of studying the remarks of 'all Advisory Committees' and reporting back to members at the next meeting. This led to another pencilled note ('I thought we'd been doing just this for years'), possibly by Barry.[26] Inglis remarks that there was by now a 'panoply' of Advisory Committees to give their views on ABC programs: 'one for each state and the ACT [Australian Capital Territory] and four for regions, others for music and the orchestras, talks, religious broadcasts and women's sessions.'[27]

The next Viewers' Committee meeting duly considered the programs agreed to on the agenda—*Market to Market*, weather reports and children's sessions—though time ran out for sport, with the meeting running until 10.30 pm. To a question about how the ABC determined public reaction to programs, Finlay replied that the ABC subscribed to ratings surveys, and periodically conducted its own surveys. It was also 'guided' by letters and telephone calls from viewers and listeners, although 'the information obtained by this means naturally tended to be more subjective'.[28]

Barry's 'general comments' on Finlay's notes of the November meeting were brief: the matter of weather reports was 'still being watched'; there was 'nothing further to report' on gardening. There had been some changes to the type of material in *Sunday Concert* (which the Committee had been informed was designed to appeal to the 'middle brow'), but suggestions that it be moved to earlier in the afternoon, or to a Thursday or Friday evening, were met with this:

> I think it is better not to enter into discussions with the Viewers' Committee about the times at which our programmes are telecast, bearing in mind there are so many factors determining this; not the least of which are the availability of studios, rehearsal times and overtime for staff.[29]

Despite some internal ABC ambivalence, in January 1960 Moses supported the formation of a Television Viewers' Committee in Melbourne 'along the lines of the body now successfully functioning in Sydney'. The selection process outlined was similar, although community organisations as well as companies were mentioned. Meetings should be held in the studio building, which enabled members to see 'behind-the-scenes' and helped maintain interest. Members should be provided with a supper of coffee and biscuits. (Inglis had assumed that Advisory Committee members might at least receive sherry and savouries in return for no payment.) The Commission now felt meetings should only be every two or three months. Although topics for the next meeting should be advised, so members could try to watch the programs, the Committee should feel free to raise others.[30]

While the Melbourne Committee was assembled with urgings from Finlay,[31] the Sydney Committee moved to meeting bi-monthly. In March, repeats were a particular source of criticism. Barry explained that repeats were screened because of the shortage of good 'films', and the great expense of these. Finlay also noted that British programs including *Dial 999* (a crime drama) and *Boyd QC* (a courtroom drama) were shown at different times on different days to maximise audiences. Asked about ratings, the pair summarised how surveys were conducted. Finlay remarked that the ABC would prefer the samples to be considerably larger than the 200 people generally used by the survey organisations.[32]

Thirty-eight people accepted the ABC's invitation to constitute the Melbourne Viewers' Committee. They were drawn from the Premier's Department, Melbourne City Council, companies (including the Myer department store and car and tyre manufacturers), and the Young Men's Christian Association. Only seven were women, including a secretary, a stenographer and Mrs C.H. Gilbert, the wife of an auditor at the Commonwealth Bank.[33]

Barry and Finlay travelled to Melbourne for the first meeting, held at the ABC's Ripponlea studios on Monday, 4 July. Speaking to the work of the Sydney Committee, Finlay remarked that 'constructive criticism was one of the best things in this world, and the A.B.C. wanted to know the views of the average viewer'. He informed the Melbournians that the ABC had 52 Advisory Committees, 'all of which were very worthwhile'.[34] But this very fact suggests that they had grown in a somewhat ad hoc fashion, so it is hardly surprising there was some uncertainty about how best to manage and delineate the role of each one. Inglis believed that whatever these groups of interested citizens thought would be heard with courtesy and passed on, but might then be ignored.[35]

Thanking Melbourne members for their attendance, Barry said that what the Commission wanted was 'an Australian view', and it was important to be frank. Programs to be discussed at the next meeting were agreed upon, and members were divided into groups to tour the studio and see the final rehearsal of *The Evie Hayes Show*, a variety show that made its debut later that night.[36]

Still limping along, *Woman's World* was put on the agenda of the new Committee as the recording alternated between Sydney and Melbourne. Members complained that demonstrations (such as of handicrafts) were too hurried, and that the program was on too late (at 4 pm), interrupted by children coming home from school. Barry conceded the point, saying that a problem with the engineering roster needed to be overcome.[37] Director of Talks Alan Carmichael also noted that the time had been raised as a problem by the Women's Session Advisory Committee,[38] indicating that the views of various Advisory Committees sometimes coincided.

Someone—probably Finlay—began noting in the margin of Melbourne Viewers' Committee meeting notes if similar issues had been raised in Sydney.[39] Renewing and supplementing the Sydney membership for another year, Finlay explained that he was looking for 'general' rather than 'expert' opinions from keen viewers ('not necessarily "fans" of Channel 2') who had television sets in their homes, and asked organisations for information on the age and interests of nominees. In a letter to the Young Women's Christian Association (YWCA), Finlay invited its original nominee, Miss J. Fletcher, to serve another term, and asked for a second nominee 'to ensure a proper balance of women on the Committee'. The YWCA enthusiastically put forward the names of two married women 'keenly interested in T.V.'[40]

In Melbourne, Ewart Chapple, the veteran ABC broadcaster now managing the Victorian branch, had been absent from the first meeting due to illness. In August 1960 he assumed his role as chair, but he was absent again in September on recreation leave. For some reason Committee meetings were scheduled for around every six weeks, rather than quarterly. Fourteen members failed to attend the September meeting, as did Chapple in October.[41] In a memo to Finlay he expressed concern at low attendance, and said that a reminder would be sent to members before each meeting. Ever hopeful, and making no mention of Chapple's own absences, Finlay asked for early advice on topics set down for discussion, so that they could try to ensure that programs were discussed by both cities' Committees. Only a third of Melbourne members attended in November, and Chapple (whose retirement was imminent) was again on recreation leave. His deputy A.J. Winter ventured to ask if the Committee was not of sufficient interest, and was 'reassured' by members that they were glad to have the opportunity to talk and learn about television.[42] The majority of members, however, seem to have been less enthusiastic, and perhaps simply too busy with work and other commitments to attend long meetings so frequently.

In spite of the cracks that were appearing in Melbourne, the federal enterprise that was the ABC moved to establish Viewers' Committees in the 'BAPH' states. Television had started in Brisbane, Adelaide and Perth in 1959, followed by Hobart in 1960. The ABC's SA manager J.S. Miller reported in July 1961 that most firms and organisations approached had nominated names. He recommended the appointment of 17 men and 11 women, aged between 17 and 55. The youngest, Miss J.M. Symington, 'seemed the most intelligent' of the girls on the staff of the SA Housing Trust and 'quite able to express herself'. Where possible, Miller summarised the nominees' 'T.V. listening' interests. Thirty-five-year-old engineer H.J. Davey had 'a Kreisler Hi-Fi TV set. Has a definite liking for "live" shows particularly musicals on Channel 2. Does general viewing on all channels, with no particular routine.' One nominee at least, Miss N. Craven, did not have her own set, giving an insight into how some Australians watched early television. She was president of the social club at the YWCA Hostel in Adelaide, which took 'a vote each evening as to the programme the residents in the Hostel wish to view, as the Hostel accommodates 85 and there are quite a few viewers each evening'. A late addition to the Adelaide Viewers' Committee was teacher Miss Merle Jenkins, who served on the National Council of Women's Radio and Television Committee.[43]

A Hobart Viewers' Committee was also assembled, with 31 people—eight of them female—nominated by the organisations approached. Two police officers were experienced at appearing on television. G.W. McCabe, Public Relations Officer to Labor Premier Eric Reece, moonlighted as Tasmanian correspondent for the Melbourne periodical *Listener In-TV*. B.K. Miller MLC (also Labor) joined the Committee, with ABC state manager F. Wilbur Reed noting that upper house members of parliament were elected and functioned on a non-party basis in Tasmania. The Electrolytic Zinc Company of Australasia proposed a supervisor, Neil C. Ashdown, who already served on the ABC's Tasmanian Advisory Committee.[44]

A free-ranging discussion took place at the first meeting, at 8 pm on Monday, 21 August 1961, followed by technical talks on production and a studio tour. Asked whether there were Committees in other states, Reid explained their evolution. Interestingly, Mrs Sheila Kerr of the Town Clerk's Department said 'she understood Melbourne meetings had been stultified by people who were aware of the professional ratings of different programs'. Reed stressed the importance of frank discussion, and the value of also conveying the opinions of friends. An internal memo conceded that one member did occasionally quote rating figures at Melbourne Committee meetings; but while such figures could be helpful to the ABC, it realised that certain types of programs and timeslots could legitimately yield quite different results. Reed assured the next meeting that if and when ratings became available for Hobart, 'they would not be permitted to handicap Committee discussions'.[45]

By August 1961 WA manager E.K. Sholl had assembled 30 names for a Perth Viewers' Committee. Twenty-seven (11 of them women, the highest proportion of any state) agreed to join. Following talks with trade unions, two further members were recruited in an effort to, as Sholl put it, 'balance the large proportion of "white collar" workers'.[46] At the first meeting, on Monday, 25 September, Arthur Povah, the Acting Program Director for Western Australia, spoke of his wish for the Committee to convey 'normal public reaction[s]' to programs generated by specialist ABC departments.[47]

On 27 September, J.S. Miller thanked members of the new Adelaide Committee for giving up their time in such a public-spirited way.[48] Seven weeks later, A.T. Read, the Director of Light Entertainment, complained that he had only just received the minutes. By this time, the second meeting had already been held. Read was annoyed not to have received timely insights into the Committee's views on light entertainment programs, and particularly wanted feedback on *The Magic of Music*,[49] a weekly program with Eric Jupp and his orchestra launched for older viewers.[50]

The November meeting, which concluded with a studio tour, included a long discussion about another new program, *Four Corners*. Inglis writes of the popularity of the Saturday-night current affairs program at a time when there was no national daily newspaper, recording that it was seen regularly by up to 10 per cent of Australians.[51] This favourable reception was reflected in the discussions of the Adelaide Viewers' Committee. Young clerk A.B. Mackew said it was the best television program he had seen, astutely summing it up as 'extremely well balanced, giving good information on matters of the moment, and yet with a lighthearted atmosphere that made it easy to take'. But Symington objected to the closing off-the-cuff interviews with 'the "man in the street", as they showed such a poor standard of Australian intelligence'. This criticism was supported by some other members, although Mackew and Mrs Spencer George from the Kindergarten Union defended the spot.[52] Members of the Melbourne Committee praised *Four Corners*' topicality, accessibility and longer segments, including one on the Box Ridge Aboriginal reserve in northern New South Wales.[53]

Even though charity worker Beryl Beaurepaire, who had married into the Olympic Tyre dynasty, had recently joined the Melbourne Committee, E.A. Whiteley, who had succeeded Chapple as Victorian manager, thought that some action needed to be taken to renew membership. A 'hard core' of members attended and participated in discussions with some enthusiasm, but membership had dwindled, he reported in November 1961. At least one member wanted the meetings—which sometimes ran until 10 pm—moved forward to around 5.30 pm, but this earlier time could not be managed by some workers.[54]

The night for the fledgling Hobart Viewers' Committee changed from Mondays to Tuesdays. University student Judith Gough, who was unable to attend the December meeting, took the trouble to send in a written report, with 'laudatory comments' on *Four Corners*. Some of the female Committee members indicated they found *Woman's World* quite interesting and instructive, but two male members reported that their wives complained the program (now at 2.30 pm) clashed with children returning from school, and it needed more entertainment. The meeting (which ran until 10.40 pm) concluded with some weighing up of programs on the ABC and Hobart's one commercial station. John Tupp, who worked in retail, ventured that TVT6 'provided entertainment for the masses whereas Channel 2 did not'. Reed argued that the ABC did schedule programs with mass appeal, but that all sections of the community needed to be catered for under the charter. W.A.A. Peters, a BP sales manager, suggested that more 'high brow' programs should be grouped together for perhaps an hour or two on a given evening rather than dispersed across peak viewing times.[55]

Charles Moses advised that Viewers' Committees should be maintained until the end of 1962, 'when we will again consider whether their value is sufficient to justify their continuance'. But he wanted the number of ABC officers in attendance reduced, as the meetings were taking up the time of too many relatively senior staff members. In a personal note, Moses added that while the 'Head Office Committee' (Sydney) had on some occasions made useful suggestions about programs, 'I would think that the[ir] main ... usefulness is in public relations'.[56] The general manager's commitment to federalism, and to audience input, only went so far.

Whiteley attempted to revitalise the Melbourne Viewers' Committee by recruiting a school-boy and school-girl and having Dr Peter Kenny, a psychologist who had been appointed head of the ABC's Research and Statistics section (which had succeeded Listener Research), speak at the April 1962 meeting. Kenny explained the mechanics of ratings surveys, and spoke about ABC Listener and Viewer Panels, which seem to have been set up in 1958. Asked whether these made the Viewers' Committees redundant, he assured members that the Committees could help frame the kind of questions to ask the Panels, while also remarking on the 'Public Relations and Publicity value' of the Committees.[57]

Then, in March, there were almost as many ABC officers (three) in attendance as Committee members (four) at the Hobart Viewers' Committee meeting.[58] Two months later, Finlay asked state managers for their 'frank views' on the value of their Committees. Whiteley reported that those members who did attend came well-prepared and were 'good communicators' who obviously watched programs to be discussed with their colleagues, friends and families: 'In a small way, they bring Channel 2 before quite a varied circle of people and could create interest in our programmes.' He also observed that they sometimes had insights into programs not conveyed by other sources, but reluctantly concluded that the small dividend was not worth the effort.[59] This view was shared by the Victorian and Tasmanian managers, with Reed in Hobart adding that he thought Committee attendance had declined because television's novelty was wearing off.[60] Sholl was the most enthusiastic defender of Viewers' Committees, explaining that discussions in Perth showed 'intelligence and insight' and brought programmers in contact with the 'ordinary viewer'. Although attendance at the most recent meeting had slipped, and servicing the meetings took time, he was keen for the Perth endeavour to continue.[61]

Finlay's memo seems to have been sent to the Queensland manager, David Felsman, who was then forced to admit that a Brisbane Viewers' Committee had not yet been formed. While claiming that the ABC's Queensland Advisory Committee had been acting as 'our T.V. Viewers' Committee', he said he would move to form a Viewers' Committee. Finlay was unimpressed, replying on 21 May that both he and Moses had pointed out that the two Advisory Committees had quite different representatives and their discussions were to be at a different level. Three days later, he told Felsman that after discussions with Moses, a decision on the future of the Viewers' Committees would not be made before the end of the year.

As a consequence, Finlay asked Felsman to form a Brisbane Committee promptly, so that it could meet twice by December. Whether it was constituted is unclear; in March 1963 Finlay complained that he had never received any meeting notes.[62]

Meanwhile, the Perth Viewers' Committee expanded to 36, with the addition of representatives of pensioners, housewives, the Country Women's Association and the Australian-American Association, as well as a married couple.[63] Committee members thought that *Four Corners* was 'first rate' and one of the ABC's best programs. When one member raised how late it was broadcast in Perth, ABC officers explained that film from Sydney and Melbourne was sometimes delayed by flight schedules. Early in 1963, the acting state manager, Malcolm Naylor, outlined the purpose of the Viewer Panel which had recently been formed in Western Australia.[64]

In May, Finlay recommended that Television Viewers' Committees in all cities but Perth be permitted to lapse on 30 June, when members' terms were to expire. He had finally come to share concerns about poor attendance, and the amount of time the Committees consumed. While he felt sure 'good public relations' had accrued from the Committees, he wondered if decisions—for sound logistical reasons—not to act on their recommendations might have been counterproductive. While the discussions of small Committees could only ever be 'subjective', the ABC's Research and Statistics section had greatly improved, and the Listener and Viewer Panels now had 5000 members. But with Perth reporting an average attendance of 17 members, that Committee could continue for another year, when the state manager would reassess its value.[65] Finlay broke the news to the Sydney Committee at its meeting on 17 June, thanking members for their service, and advising that they would be invited to join a Viewer Panel.[66] The notes of each city's final meetings do not record the reactions of the small number of members in attendance. But at least one member—Hobart's G.W. McCabe—remained keenly interested in his broadcasting work, offering himself to the ABC's Research section.[67]

Not surprisingly, a weekly program of local current affairs, *West Coast 63* (followed by *West Coast 64*), drew the attention of the one remaining Viewers' Committee. Perth members agreed that young John Penlington was a capable host, but differed over whether each half-hour program should focus on one story, or include three to four. They were pleased to learn that some stories, including on bushfires and Rottnest Island, made their way overseas.[68] The strength of Penlington's work on *West Coast 63* scored him the job of co-host of *Four Corners*.[69]

However, the Perth Viewers' Committee did not automatically applaud national success. At a meeting in 1964, one member volunteered that Diana Ward, who had moved from Perth to Sydney, was 'no longer the natural, attractive person she had been'. Asked for his comments on the meeting notes, the Director of Planning (Television), Robin Wood, defended the announcer for acquiring 'a great deal more polish and a degree of sophistication' which made her work attractive for NSW audiences. In a response to the response, WA manager Sholl noted that the criticism of Ward had been made by the Viewers' Committee, not ABC officers. Even so, 'we do feel that she was far more natural and charming when she worked for us in the West', he went on to write.[70]

The Perth Committee continued to meet beyond mid-1964, with Finlay reading meeting summaries with interest. But from that time, the number of members in attendance began being scrawled on top.[71] Only 11 people attended the November meeting, which may help to explain why there seems to have been minimal discussion of *Four Corners*' visit to Perth the previous month to report on the execution of serial killer Edgar Eric Cooke. Clem Semmler controversially declined to run the story on capital punishment. The summary of the Viewers' Committee meeting merely recorded that Malcolm Naylor (who had defended the choice of story subject) 'took the opportunity to explain the situation in respect of "Four Corners", and particularly emphasised that no political pressure whatsoever had been brought to bear on the A.B.C.'[72]

In a June 1965 memo, Sholl speculated that with television established in Perth for five years, and with a Viewer Panel of 600 WA members, the Committee may have served its purpose. Finlay was a little cautious where the state was concerned, suggesting that Naylor check with the Commissioner from Western Australia, accountant Harrie Halvorsen, to see if his view coincided.[73] It presumably did, for the Committee did not meet again.

And so the ABC's six-year experiment with Television Viewers' Committees came to an end. The Committees had had a rocky history, with a champion for the first few years in Huck Finlay. Even he had come to question their value, and how 'representative' around 30 people in each capital city could be of viewers across Australia. They were overtaken by the expansion of the ABC's Research section and the formation of Viewer as well as Listener Panels. Semmler, who was overlooked when Talbot

Duckmanton was promoted to general manager in 1965, lost responsibility for programs—just as, he would later note acerbically, the ABC's 'obsession with ratings' began.[74]

The Viewers' Committees were yet another committee for harassed ABC officers, and were just the latest incarnation of Advisory Committees stretched across the organisation, as well as Australia. The fact that the ABC's first state Advisory Committee was formed in Western Australia and that the last Viewers' Committee to be disbanded was in Western Australia 30 years later helps to highlight how unique the state was in the ABC's federal imaginings. The Commission probably also regarded the city-based Viewers' Committees of less and less value as television extended to the regions in the 1960s.

Other ABC Advisory Committees may have lasted longer, or achieved more. But how would we know? It is time for Australian historians to uncover and read the papers of these Committees, and to see something of how ABC programs were received as well as produced. The records of the Sydney, Melbourne, Hobart, Adelaide and Perth Television Viewers' Committees give us at least some qualitative insights into how viewers of early Australian television responded to topical programs (such as *Woman's World* and *West Coast 63*), iconic programs (*Six O'Clock Rock* and *Four Corners*),[75] imported and local (Australian as well as regional) programs, short-lived programs and specials; what they valued on commercial as well as ABC television; and how they watched, collectively and individually.

Notes

1. K.S. Inglis, *This Is the ABC: The Australian Broadcasting Commission, 1932–1983* (Melbourne: Melbourne University Press, 1983).
2. National Archives of Australia (NAA)/NSW: SP613/1, 2/2/7, memo from C.J.A. Moses, 14 December 1937. State Committees were formed for Western Australia in 1935 and Tasmania in 1936.
3. Inglis 1983, p. 57; Clement Semmler, *The ABC—Aunt Sally and Sacred Cow* (Melbourne: Melbourne University Press, 1981), p. 157.
4. Alan Thomas, *Broadcast and Be Damned: The ABC's First Two Decades* (Melbourne: Melbourne University Press, 1980), p. 130.
5. Thomas 1980, p. 130; Semmler 1981, pp. 59–60; NAA/NSW: SP613/1, 2/2/7, memo from Cleary to Basil W. Kirke, 29 August 1935, pp. 2–3; SP613/1, 2/2/7 PART II, memo from T.W. Bearup, 1 November 1940, p. 1.

6. NAA/NSW: SP613/1, 2/2/7, WA Advisory Committee meeting minutes, 28 May 1936, p. 1. On 28 March 1945, WA manager Conrad Charlton commented on the 'exceptionally' strong University representation on the original Committee: SP613/1, 2/2/7 PART II.
7. NAA/NSW: SP613/1, 2/2/7, memos from Kirke to Cleary, 10 September 1935; Cleary to Kirke, 11 October 1935; Kirke to Cleary, 2 November 1935.
8. NAA/NSW: SP613/1, 2/2/7, WA Advisory Committee meeting minutes, 19 August 1936, p. 1.
9. NAA/NSW: SP613/1, 2/2/7, minutes, 23 June 1937, p. 1.
10. NAA/NSW: SP613/1, 2/2/7, minutes and correspondence, 24 November–14 December 1937.
11. *News*, 13 October 1937, p. 3 and 13 April 1938, p. 9; *Advertiser*, 24 December 1937, p. 18.
12. NAA/NAA: SP613/1, 2/2/7 PART II, meeting minutes, 24 September 1941, p. 1; memo from Bearup, 1 December 1941.
13. Mark Armstrong, *Broadcasting Law and Policy in Australia* (Sydney: Butterworths, 1982), p. 37; *Australian Broadcasting Act* 1942, section 87, https://www.legislation.gov.au/Details/C1942A00033, accessed 17 December 2019.
14. Inglis 1983, p. 120.
15. NAA/NSW: SP613/1, 2/2/7 PART II, minutes and correspondence, 4 August–22 September 1943. The composition of each state Advisory Committee is listed in the *Australian Broadcasting Commission 15th Annual Report* (Sydney: ABC, 1946–47), p. 34.
16. Thomas 1980, p. 130; Inglis 1983, p. 142.
17. NAA/NSW: SP613/1, 2/2/7 PART II, minutes and correspondence, 25 July 1944–5 January 1945.
18. Armstrong 1982, p. 38.
19. NAA/NSW: C1574, TV9/5/1, ABCB agendum, May 1957; 'Television Audience Research' memo, 29 May 1957; memo from Barry, 19 June 1957.
20. NAA/NSW: C1574, TV4/1/11, memo from Finlay, 31 December 1957. For Finlay, see Inglis 1983, p. 138.
21. NAA/NSW: C1574, TV4/1/11, memos, 22 January–25 February 1958.
22. NAA/NSW: SP727/2, TV2/1/36, memo from Moses, 5 June 1959.
23. NAA/NSW: SP727/2, TV2/1/36, memo from Finlay, 31 August 1959. See also Inglis 1983, p. 213.
24. NAA/NSW: SP727/2, TV2/1/36, ABC TV Viewers' Committee (Sydney) Questionnaire Analysis, n.d. (1959).
25. NAA/NSW: SP727/2, TV2/1/36, TV Viewers' Committee Meeting (Sydney) summary, 21 September 1959.
26. NAA/NSW: SP727/2, TV2/1/36, memo from Finlay, 9 October 1959.
27. Inglis 1983, p. 208.

28. NAA/NSW: SP727/2, TV2/1/36, Sydney meeting summary, 19 October 1959.
29. NAA/NSW: SP727/2, TV2/1/36, memo 59/134 from Barry, n.d. On 18 January 1960, when some Committee members questioned the timing of *Face the People*, Finlay noted the difficulties faced by schedulers.
30. NAA/NSW: C1574, TV1/5/6, memo from Moses, 7 January 1960. See also Inglis 1983, p. 209.
31. NAA/NSW: C1574, TV1/5/6, memos from Finlay, 6 May and 7 June 1960.
32. NAA/NSW: SP727/2, TV2/1/36, Sydney meeting summary, 21 March 1960.
33. NAA/NSW: C1574, TV1/5/6, memo from Ewart Chapple, 2 June 1960; SP727/2, TV2/1/36, TV Viewers' Committee—Melbourne, 9 June 1960.
34. NAA/NSW: SP727/2, TV2/1/36, TV Viewers' Committee Meeting (Melbourne) summary, 4 July 1960, p. 1.
35. Inglis 1983, pp. 208–09.
36. NAA/NSW: SP727/2, TV2/1/36, Melbourne meeting summary, 4 July 1960, p. 1.
37. Inglis 1983, p. 213; NAA: C1574, TV1/5/6, Melbourne meeting summary, 2 August 1960, p. 2.
38. NAA/NSW: SP727/2, TV2/1/36, memo from Carmichael, 14 September 1960.
39. See, for instance, marginalia in NAA/NSW: C1574, TV1/5/6, Melbourne meeting summary, 2 August 1960.
40. NAA/NSW: C1574, TV1/5/3, correspondence with Finlay, 12 July–2 August 1961.
41. NAA/NSW: C1574, TV1/5/6, Melbourne meeting summaries, 4 July–24 October 1960.
42. NAA/NSW: C1574, TV1/5/6, memo from Chapple, 17 October 1960; Melbourne meeting summary, 28 November 1960; memo from Winter, 13 December 1960. For Chapple, see Inglis 1983, p. 245 and *Radio Active*, March 1961 (I am grateful to Guy Tranter for this article).
43. NAA/NSW: C1574, TV1/5/12, memos from Miller, 26 July 1961; Finlay, 1 August 1961.
44. NAA/NSW: C1574, TV1/5/10, memo from Reed, 5 May 1961.
45. NAA/NSW: C1574, TV1/5/9, TV Viewers' Committee Meeting (Hobart) summaries, 21 August and 2 October 1961, p. 1; memo from Darrell Miley, 5 September 1961.
46. NAA/NSW: C1574, 1/5/14, correspondence, 14–21 August 1961; inter-office memo, 24 November 1961.

47. NAA/NSW: C1574, 1/5/13, TV Viewers' Committee Meeting (Perth) summary, 25 September 1961, p. 2.
48. NAA/NSW: C1574, TV1/5/11, TV Viewers' Committee Meeting (Adelaide) summary, 27 September 1961, p. 1.
49. NAA/NSW: C1574, TV1/5/11, memo from Read, 20 November 1961.
50. Inglis 1983, pp. 206, 295. *The Magic of Music* was to run until 1974 and be sold internationally.
51. Inglis 1983, pp. 216–17.
52. NAA/NSW: C1574, TV1/5/11, Adelaide meeting summary, 15 November 1961, pp. 2–3.
53. NAA/NSW: C1574, TV1/5/6, Melbourne meeting summary, 16 October 1961, p. 1. For the Box Ridge segment, see https://www.abc.net.au/4corners/box-ridge%2D%2D-1961/2833760, accessed 26 October 2019.
54. NAA/NSW: C1574, TV1/5/6, Melbourne meeting summaries, 21 August 1961, p. 1 and 16 October 1961, p. 3; memo from Whiteley, 20 November 1961.
55. NAA/NSW: C1574, TV1/5/9, TV Viewers' Committee Meeting (Hobart) summary, 5 December 1961, p. 1.
56. NAA/NSW: C1574, TV1/5/6, memo from Moses, 19 February 1962.
57. NAA/NSW: C1574, TV1/5/6, memos from Whiteley, 26 April and 15 May 1962; TV Viewers' Committee –Meeting (Melbourne) summary, 30 April 1962. For Kenny, see Inglis 1983, p. 226.
58. NAA/NSW: C1574, TV1/5/9, Hobart meeting summary, 6 March 1962.
59. NAA/NSW: C1574, TV1/5/6, memos from Finlay, 21 May 1962; Whiteley, 6 June 1962; TV1/5/11, memo from Miller, 1 June 1962.
60. NAA/NSW: C1574, TV1/5/9, memo from Reed, 30 May 1962; TV1/5/11, memo from Miller, 1 June 1962. It is unclear if the NSW manager responded to Finlay's memo.
61. NAA/NSW: C1574, 1/5/13, memo from Sholl, 30 May 1962.
62. NAA/NSW: C1574, TV1/5/7.
63. NAA/NSW: C1574, 1/5/14, correspondence, 25 July 1962–14 May 1963.
64. NAA/NSW: C1574, 1/5/13, Perth meeting summaries, 16 April 1962, p. 1 and 18 February 1963, p. 2.
65. NAA/NSW: C1574, TV1/5/4, memo from Finlay, 31 May 1963. For Perth, see also C1574, TV1/5/13, memo from Naylor, 8 March 1963.
66. NAA/NSW: C1574, TV1/5/4, TV Viewers' Committee Meeting (Sydney) summary, 17 June 1963, p. 3.
67. NAA/NSW: C1574, TV1/5/9, memo from W.M. Foster, 2 October 1963.
68. NAA/NSW: C1574, 1/5/13, Perth meeting summaries, 24 June 1963–9 November 1964.

69. Inglis 1983, p. 222.
70. NAA/NSW: C1574, 1/5/13, Perth meeting summaries, 15 June 1964, p. 2; memos from Wood, 13 July 1964 and Sholl, 23 July 1964.
71. NAA/NSW: C1574, 1/5/13, Perth meeting summaries, 15 June 1964–6 September 1965; memo from Finlay, 8 July 1964.
72. Inglis 1983, pp. 222–24; NAA/NSW: C1574, 1/5/13, Perth meeting summary, 9 November 1964, p. 2.
73. NAA/NSW: C1574, TV1/5/13, memos, 29 June–22 September 1965.
74. Inglis 1983, pp. 257–58, 300–01; Semmler 1981, pp. 55, 62.
75. *Four Corners* remains one of the ABC's flagship television programs.

Bibliography

Advertiser (Adelaide).
Armstrong, Mark. *Broadcasting Law and Policy in Australia* (Sydney: Butterworths, 1982).
Australian Broadcasting Act 1942, https://www.legislation.gov.au/Details/C1942A00033, accessed 17 December 2019.
Australian Broadcasting Commission, *15th Annual Report* (Sydney: ABC, 1946–1947).
———, 'Box Ridge', *Four Corners*, https://www.abc.net.au/4corners/box-ridge%2D%2D-1961/2833760, accessed 26 October 2019.
Inglis, K.S. *This Is the ABC: The Australian Broadcasting Commission, 1932–1983* (Melbourne: Melbourne University Press, 1983).
National Archives of Australia (NAA)/NSW: C1574, TV1/5/3. TV Viewer's Committee—Melbourne—Nominations for Membership.
———. C1574, TV1/5/4. TV Viewer's Committee—Sydney—Minutes—General.
———. C1574, TV1/5/6. TV Viewer's Committee—Melbourne—Minutes—General.
———. C1574, TV1/5/7. TV Viewer's Committee—Queensland—Minutes.
———. C1574, TV1/5/9. TV Viewers' Committee—Hobart—Minutes.
———. C1574, TV1/5/10. TV Viewer's Committee—Tasmania—Nominations for Membership.
———. C1574, TV1/5/11. TV Viewers' Committee—Adelaide—Minutes.
———. C1574, TV1/5/12. TV Viewer's Committee—Adelaide—Nominations for Membership.
———. C1574, 1/5/13. Advisory Committees—TV Viewers Committee Perth—Minutes General.
———. C1574, 1/5/14. Advisory Committees—TV Viewers Committee Perth—Nominations for Membership.

———. C1574, TV4/1/11, Television Programmes—Programme Policy and Administration—Television Programmes—Audiences.

———. C1574, TV9/5/1. Statistics & Viewer Research—ABC Surveys—Audience Research Planning.

———. SP613/1, 2/2/7. ABC State Broadcasting Advisory Committee—Western Australia.

———. SP613/1, 2/2/7 PART II. ABC State Broadcasting Advisory Committee—Western Australia (Box 4).

———. SP727/2, TV2/1/36. TV Viewer's Committee (Box 2).

News (Adelaide).

Radio Active.

Semmler, Clement. *The ABC—Aunt Sally and Sacred Cow* (Melbourne: Melbourne University Press, 1981).

Thomas, Alan. *Broadcast and Be Damned: The ABC's First Two Decades* (Melbourne: Melbourne University Press, 1980).

CHAPTER 7

Matchmaking

Abstract This chapter traces the history of Australian broadcasting programs about romance and dating. It moves from radio in the 1930s and 1940s to dating programs on commercial television in the 1960s, teasing out notions of romantic consumerism and ordinary Australians on the airwaves. It then pays particular attention to participants and audience involvement in two popular creations of the 1980s: *Midnight Matchmaker* on Sydney radio and *Perfect Match* on network television.

Keywords Audiences • Broadcasting • Radio • Television • Romance • Game shows

This chapter considers broadcasting's role in one of the most intimate aspects of the lives of audience members: finding romance and love. It uncovers radio programs with a romantic theme, mainly on one Sydney commercial station, 2GB, since the 1930s.[1] It then traces local adaptations of American dating shows on the Ten commercial television network from the 1960s, teasing out the embrace of romantic consumerism as well as apprehensions about the role of ordinary Australians on the airwaves. The chapter moves on to concentrate on two top-rating broadcast endeavours of the 1980s: 2GB's *Midnight Matchmaker* and Ten's *Perfect Match*. It considers how and why Australians participated in the programs and, in the case of *Perfect Match*, the role of the studio audience. It looks at the shift from programs which implied a responsible interest in love and marriage, to programs with more of a focus on fun and sex. It argues that *Perfect Match* marked a transition towards later reality television programs that had the capacity to embarrass and exploit participants, and confect controversy and celebrity.

2GB's *Cupid's Conquests* was perhaps the first program to bring 'real life' romance to the Australian airwaves, at a time when the print media—particularly women's magazines—was promoting the glamour of romantic consumption.[2] 'There are many ways of announcing engagements, but Frank Sturge Harty has found another. Let the radio do it', declared a radio correspondent in 1938. The *Sun*'s columnist envisaged couples arranging Saturday-night parties at which their friends would hear the 'glad news', with appropriate fanfare and music involving announcer and singer Jack Lumsdaine.[3]

Harty was the very model of the male authority figure on radio. A returned serviceman and Church of England minister, he had begun hosting an afternoon advice program on another commercial station, 2UE, in 1934. *Between Ourselves*, Harty explained to *Wireless Weekly*, was 'designed to be intimate, so that every woman, sitting alone, will feel that it belongs to her individually'.[4] Harty moved to 2GB to host another advice session, where he was grandly described as 'The Man Who Knows the Confidence of TEN THOUSAND WOMEN'. The former minister assured radio periodicals that he met privately with each couple and checked their bona fides before announcing their engagement on *Cupid's Conquests*, and counselled against 'violent infatuations' (Fig. 7.1).[5]

The program continued into 1939,[6] when 2GB introduced *Love Time*, a nightly session of famous love songs.[7] Sydney's 2SM also gingerly launched a 'novelty audience participation' show in 1940. Listeners were asked to contact the Catholic station with ideas for marriage proposals to be dramatised. Three different versions of the winning proposal were dramatised in the studio, by the listener and partners of the opposite sex. Each participant in *Proposals*, heard on Thursday nights, was given a prize by 2SM manager and star announcer John Dunne.[8]

Back at 2GB, *Love Time* was followed by *The Romantic Hour*, featuring 'sweet music', until around 1943. Dedicated to 'all who are young enough to still believe in romance and love', the program was presented at 10.45 pm by Arthur O'Keefe, a former actor, salesman—and 'eligible bachelor'.[9] At least one retailer saw the commercial appeal of a program such as *The Romantic Hour*. Angus & Coote jewellers referred to it in newspaper

Fig. 7.1 *Australian Women's Weekly*, 19 November 1938. (Copyright Nine Radio)

advertisements for engagement rings, drawing an explicit link between romance and consumerism.[10]

Then, in 1946, came 2GB's *Blind Date*, probably Australia's first romantic game show. At 7.30 pm each Saturday, two servicemen jousted to determine which one would take out a young woman for dinner and dancing at Romano's nightclub, chaperoned by announcers. The servicemen each spoke to the woman over a telephone connected to the studio, so the audience could hear the men's wooing and her decision. The woman was typically a model or actress, with the possibility of an ordinary person being matched with a celebrity to emerge as quite common in programs with a romantic theme.[11] The reward, paid for by the station, reflected a conception of consumerist dating and gift-giving that the presence of American servicemen in Australia during World War II had entrenched.[12] *Blind Date* was sufficiently novel to feature in a Cinesound newsreel.[13] 2GB's next undertaking, in 1947, involved listeners even more. *Boy Meets Girl* was hosted by comedian George Foster, who had appeared in the station's recent production of the Hollywood screwball comedy of the same name. Each episode saw three men and four women, chosen from applications from listeners, vying for dates. The ultimate loser got a date with Foster himself as a prize.[14]

2GB then seems to have stepped back from a decade of romantic programming, generally on Saturday nights. Then, in 1958, another Sydney commercial radio station, 2UE, launched a program, also called *Blind Date*, on Friday nights. It seems to have involved listeners (reportedly in their hundreds each week) sending in photographs of themselves. Host Tony Withers chaperoned the winning couples on dates to another nightclub, Chequers.[15]

'No topic in print, radio or film sells better than "Romance"', declared a South Australian newspaper in the lead-up to Valentine's Day, 1960.[16] In 1966 producer Reg Grundy created *The Marriage Game* for Sydney's newest commercial television station, TEN10. At lunchtime from Mondays to Thursdays, it tested how much newly married couples knew about each other. Winners competed for the main prize (a washing machine in the first week) on Friday nights. The show was based on *The Newlywed Game*, which had recently been launched on the American Broadcasting Corporation.[17] The local adaptation was further evidence of one cultural narrative of romantic love becoming increasingly hegemonic through the American-dominated global economy.[18]

Sun-Herald television writer Valda Marshall reflected on how host, actor John Bonney, had to contend with the 'old' problem of the 'inarticulate Australian', rarely getting anything more out of contestants than 'gee', 'golly' or maybe 'omigosh'.[19] It is worth noting that this view of 'ordinary' Australians was shared by officials at the Australian Broadcasting Control Board (ABCB), which as we saw in Chap. 5 was reluctant to allow dial-in talkback radio. There were concerns about 'poorly spoken' individuals like 'Fred of Coburg' going to air, before the commercial radio industry's agitations led to the overturning of a ban on the recording of telephone conversations in 1967. A Queensland Board officer predicted that it might take time for listeners to become accustomed to 'untrained voices carrying on conversations with polished announcers'.[20]

Taking another look at *The Marriage Game* in 1967, when it had moved to Tuesday nights over summer, Marshall thought the production had improved somewhat, though she was still struck by 'The Great Australian Silence'.[21] Producers tried to liven it up by featuring well-known personalities, including a group of cartoonists. Another television writer was unimpressed, 'yawning' in response to what was revealed about the 'Press gents', such as Frank Benier not being able to get his wife out of bed in the mornings.[22]

When Malcolm Searle, who replaced Bonney as host, was interviewed about *The Marriage Game* in 1969, he hinted at difficulties with the Australian contestants, indicating that they were more reserved than their 'gregarious', 'marvellous' and amusing English counterparts. Husbands were also more reticent than their wives, Searle said, with men often talked into appearing on the show. He observed that couples were generally in good spirits when they arrived at the studio, and knew each other well. But even though the show's questions were intended to be harmless, some occasionally revived old tensions and led to dramas after filming ended.[23] *The Marriage Game*, which had extended to ATV0 in Melbourne, seems to have continued until 1972. One of the last episodes featured fictional couples from the soap opera *Number 96*, in an early instance of cross-promotion by the Ten Network.[24]

By now TEN10 had launched *Blind Date*, based on another American series, *The Dating Game*. It was hosted by radio disc jockey Graham Webb at 5.30 pm on Tuesdays and Thursdays. Aimed at teenagers, the new Grundy production apparently started as a fill-in early in 1967. The format involved pairing off girls and boys with sets of matching questions, with the prize a chaperoned dinner for two. Marshall described early episodes as 'loose, sloppy and boring', but found the format tightened a few months later. Celebrities such as pop stars were sometimes involved. As *Blind Date* took off, Grundy hit on the idea of licensing his programs to other commercial broadcasters. *Blind Date* was sold to ATV0 and eight other stations around Australia, with the press starting to refer to Ten as 'Network G'. The prizes became weekends away (also chaperoned) at the Barrier Reef and the Snowy Mountains.[25]

There was added interest in 1968, when Webb's brother Mike competed and then became an announcer on *Blind Date*. Graham Webb also reportedly met his own wife on the program, saying he knew of around ten couples 'keeping company'. The questions he asked, on moods, appearances and boyfriends, against a background of flashing hearts and cupids, were hardly profound. But contestants could toy with expectations, as when one 'jolly, blonde nurse' was asked 'What time do you get home after a late night?' She replied that she got home at 4 am after a night out with the girls, but after a night out with a boy, about 2 am.[26]

After Webb, now a television star, left for the United States in late 1969, auditions were reportedly held around the country. By the time Jeremy Cordeaux was appointed, ratings had begun to slide, along with the prizes: dates to Luna Park, and deodorants for runners-up. *Blind Date* was dropped in 1970.[27]

Reg Grundy Enterprises resurrected *Blind Date* for the Seven Network in 1974. Scottish-born singer Bobby Hanna, now resident in Australia, successfully auditioned as host. Each episode, at 5.30 pm weekdays, featured three boys and three girls—'nice, ordinary kids' aged between 16 and 25—competing for a date with a mystery showbusiness personality.[28] The program seems to have ceased production in 1975.

Two of Australia's best-known romance programs—*Midnight Matchmaker* on 2GB and *Perfect Match* on the Ten Network—emerged in the 1980s. One evening, while waiting to conduct a talkback counselling session on 2GB, an American-born psychologist penned a proposal for a matchmaking program, inspired in part by a successful New York radio undertaking. Dr Fred Orr, who was interested in problems of social interaction and ran a shyness clinic, thought that the initial anonymity radio afforded listeners might allow it to help bring people looking for relationships together. 2GB's manager, who was sceptical, believing that Australians would be too reticent to ring in, showed the proposal to various people, including late-night host Brian Wilshire. Purely by coincidence, a woman rang in one night to express her desire for a relationship, and the switchboard lit up. Wilshire began swapping the telephone numbers of callers over the next few nights, and *Midnight Matchmaker* was born in 1982.[29]

The program began with the seductive jingle, 'If you're there on your own, I'm here on the phone, Brian Wilshire on 2GB'. People aged over 17 rang in to talk about themselves and the type of person they wanted to meet. Anyone interested was to write to the caller via 2GB, as its switchboard had become overloaded during the experiment with swapping numbers. There were two rules in an effort to ensure the bona fides, and guarantee the safety, of participants: male callers had to be listed in the telephone book, and women had to initiate personal contact.[30]

Callers adopted names—'Sailor', 'Cookie' and 'Bunny' were popular—and provided details about themselves and what they wanted in a mate: age, height and weight; whether they were turned off by beards, tattoos or garlic; whether they were morning or night people; and whether they were looking for someone of any particular race, religion or star sign. A kind of linguistic code was deployed: 'spare parts' referred to spectacles and hearing aids; 'NCT' meant neat, clean and tidy. The show was resolutely heterosexual, and spelling out racial preferences was encouraged: one caller wanted 'a native, normal Australian'; another did not want Asians or Muslims to apply.[31]

Within five months *Midnight Matchmaker* had acquired an audience share of 21 per cent, greater than for any other session in Sydney; it had received 3000 letters; and it took credit for arranging two marriages. Wilshire ('a happily married father of four') took 10–12 calls each program, and calculated that anyone ringing in had at least a 50 per cent chance of meeting four people. A sprinkling of callers and correspondents were from as far away as Queensland and Tasmania.[32]

As we have seen in earlier chapters, the perception of radio as the most intimate and companionable of media has long had currency in writings about broadcasting.[33] Within the industry, late-night programs are regarded as the most intimate of all. The findings of a 1979 study of late-night Chicago radio were consistent with the hypothesis that those who called in were seeking human contact; those who were unmarried made up almost three-quarters of the people who had most recently called a talk show.[34] *Midnight Matchmaker* ran from midnight until 1 am Mondays to Fridays and from 8 to 10 pm on Saturdays, 'the loneliest night of the week' in the words of the *Sydney Morning Herald*'s Doug Anderson.[35]

The broadcasting correspondent was an early admirer of 2GB's venture. With 'radio's role as a late night companion' well established, Anderson wrote, it seemed logical to extend its function to bringing together people who were listening to the same program. A subsequent column described the 'Lonely Heart's Club of with a bit of style' as 'a vast improvement on the blatant spruiking of massage parlours'. *Midnight Matchmaker* provided a free 'potential remedy to one of the most depressing social problems of our time': isolation.[36]

Divorced journalist Margaret Morrison found out about the program through Anderson's column. As most of the men who called in bored her, she decided to go on *Midnight Matchmaker* herself. In her article about the experience, she recounted coming up with a list of her key characteristics, and what she was looking for, as something of an 'ordeal'. The 47-year-old ('attractive enough to have been a TV compere') found the 2GB telephonist helpful and cheerful, and Wilshire 'masterly' in his command of their interview. Following her appearance, she received several replies and had two quite successful dates at a local restaurant. 'Have a go!', she advised readers.[37]

A few days later, the *Sun-Herald* featured the story of another divorcee. Thirty-six-year-old postal worker Neville Broome was a shy teetotaller and 'not the type to chat up women at pubs or parties'. He had experimented with an introduction agency and newspaper singles advertisements, with little success. Perhaps he wasn't 'flash enough', Broome mused. Arriving home from a second job, he would turn on the radio to help him drift off to sleep. One night he heard Denise Barry-Dunn call in to *Midnight Matchmaker* and was attracted by her voice. He wrote to the 36-year-old divorced mother of two via 2GB. Although she thought he was a 'lousy letter writer', they arranged to meet at the Newtown Leagues Club. Three weeks later they were engaged, with Broome telling the newspaper that 'hearing what someone is like [on radio] gives you an excellent insight into their character'.[38]

Most callers to *Midnight Matchmaker* came from Sydney's populous, generally blue-collar western suburbs. An occupation breakdown revealed many shift-workers (nurses and chefs), as well as receptionists and electricians. Almost twice as many women as men rang in, and many callers were divorced or widowed.[39] Wilshire told a journalist that the 'depressing truth' was that half the women in Australia over 50 were living alone.[40]

2GB staff struggled to keep up with the 400 to 500 letters that poured in each week until the station's head technician developed a computer program to process the information. By 1984, *Midnight Matchmaker* was boasting of nearly 40 marriages, including one between divorced truck-driver Emmanuel Borg ('Peacemaker') and Maura O'Riordan, who had emigrated from Ireland after leaving the convent.[41] A 'Long Lost Lovers' segment was introduced, enabling listeners to ring in to try to find out if old flames were single, separated, divorced or back on the market.[42] Wilshire was unflappable, keeping a straight face when a woman rang in seeking a man who looked like Jesus Christ so they could rewrite the Bible in 'dingo-lingo'.[43]

2GB organised a Midnight Matchmaker Ball in 1988, with four of the more than 100 couples the program had brought together as guests-of-honour.[44] A second ball was held a year later, with Wilshire dreaming of commercial spin-offs from the show. By 1991, 2GB was hosting singles cruises on Sydney harbour. One attendee, a 56-year-old with a gold chain under his unbuttoned shirt, admitted that he had met about 30 women through the program but still hadn't found a partner: 'I'd like them younger.'[45]

Midnight Matchmaker's ratings spawned similar programs on commercial radio stations—most of them part of the Macquarie Network, headed by 2GB—in other cities. At 4BC in Brisbane, Stuart Robertson tried to make *Matchmaker* fun, attracting mainly teenagers at 10.30 pm Mondays to Thursdays. With a current affairs background, Robertson found talking to people who were shy the opposite of what he was used to, although he concluded that most seemed to be 'fairly truthful about themselves which is a good start'.[46]

2CA in Canberra struggled to hit the right note with a matchmaking program at 11 pm on Wednesdays in 1984, even though Peter Henry thought the federal capital needed an aid to meeting people. In 1988, the Macquarie station began relaying Wilshire's original offering. After 7HO had a good response to a matchmaking program in 1984, rival Hobart station 7HT launched a segment on Keith Neil's Saturday-night rock music show. Each week four couples were awarded a dinner out with Neil and his wife. In Perth, 6PR dropped a matchmaking program after a few months, conceding that people were too busy to commit to the program during the awkward time it had been scheduled (5.30 to 8 pm).[47]

In Melbourne, *Midnight Matchmakers* was short-lived, perhaps because it did not fit 3KZ's music-driven format. In 1983 2GB's sister station, 3AW, launched 'Matchmakers' as part of the *Helen Jackson Show*. During her Saturday-night program, the journalist allowed callers seeking a mate to swap numbers. More women than men rang in, possibly taking advantage of their initial anonymity to move away from the tradition that men should make the first move. Jackson persuaded a 25-year-old onto the program who had never been asked out:

> She was an accountant, bright, witty, a lovely person. ... It emerged that she had been to an all-girls school. She was the only child of a not too social family and admittedly, had slightly idealistic ideas about men. We stopped counting the calls [in response] after 24.

'Matchmakers' was reportedly responsible for at least one marriage, between Kevin Clarke and 'Maureen', both 33-years-old, divorced, and supporters of the same football team.[48]

The 3AW program featured a series on 'Successful Singles', including entertainer Don Lane and journalist George Negus. Jackson was interested in addressing all relationship issues, including sex, which upset some listeners but attracted others. She featured news items on sex and sexual health, and did talkback with a sex therapist. Jackson's listeners had an average age of 34, and were more white-collar than the callers to *Midnight Matchmaker*.[49]

While continuing to host the 3AW program, Jackson also edited *Australian Singles News*, a monthly which launched in Melbourne and then went national. 2GB did a deal with 'The Magazine for Unattached People' that enabled *Midnight Matchmaker* callers to have their details published for free in the classified advertisements.[50] 'The singles are the baby boom children, the divorced and the professionals who have been busy with their careers until their early 30s', wrote the *Bulletin*'s Susan Molloy.[51] As the scene grew, current affairs star Michael Willesee went on a singles holiday to Club Med in Noumea in a special for the Seven Network in 1983. 'Singles Play Doubles' showed him doggedly in pursuit of 'the greatest product imaginable—true love.'[52]

Meanwhile, on 2KY, a Sydney commercial radio station affiliated with the labour movement, 'ocker' morning presenter John Singleton introduced a segment that sent up *Midnight Matchmaker*. In 'Dinner with Sally', Sally—on the line somewhere else—vetted a selection of potential suitors who called her to try to persuade them to have dinner with her. She and 'Singo' made mincemeat out of most of the men who called in, although there seems to have been a certain degree of recognition of the send-up by at least some of the callers.[53]

Midnight Matchmaker quietly faded away in 1991, having lost its novelty value and its unique place in the Australian media landscape. By now 2WS, a commercial station in western Sydney, ran *Love Song Dedications*, suitable to its music format, from 8 pm to midnight. When host Filomena Leone introduced a lonely-hearts segment, she attracted calls from more young men than women.[54]

Two years after *Midnight Matchmaker*'s launch, *Perfect Match* had debuted on Australian television. In 1984 Bill Mason at Grundy Entertainment developed the idea for a program based in part on *Blind Date* and *The Dating Game*. Melbourne radio host Greg Evans was chosen as compere, assisted by Debbie Newsome. *Perfect Match* involved Evans and a contestant asking questions of three potential suitors of the opposite sex on the other side of a screen. Each of the three was defined by first name, occupation and interests, often facetiously: 'a Mechanical Engineering student who's into rap dancing and playing the bagpipes.' Following their answers, the contestant selected one of the three for a weekend away. A computerised robot called Dexter then revealed the partner with the highest 'compatibility score' based on its calculations, although this did not change the end result. Each episode featured two rounds, one with a male and one with a female contestant, and a recap of the holiday taken by an earlier couple.[55]

As the Ten Network scheduled *Perfect Match* at 5.30 pm weekdays, producers had to be careful that questions did not contain too much innuendo for children who might be watching. Launched in January 1984, the program quickly ascended the ratings, attracting adults as well as teenagers. In a *Perfect Match* book-come-magazine (costing $2.95) in 1985, producer Michael Boughen claimed that the show was for people of all ages, from 18 to 70. However, a contemporary observer thought that most participants in the narrative of heterosexual seduction were in their twenties.[56] The program had a light touch, finding humour in the candid replies of contestants, unintentional bumbling and the awkward moments when a couple first saw each other. Then there were the 'perfect clangers' from couples returning after their weekends away, and being interviewed separately: 'What I thought when I first saw him? I've always been unlucky'; 'She didn't say a word—it was like talking to Marcel Marceau all weekend'; 'It was a good time, but not with him' (Fig. 7.2).[57]

The *Perfect Match* book included a feature on how to become a contestant: 'you've watched enough people being matched up with delectable (or at least interesting!) partners and heading off for fun-filled tropical holidays.' Prospective contestants rang or wrote to Grundy House in Sydney, completed a questionnaire and attached a photograph. They were auditioned and informally interviewed. If they were chosen to go on the show, filming generally took most of a day. On returning from their weekend getaway, contestants went back to Grundy House on the Tuesday for an interview. If their interview was chosen to go to air, they returned to the studio (together or separately with their partner, depending on the status of their relationship) the following Saturday to recap their experiences.[58]

Fig. 7.2 From *Grundy Entertainment's Perfect Match* (1985). (Copyright Loui Silvestro)

The book featured brief accounts by around 30 participants on why they had gone on the show. Of those who were photographed, only one, Carole, was not white, and only two appeared to be aged over 40. Many were attracted by a free holiday. Several wanted to meet new people, especially if they had recently moved. Some had been dobbed in or dared to appear on the show. Ray, from Bathurst in the central west of New South Wales, revealed that his friends had solicited an application form and persuaded him to appear on the show, even though they were unable to proceed with plans to travel to the recording in a bus as they could not get enough tickets for the studio audience. Most seemed to want to enjoy fun and adventure ('everyone seems to have such a good time', said Sean) and possibly meet someone 'nice', though they did not necessarily expect to meet their life partner. 'Just to say I've done it is a big thing—and it's really trendy at the moment if you've been on Perfect Match!', admitted Sue. One woman wanted to experience the excitement of being in a television studio, and another looked forward to having her hair and makeup professionally done.[59]

Craig, an apprentice metal worker, almost had to justify his determination 'to find my perfect match: I want to find out who it is, that's why I came on.'[60] 'Success, in the achievement of a perfect match', wrote cultural studies scholar Graeme Turner, 'is an unlooked for bonus that occurs very rarely.' The professed object of *Blind Date* and its predecessors had been romance and marriage. While the success of *Midnight Matchmaker* was still being promoted as lying in the number of marriages it seeded (as well as ratings), *Perfect Match* adopted a romantic game show format which it then subverted.[61] Publicity did not boast of couples claiming to be in love after weekends away, or of marriages.[62]

As another scholar, John Fiske, observed, each episode equalised the genders, with both a woman and a man choosing a partner. Feminine sexuality was freed from the respectability of marriage, with women able to have fun when choosing their mates, and pleasure on their dates. *Perfect Match* trod a fine line, never directly asking returning couples whether they had had sex, and leaving it to the audience to try to infer the answer. The program's title sequence had the traditional trimmings of romance—soft focus, pulsating hearts and romantic music—but were so exaggerated as to parody them.[63]

The book also addressed the role of the studio audience:

> A fun audience creates a good atmosphere and an appreciative audience keeps the show on a 'high' that is relayed to viewers at home.
> The audience likes to react particularly to sexy or good-looking contestants with loud cheers and whistles. As a group the audience decides who will be their favourite.

Perfect Match had a warm-up comic, Keith Scott (who also voiced Dexter), tasked to keep the audience at 'fever pitch'.[64] Friends in the audience sometimes used sign language and miming to try to signal the attributes of the people on the other side of the screen.[65] The show could shock or disgust audience members, at home as well as in the studio, at least as much as it could reinforce cosy images of love and marriage.[66] Viewers were engaged in the voyeurism of the blind-date, occupying a privileged position with information about the three contestants' jobs and interests that was not heard by the man or woman asking questions of them.[67]

Grundy Entertainment and Ten seized the opportunity for more spin-offs, releasing a board game 'Based on Television's Hit Game Show!', and an electronic game for teenagers.[68] In 1985 came the *Perfect Match Guide to Wedding Etiquette*.[69] While the show itself was not centred on the experience of marriage, producers spotted a gap in the market. One journalist wrote about finding a copy at her daughter's house and discovering she was engaged. The young woman was in turn pleased by what the book revealed: 'Poor Nige [her fiancé] cops the church costs and the cars and the flowers.'[70]

Seeing the popularity of *Perfect Match*, Seven responded with the *Love Game*, at 6 pm weeknights, from 30 July 1984. The format was similar to that of *Perfect Match*, although here a panel of celebrities matched the contestants. The Love Machine (a computerised column of lights known backstage as the 'Orgasmatron' or the 'Phallus Palace') then assessed how 'hot' the match was and awarded a holiday accordingly. 'Who'll score tonight?' a newspaper advertisement asked suggestively. With *Perfect Match* inundated by people wanting to be on the show, 600 young hopefuls began turning up for Seven's auditions. Ten's director of programming thought the original would be hard to beat, while anticipating that *Perfect Match* would run for another couple of years before running out of steam. Within weeks the *Love Game* was struggling in the ratings, and viewers were complaining about advertisements during children's cartoon shows. The celebrity panel shrank and host Mark Holden was replaced. The program was axed in October.[71]

Perfect Match provided a strong lead-in for Ten's evening schedule and helped take TEN10, for the first time, to the top of the ratings.[72] One Valentine's Day special featured Guy Pearce, from Ten's *Neighbours*. The hosts later recalled that the woman who won dinner with the heartthrob almost fainted with excitement.[73] The fun continued in the lead-up to the 1986 wedding of Prince Andrew and Sarah Ferguson. Ten programmed a 'Royal day' which included a special episode of *Perfect Match* with Andrew and Sarah lookalikes dressed in naval uniforms and wedding dresses.[74] The *International TV & Video Guide 86* described *Perfect Match* as 'the most important programme made in Australia in the past year'.[75]

In 1986 Nine seems to have obtained the Australian rights to *The Newlywed Game*. Host Ian Turpie initially feared that Australian contestants would not be as gregarious as their American counterparts, but was soon pleasantly surprised. Television critic Richard Coleman, who found that the program had 'a voyeuristic quality that keeps you in front of the set in spite of your better instincts', also remarked on the husbands and wives 'who took questions and answers without any embarrassment and considerable hilarity'.[76]

Critic Richard Glover was disturbed by how *The Newlywed Game* made love:

> into something smutty and nasty and small; going out of its way to force people to belittle their partners and relationship in order to win prizes.
>
> In this, it is a much more insidious and damaging program than *Perfect Match* which at least doesn't seek to destroy a relationship which already exists.

Glover wondered if, after Ten paired off couples, and Nine sowed the seeds of doubt, Seven would enter the fray with '*Custody Battle* or *The Big Split*'.[77] Another critic was less than impressed by husbands being asked to estimate their wives' chest size.[78] The Australian version of *The Newlywed Game* lasted less than a year.

Perfect Match continued until 1989, longer than Ten expected.[79] Doug Anderson, who was considerably more negative about the program than about *Midnight Matchmaker*, was unimpressed by the prospect of a 'best of' series of 'saccharine inanity' over the summer.[80] A short-lived reprise with Greg Evans, reverting to the name of *Blind Date*, followed in 1991.[81]

The Seven Network went into the new ratings year in 2002 with an Australian version of *Temptation Island*, in which couples agreed to live with a group of singles in order to test the strength of their relationships. Based on a controversial American show that had premiered in 2001,[82] this was the first Australian foray into reality television with a 'romantic' theme. Still finding its feet in this arena, Seven also relaunched *Perfect Match* in 2002. This time it was on Saturday nights, and the host was a woman, travel presenter Shelley Craft.[83] Friends and relatives increased the embarrassment factor by revealing the contestant's habits, plus likes and dislikes in new partners.[84] Journalist Brett Debritz joked that 'maybe there's a genuine desire to bring people together—in front of the television'.[85] The series was not renewed.

A range of other 'reality romance' programs followed on the commercial networks, mostly franchised from overseas and stripped over several nights a week, including *Beauty and the Geek Australia* (Seven), *Farmer Wants A Wife* and *Married at First Sight* (Nine), and *The Bachelor* and *The Bachelorette* (Ten).

In a 2001 study of participants in *Reisesjekken*, a Norwegian dating game, Trine Syvertsen found that most yearned for attention, and that they generally received it from family, friends, colleagues and neighbours. She also suggested that programs like *Reisesjekken* provided an opportunity for ordinary people to be on television, with 'being on television' turning into a leisure activity for some people.[86] This observation resonates with some of the comments made by *Perfect Match* contestants, none of whom had (or it seemed wanted) the anonymity offered by radio's *Midnight Matchmaker*.

Examining the Australian version of *Married at First Sight* (which in 2016 featured its first same-sex couple), Lara McKenzie and Laura Dales observed that singles who were 'matched' celebrated their weddings with all of the associated rituals of romance and marriage, and that the format reflected viewers' appetites for love stories that juxtaposed weddings, fantasy and fate with mundane daily life.[87] In a 2018 study of the American and Australian iterations of *The Bachelor/ette* franchise, Jodi McAlister concluded that the romances as presented by the show resonated with what the local audience expected love to look like, even if that did not match up with reality.[88]

In the late 1930s, Australian radio had begun to try to attract listeners with programs with a romantic theme, while heterosexual romantic love was framed as a cultural ideal. In the 1940s, the industry had begun to turn efforts to find a mate into a game. But for the next 40 years, broadcast endeavours in this field were largely centred on romance, love and marriage. *Perfect Match* (1984–1989) marked a turning point, with fun and by implication sex, and no real expectations of marriage, seen (and apparently embraced) as the motivating factors for contestants. Psychologist Fred Orr, who had seeded the idea for *Midnight Matchmaker*, was unimpressed by the lure of holidays and gifts, and people being 'abused for the sake of entertainment'.[89] If there had long been a nexus between ordinary people and celebrities in romance programs on Australian radio and television, in the global discourse of big-budget reality romance shows, participants could become not just national celebrities themselves, but villains.

Notes

1. Radio is not considered in Hsu-Ming Teo (ed.)'s *The Popular Culture of Romantic Love in Australia* (North Melbourne: Australian Scholarly Publishing, 2017). Two chapters consider depictions of World War II in television and film, and romance in television mini-series, but not audiences.
2. Hsu-Ming Teo, 'The Americanisation of romantic love in Australia' in Ann Curthoys and Marilyn Lake (eds.), *Connected Worlds: History in Transnational Perspective* (Canberra: ANU E Press, 2006), pp. 181–84.
3. *Sun*, 13 November 1938, p. 17.
4. *Wireless Weekly* (*WW*), 13 November 1936, xvii–xix.
5. *Australian Women's Weekly* (*AWW*), 19 November 1938, p. 50; Julia Gordon, 'Ten thousand women and Frank Sturge Harty', *WW*, 9 December 1938, p. 17; *Radio Pictorial of Australia* (*RPA*), February 1939, p. 44 and September 1939, pp. 27, 64.
6. *World's News*, 18 February 1939, p. 31.
7. *WW*, 23 August 1939 and 13 July 1940, p. 12.
8. *Catholic Press*, 29 February 1940, p. 27; *RPA*, 1 April 1940, p. 14.
9. Julia Gordon, 'The man with the hairless chest', *WW*, 6 May 1938, p. 7; *Cumberland Argus and Fruitgrowers Advocate*, 15 May 1940, p. 6; *WW*, 18 May 1940, p. 11; *RPA*, June 1940, p. 28; *AWW*, 18 October 1941, p. 15.
10. *Daily Telegraph*, 2 January 1941, p. 1; Teo 2006, p. 181.
11. *Truth*, 24 February 1946, p. 35; George Hart, 'Radio roundup', *Sun* (Sydney), 16 September 1946, p. 6 and 28 September 1946, p. 2; *ABC Weekly*, 5 October 1946, p. 8.
12. Teo 2006, pp. 186–89.
13. *Truth*, 17 March 1946, p. 32. It has not been possible to locate the Cinesound footage.
14. *ABC Weekly*, 28 December 1946, p. 22; George Hart, 'Radio roundup', *Sun* (Sydney), 27 February 1947, p. 6.
15. *ABC Weekly*, 6 August 1958, p. 42. *Blind Date* was listed in radio program guides in the *Sydney Morning Herald* (*SMH*) until mid-1959.
16. *Victor Harbor Times*, 5 February 1960, p. 1.
17. 'The Marriage Game', Internet Movie Database, https://www.imdb.com/title/tt4024166/, accessed 22 January 2020; Valda Marshall, 'A game of wedded bliss', *Sun-Herald*, 25 September 1966, p. 90; Albert Moran, *TV Format Mogul: Reg Grundy's Transnational Career* (Bristol/Chicago: Intellect, 2003), pp. 81, 86, 88.
18. Teo 2006, p. 192.
19. Valda Marshall, 'Traps of wedlock', *Sun-Herald*, 16 October 1966, p. 109.

20. Bridget Griffen-Foley, 'Voices of the people: Audience participation in Australian radio', *Media International Australia*, 137 (November 2010), pp. 12–13.
21. Valda Marshall, 'The great Aust. silence', *Sun-Herald*, 1 January 1967, p. 55.
22. Harry Robinson, 'The morbid game', *SMH*, 28 June 1967, p. 17.
23. Geoff Allen, 'Comperes search for perfect couple', *SMH*, 27 October 1969, p. 20.
24. Valda Marshall, 'Coming up soon', *Sun-Herald*, 16 July 1972, p. 103.
25. Valda Marshall, 'Blind dates with Graham', *Sun-Herald*, 2 April 1967, p. 92 and 'A bright man in a dull spot', *Sun-Herald*, 9 July 1967, p. 92; Geoff Allan, 'Blind Date now in Melbourne', *SMH*, 27 May 1968, p. 14; Reg Grundy, *Reg Grundy* (Sydney: Pier 9, 2010), pp. 132–33; Moran 2003, pp. 81, 87, 104.
26. Geoff Allen, 'Vast world audience', *SMH*, 30 June 1969, p. 14; Lenore Nicklin, 'TV's cupid bows out', *SMH*, 6 November 1969, p. 6; Valda Marshall, 'It's a happening world', *Sun-Herald*, 9 November 1969, p. 116.
27. *Age*, 1 December 1969, p. 2; Valda Marshall, 'Blind Date gets off to another flying start', *Sun-Herald*, 24 March 1974, p. 90. *Blind Date* could (inadvertently) take credit for at least one marriage; see Jenny Cullen, 'Marriage comes first for Joanna', *AWW*, 24 September 1980, pp. 24–25.
28. Marshall 1974; *TV Week*, 17 August 1974, p. 35.
29. Scott Exmann-Moloney, '2GB's Midnight Matchmaker: Commercialism and community service hand in hand', *Media Information Australia*, 41 (August 1986), pp. 58–59; telephone interview with Fred Orr, 31 March 2004; Sandra Moore, 'Loneliness—the modern epidemic', *AWW*, 17 November 1982, p. 88; Carolyn Dunne, 'Sex and the single radio', *Look & Listen*, 1(6) (January 1985), pp. 61–62.
30. Louisa Costa, 'Airwaves of the night', *Australian* (Magazine section), 19 August 1989, pp. 34–36; Doug Anderson, 'Lonely hearts', *SMH*, 5 July 1982, p. 17; Yvonne Preston, 'Tune in and hear the prejudiced society', *SMH*, 3 November 1982, p. 22; Glenda Thompson, 'Matchmakers of the airwaves', *Bulletin*, 6 November 1984, pp. 38–40.
31. Anderson 1982, p. 17; Sally McInerney, 'The joys of listening in to others' conversations', *SMH*, 3 September 1983, p. 32; Costa 1989, pp. 34–36, 39–40; Preston 1984, p. 22; Thompson 1984, pp. 38–40.
32. Moore 1982, p. 88; Dunne 1985, p. 61.
33. See also Bill Kirkpatrick, '"A blessed boon": Radio, disability, governmentality, and the discourse of the "shut-in," 1920-1930', *Critical Studies in Media Communication*, 29(3) (2012), pp. 165–84.
34. Jeffrey Bierig and John Dimmick, 'The late night radio talk show as interpersonal communication,' *Journalism Quarterly*, 56(1) (Spring 1979),

pp. 92–96; Bridget Griffen-Foley 'Midnight to dawn programs on Australian commercial radio', *Journal of Radio Studies*, 11(2) (Winter 2004), pp. 239–53.
35. Doug Anderson, 'Is it 2GB or not 2GB?', *SMH*, 10 May 1982, p. 31.
36. Anderson 1982, 'Is it 2GB', p. 31 and 'Lonely hearts', p. 17.
37. Margaret Morrison, 'Looking for a man? Listen to this ...', *SMH* (The Guide), 20 September 1982, p. 4.
38. Jacky Hyams, 'Dial M for marriage', *Sun-Herald*, 26 September 1982, p. 158.
39. Nick Yardley, 'Walking on air for love', *Sun-Herald*, 4 July 1982, p. 90; Margaret O'Sullivan, 'Radio romance', *People*, 31 August 1982, pp. 16–17; McInerny, p. 32; Dunne 1985, pp. 61–62.
40. Emily Gibson, 'Desperately dateless', *SMH* (Metro section), 15 February 1991, p. 2.
41. Margaret O'Sullivan, 'Radio romance', *People*, 31 August 1982, pp. 16–17; Harry Robinson, 'The matchmaker woos midnight droolers', *SMH*, 30 January 1984, p. 43; Adrian Swift, 'Matchmaking doesn't take much brains', *SMH*, 6 August 1984, p. 16; Chris Purcell, 'Love the order of the day for a former nun', *Sun-Herald*, 4 January 1987, p. 3.
42. Dunne 1985, p. 62.
43. Deidre Macken, 'Radio straight from the heart', *Age* (Green Guide section), 3 February 1983, p. 16.
44. *Sun*, 20 November 1987, p. 3; Ian Horner, 'Matchmakers is a late-night success', *Sun-Herald*, 17 July 1988, p. 55.
45. Macken 1983, p. 16; Wanda Jamrozik, 'Some ship mates find love's just not for sail', *SMH*, 15 April 1991, p. 2.
46. Thompson 1984, pp. 38–40.
47. Rohan Greenland, 'Radio', *Canberra Times*, 25 June 1984, p. 26; Thompson 1984, pp. 38–39. *Midnight Matchmaker* was listed in radio program guides in the *Canberra Times* in 1988.
48. Thompson 1984, p. 39; Barbara Hooks, 'Game, set and match', *Herald* (Melbourne), 16 February 1984, p. 6.
49. Thompson 1984, pp. 38–40; Dunne 1985, pp. 61–64.
50. Thompson 1984; pp. 38–40.
51. Susan Molloy, 'How a single can get to mingle', *Bulletin*, 26 June 1984, p. 59.
52. *SMH*, 26 June 1983, p. 47; Glen Lewis, *Real Men Like Violence: Australian Men, Media and Violence* (Sydney: Kangaroo Press, 1983), p. 66.
53. Lewis 1983, pp. 66–67.
54. Bronwyn Watson, 'It's just a little love on the air', *SMH* (The Guide), 9 September 1991, p. 7s.

55. Michelle Smith (ed.), *Grundy Entertainment's Perfect Match* (Sydney: Federal Publishing Company, 1985), pp. 4–5; Stephen Crofts, 'The construction of sexuality in Perfect Match', *Australian Journal of Cultural Studies (AJCS)*, 4(2) (May 1987), p. 102.
56. Smith 1985, pp. 4–5; John Fiske, 'Everyday quizzes, everyday life' in Tulloch and Turner 1989, p. 83.
57. Smith 1985, pp. 5, 60.
58. Smith 1985, pp. 18–19.
59. Smith 1985, pp. 21–24. Crofts 1987, p. 103, also alludes to the lack of diversity—particularly regarding ethnicity and disability—of contestants.
60. Smith 1985, p. 22.
61. Graeme Turner, 'Perfect Match: Ambiguity, spectacle and the popular', *AJCS*, 4(2), (May 1987), pp. 80, 85 and 'Transgressive TV: From *In Melbourne Tonight* to *Perfect Match*' in John Tulloch and Graeme Turner (eds.), *Australian Television: Programs, Pleasures and Politics* (Sydney: Allen & Unwin, 1989), p. 30.
62. Twenty years later, a couple that had met on *Perfect Match* ran into each other and got married. See National Film and Sound Archive (NFSA): 700796, ATV10 news story, 12 May 2006.
63. Fiske 1989, p. 84 and 'Women and quiz shows: Consumerism, patriarchy and resisting pleasures' in Mary Ellen Brown (ed.), *Television and Women's Culture: The Politics of the Popular* (Sydney: Currency Press, 1990), pp. 139–40.
64. Smith 1985, pp. 58–59.
65. Leonie Lamont, 'Making up for matchmaking', *Sun-Herald*, 12 February 1984, p. 13.
66. Turner 1987, p. 82.
67. Crofts 1987 pp. 107–09.
68. These 'vintage' or 'retro' games are for sale on eBay.
69. Leone Hendry, *Perfect Match Guide to Wedding Etiquette* (Sydney: Ellsyd Press in association with Grundy Entertainment, 1985).
70. Susan Nichols, 'Books for good living', *SMH*, 20 August 1985, p. 47; Judy Johnson, 'Up tempo', *Sun-Herald*, 20 October 1985, p. 192.
71. Swift 1987, p. 16; *Sun-Herald*, 29 July 1984, p. 57; Robyn Ferrell, 'The Love Machine v Dexter the Robot', *SMH* (The Guide section), 30 July 1984, p. 3; *SMH* (The Guide), 20 August 1984, p. 16; Richard Coleman, 'TV extra', *SMH*, 13 October 1984, p. 38; Moran 2003, p. 144.
72. Jacqueline Lee Lewes, 'A perfect ten', *Sun-Herald*, 18 November 1984, p. 65. This article relates to Sydney television ratings and not the national Ten Network.
73. Jackie Brygel, 'Kerrie and Greg: We're still a Perfect Match', *Woman's Day*, 19 September 2011, p. 32.

74. Amruta Slee, 'Run for the hills, it's That Wedding week', *SMH* (The Guide), 21 July 1986, p. 6.
75. Crofts 1987, p. 95.
76. Richard Coleman, 'TV extra', *SMH*, 13 December 1986, p. 37; Moran 2003, p. 168.
77. Richard Glover, 'On television', *SMH*, 10 December 1986, p. 16.
78. Joanmarie Kalter, 'Sleaze unlimited', *SMH* (The Guide), 2 November 1987, p. 11.
79. Helen O'Neill, 'The non-ratings reshuffle', *SMH* (The Guide), 13 November 1989, p. 2.
80. Doug Anderson, 'Best of Perfect Match', *SMH* (The Guide), 20 November 1989, p. 17.
81. Moran 2003, p. 178; Candace Sutton, 'Armchair critic', *Sun-Herald*, 24 February 1991, p. 119.
82. Michael Idato, 'Let the fight begin', *SMH* (The Guide), 11 February 2002, p. 3.
83. Melissa Ken, 'Return match for love game', *West Australian*, 23 August 2002.
84. Sue Yeap, 'Review—TV BITES', *West Australian*, 8 November 2002.
85. Brett Debritz, 'Match made in heaven', *Brisbane News*, 21 August 2002, p. 29; Jenny Dillon, 'TV PICK: Perfect Match Seven', *Daily Telegraph*, 30 November 2002, p. 10.
86. Trine Syvertsen, 'Ordinary people in extraordinary circumstances: A study of participants in television dating games', *Media, Culture & Society*, 23(3) (May 2001), pp. 331–34.
87. Lara McKenzie and Laura Dales, 'Choosing love? Tensions and transformations of modern marriage in *Married at First Sight*', *Continuum*, 31(6) (2017), pp. 857–67.
88. Jodi McAlister 'What we talk about when we talk about love: Declarations of love in the American and Australian *Bachelor/ette* franchises', *Continuum*, 32(5) (2018), pp. 643–56, DOI: 10.1080/10304312.2018.1500523.
89. In Thompson 1984, p. 40.

Bibliography

ABC Weekly.
Age (Melbourne).
Allen, Geoff. 'Blind Date now in Melbourne', *Sydney Morning Herald* (*SMH*), 27 May 1968, p. 14.
———. 'Vast world audience', *SMH*, 30 June 1969a, p. 14.
———. 'Comperes search for perfect couple', *SMH*, 27 October 1969b, p. 20.
Anderson, Doug. 'Is it 2GB or not 2GB?', *SMH*, 10 May 1982a, p. 31.

———. 'Lonely hearts', *SMH*, 5 July 1982b, p. 17.
———. 'Best of Perfect Match', *SMH* (The Guide), 20 November 1989, p. 17.
Australian Women's Weekly (AWW).
Bierig, Jeffrey and Dimmick, John. 'The late night radio talk show as interpersonal communication,' *Journalism Quarterly*, 56(1) (Spring 1979), pp. 92–96.
Brygel, Jackie. 'Kerrie and Greg: We're still a Perfect Match', *Woman's Day*, 19 September 2011, p. 32.
Catholic Press (Sydney).
Coleman, Richard. 'TV extra', *SMH*, 13 October 1984, p. 38.
———. 'TV extra', *SMH*, 13 December 1986, p. 37.
Costa, Louisa. 'Airwaves of the night', *Australian* (Magazine section), 19 August 1989, pp. 34–36, 39–40.
Crofts, Stephen. 'The construction of sexuality in Perfect Match', *Australian Journal of Cultural Studies (AJCS)*, 4(2) (May 1987), pp. 95–115.
Cullen, Jenny. 'Marriage comes first for Joanna', *AWW*, 24 September 1980, pp. 24–25.
Cumberland Argus and Fruitgrowers Advocate (Parramatta).
Daily Telegraph (Sydney).
Debritz, Brett. 'Match made in heaven', *Brisbane News*, 21 August 2002, p. 29.
Dillon, Jenny. 'TV PICK: Perfect Match Seven', *Daily Telegraph*, 30 November 2002, p. 10.
Dunne, Carolyn. 'Sex and the single radio', *Look & Listen*, 1(6) (January 1985), pp. 61–62.
Exmann-Moloney, Scott. '2GB's Midnight Matchmaker: Commercialism and community service hand in hand', *Media Information Australia*, 41 (August 1986), pp. 58–59.
Ferrell, Robyn. 'The Love Machine v Dexter the Robot', *SMH* (The Guide section), 30 July 1984, p. 3.
Fiske, John. 'Everyday quizzes, everyday life' in John Tulloch and Graeme Turner (eds.), *Australian Television: Programs, Pleasures and Politics* (Sydney: Allen & Unwin, 1989), pp. 72–87.
———. 'Women and quiz shows: Consumerism, patriarchy and resisting pleasures,' in Mary Ellen Brown (ed.), *Television and Women's Culture: The Politics of the Popular* (Sydney: Currency Press, 1990), pp. 134–43.
Gibson, Emily. 'Desperately dateless', *SMH* (Metro section), 15 February 1991, p. 2.
Glover, Richard. 'On television', *SMH*, 10 December 1986, p. 16.
Gordon, Julia. 'The man with the hairless chest', *Wireless Weekly (WW)*, 6 May 1938a, p. 7.
———. 'Ten thousand women and Frank Sturge Harty', *WW*, 9 December 1938b, p. 17.
Greenland, Rohan, 'Radio', *Canberra Times*, 25 June 1984, p. 26.

Griffen-Foley, Bridget. 'Midnight to dawn programs on Australian commercial radio', *Journal of Radio Studies*, 11(2) (Winter 2004), pp. 239–53.

———. 'Voices of the people: Audience participation in Australian radio', *Media International Australia*, 137 (November 2010), pp. 5–19.

Grundy, Reg. *Reg Grundy* (Sydney: Pier 9, 2010).

Hart, George. 'Radio roundup', *Sun* (Sydney), 16 September 1946a, p. 6.

———. 'Radio roundup', *Sun* (Sydney), 28 September 1946b, p. 2.

Hendry, Leone. *Perfect Match Guide to Wedding Etiquette* (Sydney: Ellsyd Press in association with Grundy Entertainment, 1985).

Hooks, Barbara. 'Game, set and match', *Herald* (Melbourne), 16 February 1984, pp. 6–7.

Horner, Ian. 'Matchmakers is a late-night success', *Sun-Herald*, 17 July 1988, p. 55.

Hyams, Jacky. 'Dial M for marriage', *Sun-Herald*, 26 September 1982, p. 158.

Idato, Michael. 'Let the fight begin', *SMH* (The Guide), 11 February 2002, p. 3.

Jamrozik, Wanda. 'Some ship mates find love's just not for sail', *SMH*, 15 April 1991, p. 2.

Johnson, Judy. 'Up tempo', *Sun-Herald*, 20 October 1985, p. 192.

Kalter, Joanmarie. 'Sleaze unlimited', *SMH* (The Guide), 2 November 1987, p. 11.

Ken, Melissa. 'Return match for love game', *West Australian*, 23 August 2002.

Kirkpatrick, Bill. '"A blessed boon": Radio, disability, governmentality, and the discourse of the "shut-in," 1920–1930', *Critical Studies in Media Communication*, 29(3) (2012), pp. 165–84, https://doi.org/10.1080/15295036.2011.631554.

Lamont, Leonie. 'Making up for matchmaking', *Sun-Herald*, 12 February 1984, p. 13.

Lewes, Jacqueline Lee. 'A perfect ten', *Sun-Herald*, 18 November 1984, p. 65.

Lewis, Glen. *Real Men Like Violence: Australian Men, Media and Violence* (Sydney: Kangaroo Press, 1983).

Macken, Deidre. 'Radio straight from the heart', *Age* (Green Guide section), 3 February 1983, p. 16.

Marshall, Valda. 'A game of wedded bliss', *Sun-Herald*, 25 September 1966a, p. 90.

———. 'Traps of wedlock', *Sun-Herald*, 16 October 1966b, p. 109.

———. 'The great Aust. silence', *Sun-Herald*, 1 January 1967a, p. 55.

———. 'Blind dates with Graham', *Sun-Herald*, 2 April 1967b, p. 92.

———. 'A bright man in a dull spot', *Sun-Herald*, 9 July 1967c, p. 92.

———. 'It's a happening world', *Sun-Herald*, 9 November 1969, p. 116.

———. 'Coming up soon', *Sun-Herald*, 16 July 1972, p. 103.

———. 'Blind Date gets off to another flying start', *Sun-Herald*, 24 March 1974, p. 90.

'The Marriage Game', Internet Movie Database, https://www.imdb.com/title/tt4024166/, accessed 22 January 2020.

McAlister, Jodi. 'What we talk about when we talk about love: Declarations of love in the American and Australian *Bachelor/ette* franchises', *Continuum*, 32(5) (2018), pp. 643–56, https://doi.org/10.1080/10304312.2018.1500523.

McInerney, Sally. 'The joys of listening in to others' conversations', *SMH*, 3 September 1983, p. 32.

McKenzie, Lara and Dales, Laura. 'Choosing love? Tensions and transformations of modern marriage in *Married at First Sight*', *Continuum*, 31(6) (2017), pp. 857–67, https://doi.org/10.1080/10304312.2017.1334873.

Molloy, Susan. 'How a single can get to mingle', *Bulletin*, 26 June 1984, pp. 58–59.

Moore, Sandra. 'Loneliness—the modern epidemic', *AWW*, 17 November 1982, pp. 88–89.

Moran, Albert. *TV Format Mogul: Reg Grundy's Transnational Career* (Bristol/Chicago: Intellect, 2003).

Morrison, Margaret. 'Looking for a man? Listen to this...', *SMH* (The Guide), 20 September 1982, p. 4.

National Film and Sound Archive (NFSA): 700796, ATV10 news story, 12 May 2006.

Nichols, Susan. 'Books for good living', *SMH*, 20 August 1985, p. 47.

Nicklin, Lenore. 'TV's cupid bows out', *SMH*, 6 November 1969, p. 6.

O'Neill, Helen. 'The non-ratings reshuffle', *SMH* (The Guide), 13 November 1989, p. 2.

O'Sullivan, Margaret. 'Radio romance', *People*, 31 August 1982, pp. 16–17.

Preston, Yvonne. 'Tune in and hear the prejudiced society', *SMH*, 3 November 1982, p. 22.

Radio Pictorial of Australia (RPA).

Purcell, Chris. 'Love the order of the day for a former nun', *Sun-Herald*, 4 January 1987, p. 3.

Robinson, Harry. 'The morbid game', *SMH*, 28 June 1967, p. 17.

———. 'The matchmaker woos midnight droolers', *SMH*, 30 January 1984, p. 43.

Slee, Amruta. 'Run for the hills, it's That Wedding week', *SMH* (The Guide), 21 July 1986, p. 6.

Smith, Michelle (ed.). *Grundy Entertainment's Perfect Match* (Sydney: Federal Publishing Company, 1985).

Sun (Sydney).

Sun-Herald.

Sutton, Candace. 'Armchair critic', *Sun-Herald*, 24 February 1991, p. 119.

Swift, Adrian. 'Matchmaking doesn't take much brains', *SMH*, 6 August 1984, p. 16.

Sydney Morning Herald (SMH).

Syvertsen, Trine. 'Ordinary people in extraordinary circumstances: A study of participants in television dating games', *Media, Culture & Society*, 23(3) (May 2001), pp. 319–37.

Teo, Hsu-Ming. 'The Americanisation of romantic love in Australia' in Ann Curthoys and Marilyn Lake (eds.), *Connected Worlds: History in Transnational Perspective* (Canberra: ANU E Press, 2006), pp. 171–92.

———. (ed.). *The Popular Culture of Romantic Love in Australia* (North Melbourne: Australian Scholarly Publishing, 2017).

Thompson, Glenda. 'Matchmakers of the airwaves', *Bulletin*, 6 November 1984, pp. 38–40.

Truth (Sydney).

Turner, Graeme. 'Perfect Match: Ambiguity, spectacle and the popular', *AJCS*, 4(2) (May 1987), pp. 79–92.

———. 'Transgressive TV: From *In Melbourne Tonight* to *Perfect Match*' in Tulloch and Turner 1989, pp. 25–38.

TV Week.

Victor Harbor Times.

Watson, Bronwyn. 'It's just a little love on the air', *SMH* (The Guide), 9 September 1991, p. 7s.

Wireless Weekly (*WW*).

World's News (Sydney).

Yardley, Nick. 'Walking on air for love', *Sun-Herald*, 4 July 1982, p. 90.

Yeap, Sue. 'Review—TV BITES', *West Australian*, 8 November 2002.

CHAPTER 8

Conclusion

Abstract The concluding chapter brings together this book's case studies by considering the long history of Australian listeners and viewers interacting with broadcast media. It highlights how Australian radio and television stations and networks have been integral parts of the social, cultural, educational and financial fabric of their communities. And it summarises some of the ways to locate and uncover the voices of earlier generations of Australian broadcast audiences, pointings to potential new research directions.

Keywords Media audiences • Radio • Television • Broadcasting • Australia

'What's the most unforgettable Australian TV moment?', the *Guardian Australia* began asking in January 2020. It wanted readers to nominate the moments they would never forget, receiving more than a thousand nominations in response. Then the newspaper chose the 50 most popular as the basis for a poll, attracting 13,000 votes.[1]

There are now so many ways to gauge audience reactions to radio and television content, with online polls and 'comments', social media, blogs, podcasts and vodcasts, as well as, since 2015, *Gogglebox Australia*. But long before 'the people formerly known as the audience' were recognised as producing their own media content, and having some power in the

© The Author(s) 2020
B. Griffen-Foley, *Australian Radio Listeners and Television Viewers*, Palgrave Studies in the History of the Media,
https://doi.org/10.1007/978-3-030-54637-3_8

media landscape.[2] Australian listeners and viewers were interacting with broadcast media: through clubs, community singing and talkback radio, and as participants in excursions, events, fund-raising and studio audiences. So ubiquitous were these endeavours that they were sent up by broadcasters Jack Davey in the 1930s, Keith Walshe in the 1950s (as we saw in Chap. 3) and John Singleton in the 1980s (Chap. 7).

This book has shown something of the extracurricular reach of Australian Broadcasting Commission (ABC) and commercial broadcasting across metropolitan and regional Australia. As we saw in Chaps. 2 and 3, around 150,000 women, and 450,000 children, belonged to radio clubs in 1942. Most of the more than 100 clubs formed by the Australian radio industry by this time each raised tens of thousands of dollars for local and charitable works. More radio clubs were to emerge after World War II, and were to be followed by television clubs. Through their audience outreach, Australian radio and television stations and networks were integral parts of the social, cultural, educational and financial fabric of their communities.

Traces remain of Australians' broadcast consumption and engagement, including fan cards, fan mail, letters of complaint (to regulators, stations, networks and periodicals), club records, advisory committee minutes and online marketplaces such as eBay. I hope my book gives some clues for tracing the voices of media audiences between the 1920s and the 2000s, from regulatory records to private archives. Qualitative research can augment and complement the quantitative work, and extant records, of survey and ratings organisations since the 1930s.[3] My six 'perspectives' barely acknowledge cultural diversity, with much more work to be done on how migrants[4] and Indigenous Australians listened to, watched and engaged with radio and television, including SBS.

Researching the reception as well as production of broadcast content can clearly enlarge and enrich our understanding of Australian media history. And by recovering some more of the quotidian voices of Australians, other historians and sociologists can learn more about their education, their professions, their lives, their loves, their anxieties and their dreams over the last century.

Notes

1. 'Unforgettable Australian TV', *Guardian Australia*, https://www.theguardian.com/tv-and-radio/ng-interactive/2020/jan/24/whats-the-most-unforgettable-australian-tv-moment-vote-in-the-guardians-poll, accessed 23 March 2020. Prime Minister Julia Gillard's 2012 parliamentary 'misogyny speech' topped the poll.
2. Jay Rosen, 'The people formerly known as the audience', Pressthink, http://archive.pressthink.org/2006/06/27/ppl_frmr_p.html, 27 June 2006, accessed 23 March 2020.
3. Murray Goot, 'Audience Research', in Bridget Griffen-Foley (ed.) *A Companion to the Australian Media* (North Melbourne: Australian Scholarly Publishing, 2014), pp. 31–34.
4. A team of researchers, led by Kate Darian-Smith, is currently completing a major research project on 'Migration, Cultural Diversity and Television: Reflecting Modern Australia'.

Bibliography

Goot, Murray. 'Audience Research', in Bridget Griffen-Foley (ed.) *A Companion to the Australian Media* (North Melbourne: Australian Scholarly Publishing, 2014), pp. 31–34.

Rosen, Jay. 'The People Formerly Known as the Audience', Pressthink, http://archive.pressthink.org/2006/06/27/ppl_frmr_p.html, 27 June 2006.

"Unforgettable Australian TV", *Guardian Australia*, https://www.theguardian.com/tv-and-radio/ng-interactive/2020/jan/24/whats-the-most-unforgettable-australian-tv-moment-vote-in-the-guardians-poll, accessed 23 March 2020.

Index[1]

A
ABC Children's TV Club, 37, 38
ABC Weekly, 59
Aborigines, 61, 117, 154
A-class stations, 7–9, 52, 76, 78
Adams, J.H., 60
Adams, Phillip, 64
Adventures of Harry and Grace Smith, The, 53
Allen, Joan
 'Aunt Mary,' 16–17
Amalgamated Wireless Australasia Ltd (AWA), 10, 13, 30, 52
American Broadcasting Corporation, 130
America's Town Meeting of the Air, 58
Anderson, Doug, 133, 141

Angel, Isabel, 40
Angus & Coote, 128
Anthony, H.L., 85
Archer, Janet, 34
Archers, The, 61
Argonauts, 2, 8, 12, 13, 19–21, 37, 38, 58
'Argosy' magazine, 20
Armstrong, D.R., 56
Ashley, W.P., 81, 108
Atlantic Show, 84
Audience measurement, 106, 108, 109, 112, 113, 154
 See also Ratings
Aunts, 7, 8, 52
 'Aunt Eva' (4BC), 14
 'Auntie Amelia' (6KG), 17
 'Aunt Topsy' (7ZL), 13
 'Aunt Willa' (2FC), 10

---

[1] Note: Page numbers followed by 'n' refer to notes.

Australian Broadcasting Commission
  (ABC), 1, 2, 7, 10–12, 16, 19,
  30, 32, 52, 53, 57, 58, 60, 62,
  63, 75, 79, 83, 105, 154
  Advisory Committees, 2, 105–108,
    110, 112, 113, 121; State
    School Broadcast Advisory
    Committees, 106; Talks
    Advisory Committee, 106;
    Women's Session Advisory
    Committee, 114
  Audience Research section, 90
  Listener and Viewer
    Panels, 118–120
  Listener Research section, 108, 118
  National Children's Session, 19
  Research and Statistics
    section, 118–120
  State Advisory Committees;
    Queensland Advisory
    Committee, 118; South
    Australian Advisory Committee,
    107; Tasmanian Advisory
    Committee, 115; Western
    Australian Advisory
    Committee, 106
  Television Viewers' Committees, 2,
    105; Adelaide Viewers'
    Committee, 115; Brisbane
    Viewers' Committee, 118;
    Hobart Viewers' Committee,
    115, 117, 118; Melbourne
    Viewers' Committee, 112, 118;
    Perth Viewers' Committee,
    116, 119; Sydney Viewers'
    Committee, 110
Australian Broadcasting Company, 31
Australian Broadcasting Control Board
  (ABCB), 2, 16, 36, 38, 39, 76,
  83–96, 109, 130
  Advisory Committee on Children's
    Television Programs, 87

Program Services Division, 89, 109
Television Program
  Standards, 87, 90
Australian Broadcasting Tribunal
  (ABT), 75, 95
Australian Singles News, 136
Australian Women's Weekly, 54,
  110, 129
Australia's Amateur Hour, 58
AWA network, 58
AWA Tower, 83

B
Bachelor, The, 141, 142
Bachelorette, The, 141, 142
Ball, W. Macmahon, 80
Banks, Norman, 57, 92
Barry, Dr Keith, 19, 109, 111–114
Battye, Dr J.S., 106–108
Baume, Eric, 58
B-class stations, 7–9, 11, 12, 76
Bearup, T.W. (Bill), 11, 12,
  107, 121n5
Beaurepaire, Beryl, 117
Beauty and the Geek Australia, 141
Bennett, Lewis, 86
Berryman, Laurel
  'Aunty Laurel,' 16
Bessemer, Eric
  'Sunshine Sam,' 9
Between Ourselves, 128
Bird, Alan, 88
Birthday calls, 7, 9, 11, 16, 40, 54
Blair, Megan, 61
Blind Date, 139
Blind Date (Seven Network), 132
Blind Date (TEN10), 131, 132, 141
Blind Date (2GB), 129, 130
Blind Date (2UE), 130
Blue Hills, 3, 61, 66
Blundell, Graeme, 94

Bobby Limb Show, 112
Bobo Show, The, 41
Bobo the Clown, 41
Bonney, John, 130
Bonython, Lady (Constance), 107
Book Club, The, 42
Boughen, Michael, 137
Box, The, 93
Boyd QC, 113
Boyer, Sir Richard, 111
Boy Meets Girl, 130
Bradman, Donald, 16
British Broadcasting Corporation (BBC), 11, 56, 61, 108
Broadbent, Mrs Jack
  'Smiler,' 33
Broadcasting Business Year Books, 34
Brown, H.P., 76
Burr, Raymond, 63
Burt, Professor Cyril, 56
Byrne, Lorna, 61

C
Callsigns, v
Calwell, Arthur, 82, 84, 90, 92, 108
Cameron, Senator Donald, 82
Capital Television, 64
Captain Fortune Show, 36
Captain Fortune's Saturday Party, 36
Carmichael, Alan, 114
Celebrity, 128, 129, 131, 140, 142
Censorship, 79, 90, 93
Channel Niners, The, 41, 63
Chapple, Ewart, 114, 117
Charlton, Conrad, 107
Chater, Gordon, 90
Chatterbox Corner, 17
Cheerio calls, 16, 19
Cheyenne, 63
Children's Hour, 11–13, 19
Clark, S.R.I., 91
Cleary, W.J., 59, 79, 106, 108

Clewlow, Frank D., 11, 19, 20
Club Buggery, 66
Cochrane, A.S., 10
  'Hello Man,' 9
Coffey, Ida
  'Penelope,' 32
Colefax, Alan, 58
Colgate-Palmolive Radio Production Unit, 81–83
Collignon, Madelaine, 41
Columbia Broadcasting System (CBS), 60, 111
Commercial Broadcasting, 56
Commercial radio, 56, 78, 79, 83, 87–89, 92, 95, 130, 135, 136
Commonwealth Broadcasting Network, 84
Community radio, 95
Community singing, 13, 31, 85, 154
Complaints, 2, 16, 95, 154
  advertising, 54, 76, 83, 88
  bad language, 95
  competitions, 84
  disc jockeys, 88
  music, 80, 88
  news, 83
  news dramatisation, 86
  nudity and sex, 76, 79, 92, 93, 95
  political matter, 83
  radio changes, 88, 89
  religious broadcasting, 76, 79
  talkback, 91
  thrillers, 54
  violence, 76, 95
Concerts, 31, 54, 59
Conder, W.T., 12, 13
Cooke, Edgar Eric, 120
Cop the Lot, 85
Cordeaux, Jeremy, 132
Cormac, Mabel
  'Little Miss Sunshine,' 8
  'Miss Mabel Sunshine,' 8
Country Hour, 59

Country Women's Session, 61
Cracknell, Ruth, 64
Craft, Shelley, 141
Crawford, Hector, 93
Crease, Kevin, 63
Crease, Tony, 63
Crime Game, The, 78
Critics, The, 111
Cross, C.J.
   'Uncle Jim,' 17
Cupid's Conquests, 128

D

Dad and Dave, 82
Dalton, Lara, 41
Dating Game, The, 131, 136
Davey, Jack, 17, 32, 55, 81, 154
David Jones, 31
Davidson, Sir Charles W., 87
Dawson, Dorothy, 29
Dearth, Harry, 58
Department of Information (DoI), 80
Department of the Media, 95
Desmond, Therese, 60
Dexter, 137, 139
Dial 999, 113
Dickinson, Howard, 52
Dixon, Arthur L.
   'Master Dixie,' 14
Donald, Eric L.
   'Uncle Eric,' 16
Donikian, George, 63
Doopa Dog, 41
Doyle, John
   'Roy Slaven,' 65, 66
Duckmanton, Talbot, 91, 120–121
Dudley, Maurice
   'Billy Bunny,' 9
Dunne, John, 16, 19, 54, 128
   'Uncle Tom,' 8, 14
Durant, Will, 56
Dyer, Bob, 84, 85

E

Eastlake, Darryl, 65
eBay, 63, 154
Empire Broadcasts, 52
Errington, Betty, 34
Evans, Greg, 136, 141
Evans, Lindley
   'The Melody Man,' 20
Evie Hayes Show, The, 114

F

Fair, Dick, 58
Fair, Roger, 13
   'The Smileman,' 13
Fan cards, 39, 62, 154
Fan mail, 2, 52, 54, 60, 63–66, 75, 79, 82, 154
Farmer & Co., 9
Farmer Wants A Wife, 141
Federation of Australian Radio Broadcasters (FARB), 80, 85, 86, 89
Felsman, David, 118
Fields, Gracie, 32
Finlay, A.N., 109, 111–114, 118–120, 125n71
Fisk, Sir Ernest, 30
Fitz-Henry, L., 54
For Men Only, 57
Foreign-language broadcasting, 80
Foster, George, 130
Four Corners, 116, 117, 119–121
Fred and Maggie Everybody, 60
Fuller, W.E., 53
Funicello, Annette, 37

G

Gainford, Rod
   'Uncle Rod,' 14
George Wallace Show, 82
Gibson, Marcus, 53

INDEX

Gibson Committee, 35, 80–82, 108
Glover, Richard, 141
Gogglebox Australia, 153
Golden West Network (GWN), 41
   Doopa's Club, 41
   GWN Saturday Club, 41
Good Film and Radio Vigilance
   League of New South
   Wales, 80, 83
Goodnight segments, 41
Gorman, Frank W.
   'Kanga,' 9
Grace, Isabelle, 54
Graham, Dorothy, 32
Graham Kennedy Show, The, 93, 94
Great Depression, 10, 11, 29, 31
Green, F.C., 62
Greig, E.L., 81, 85
Grey, Kathleen, 35
Grose, Frank
   'Uncle Frank,' 31
Grundy, Reg, 130, 131
Grundy Entertainment, 136, 139
Guest of Honour, 62
Gyngell, Bruce, 91

H

Handyman, The, 111
Hanna, Bobby, 132
Hardin, Ty, 63
Harty, Frank Sturge, 128
Hatherley, Frank, 33
   'Bobby Bluegum,' 9
Hector Crawford Productions, 59
Heffron, R.J., 79
Heinze, Professor Bernard, 59
Heming, Dick, 89
Henry, Peter, 135
Herbert, Alan, 36
Herd, Margaret
   'Fairy Godmother,' 10, 20
Hickey, Helen, 40

Holden, Mark, 140
Hope, A.D.
   'Anthony Inkwell,' 20
Hordern, Anthony, 9–10
Horner, H.G., 20, 58, 82
How to Murder in Your Own Home, 32
Howell, Edward, 60
Howson, Denzil, 39
   'Barney Sludge,' 39
Hughes, W.M., 30
Hulme, Alan, 91
Hume Broadcasters, 14
Hume, Stella, 9
   'Auntie Stella,' 9
   'Miss Leonora Starr,' 9

I

I Love Lucy, 112
Inglis, Ken, 11, 106, 111–113, 116
In Melbourne Tonight (IMT), 62, 88
In Sydney Tonight, 39

J

Jackson, Helen, 135
   Helen Jackson Show, 135
James, Sir Walter, 106
Jones, Charles Lloyd, 80
Jose, Adrian, 85, 89, 92
Jupp, Eric, 116

K

Katy and John, 56
Katz, Elihu, 56
Kennedy, Graham, 62, 63, 85,
   88, 92–94
Kenny, Dr Peter, 118
King, Catherine, 60
Kipling, Rudyard, 16
Kirke, Basil W., 56, 106, 121n5
Knight, Hattie, 31

L

Lamport, Nellie, 61
Landon, Marie
  'Aunt Marie,' 14
Lane, Don, 63, 136
Lange, Bob, 19
Larkin, Mike, 64
Late Show, The, 62
Laws, John, 64
Lawsons, The, 61
Lee, Alicia, 63, 90
Le Garde Twins, 62
Lehman, Val, 64
Leone, Filomena, 136
Lindgren, Kathleen
  'Nancy Lee,' 17
Lisner, Panda, 62
Listener In-TV, 10, 115
Logie Awards, 40, 64
Love Game, 140
Love Song Dedications, 136
Love Time, 128
Lumsdaine, Jack, 128
Lunn, Lionel
  'Uncle Lionel,' 8
Lux Radio Theatre, 58
Lynn, Nancye, 35
Lyons, Dame Enid, 31, 58
Lyons, Gerald, 62
Lyons, J.A., 58

M

Macquarie Network, 17, 31, 33, 34, 58, 91, 135
Magic Circle Club, The, 40
Magic of Music, The, 116
Magor, Wilfred
  'Reverend Dixie,' 14
Mark Foys, 31
Market to Market, 112
Marriage Game, The, 130, 131

Married at First Sight, 141, 142
Marsh, Gordon, 14
Marshall, Denny
  'Cousin Denny,' 9
Marshall, Dr A.J., 58
  'Jock the Backyard Naturalist,' 20
Marshall, Valda, 130, 131
Martin, J.M., 82
Mason, Bill, 136
Maude, Hazel
  'Little Miss Kookaburra,' 9
Mavis Bramston Show, The, 90
McCabe, G.W., 115, 119
McClelland, Douglas, 93, 95
McEachern, Mary
  'Mary Lou,' 19
McNair Survey, 87
McNair, W.A., 53
Men at the Top, 111
Meredith, Gwen, 61
Meredith, Si, 56
  'Uncle Si,' 54
Mickey Mouse Club, The, 37, 39
Midnight Matchmaker, 2, 127, 132–136, 139, 141, 142
Miethke, Adelaide, 107
Migrants, 94, 154
Miller, B.K., 115
Miller, J.S., 115, 116
Moore, Richard
  'Uncle Dick,' 16
Morrisby, Rex, 86
Morrison, Margaret, 133
Morse, Carlton, 53
Morse, Hilda, 55
Morton, Tex, 58
Moses, Charles, 19, 107, 110, 112, 117, 118
Mother and Son, 64
Murdoch, Nina, 12, 13
Murdoch, Professor Walter, 107
Murdoch, Sir Keith, 80

Musgrove, Nan, 63
Myer, Norman, 57, 113
Myer Musicale, 57

N
National Archives of Australia, 94, 105–106
National Council of Women, 107, 115
Naylor, Malcolm, 119, 120
Negus, George, 136
Neighbours, 63, 140
Neil, Keith, 135
New York Philharmonic Symphony Orchestra, 60
Newlywed Game, The, 130, 140, 141
News, 63, 79, 86, 111
Newsbeat, 86
Newsome, Debbie, 137
Newton, Bert, 21, 62
Nichols, Joy, 20
Nine Network, 65, 140, 141
NSW Council for Film and Television, 38
NSW Council of Churches, 10, 82
Number 96, 93, 131

O
O'Keefe, Arthur, 128
O'Kelly, Joseph, 88
Olden, Colonel A.C.N., 106
One Man's Family, 53, 60
Opera for the People, 59
Orr, Dr Fred, 132, 142
Osborne, R.G., 88, 89, 92
Osbourne, Ida, 19

P
Packer, Sir Frank, 37
Parish, H.R.
 'Uncle Cliffe,' 19

Park, Ruth, 20
Parliamentary Standing Committee on Broadcasting (PSCB), 82, 108
Patterson, George, 80
Pearce, Eric, 85
Pearce, Guy, 140
Penlington, John, 119
Perfect Match (Seven Network), 141
Perfect Match (Ten Network), 2, 3, 127, 128, 132, 136–142
Perry Mason, 63, 111
Peters Pals, 20
Phil Silvers Show, The, 111
Pickhaver, Greig
 'H.G. Nelson,' 65, 66
Pop Opera, 63
Postmaster-General's (PMG's) Department, 16, 76, 79, 81, 82, 85, 87, 109
Povah, Arthur, 116
Prentice, J.M.
 'Uncle Jack,' 8, 54
Prider, Dorothy
 'Aunty Ruby,' 33
Prime Network
 Possum's Club, 41
 Prime Saturday Club, 41
Prime Possum, 41
Princeton Radio Research Project, 58
Prisoner, 64
Proposals, 128

Q
Queensland Radio News, 8
 'Uncle Ben's Corner,' 8

R
Radio clubs, 2, 11, 29, 31, 33–35, 39, 41, 42, 154
 See also Radio stations
Radio exhibitions, 11

164 INDEX

Radio Pictorial of Australia, 15, 17, 55, 57
Radio stations
5AD, 34; 5AD Kangaroo Club, 16, 34
5CK, 13
5CL, 13; 5CL Bluebird Girls' Club, 8; 5CL Twinklers' Boys Club, 8
5DN, 9; 5DN Happiness Club, 31; 5DN Kangaroo Club, 16; 5DN Kipling Boys' Club, 14
5KA, 85
5RM, 16, 86
4BC, 52, 135; 4BC Bunny Club, 14; 4BC Happiness Club, 14
4BH, 14, 78; 4BH Lonely Listeners' Club, 29; 4BH The Nothing Under 60 Club, 33
4BK, 92; 4BK Association of Friends, 32; 4BK Dixie Radio Club, 14
4CA, 34
4KQ, 60
4QG, 8
4WK, 34
7BU; 7BU Sunpolishers' Club, 19
7DY; 7DY Sunpolishers' Club, 19
7EX; 7EX Gardening League, 33
7HO, 135; 7HO Pals Club, 19; 7HO Women's Club, 35
7HT, 135
7LA, 35; 7LA Women's Association, 35, 41
7QT; 7QT Chums Club, 19; 7QT Queenstown Children's Hour, 19
7ZL, 9; 7ZL Children's Radio Club, 13
6AM, 17, 34
6IX, 17
6KG, 9, 17; 6KG Goldfields Boys' Club, 17
6LM, 11
6ML, 16, 79; 6ML Cheerio Club, 30, 32; 6ML Fox Hoyts Radio Club, 30; 6ML Junior Cheerio Club, 17, 34
6PR, 11, 16, 135
6WF, 11, 16; 6WF Women's Association, 32
3AR, 53
3AW, 17–19, 92, 135, 136; 3AW Night Owls' Club, 33
3BO, 13, 34
3DB, 59, 82
3KZ, 57, 79, 82, 135; 3KZ Friendship Circle, 32
3LO, 11, 53
3SH; 3SH Microphone Ball, 33; 3SH Women's Club, 33
3UL; 3UL Breakfast Club, 33
3UZ, 85; 3UZ Look Up and Laugh Club, 32
3XY, 89, 92; 3XY Fisherman's Club, 33
3YB; 3YB Breakfast Club, 33
2AY, 13
2BH; 2BH Smilers' Club, 33
2BL, 8, 9
2CA, 86, 135; 2CA Night Owls' Club, 33
2CH, 10, 13, 53, 54, 56; 2CH Crusaders' Club, 20; 2CH Smile Club, 13
2CN, 64
2FC, 9, 10, 13, 52; 2FC Children's News Radio Birthday Club, 9; Bluegum Sunshine Soldiers, 13
2GB, 10, 16, 20, 53, 54, 56, 57, 77, 79, 81, 127, 128, 130, 132, 134, 136; 2GB Happiness Club, 30, 31, 34, 35; 2GB MGM Radio Movie Club, 30; 2GB Miserable Club, 32

INDEX 165

2GF; 2GF Smile Club, 13, 34
2GZ; 2GZ Country Service Club, 34
2HD, 9, 34; 2HD Joy Club, 13
2KA; 2KA Radio Service Club, 34
2KO, 80
2KY, 82, 84, 136
2LM, 59
2MW, 34
2NZ; 2NZ Country Service
  Club, 35
2SM, 8, 14, 54, 128; 2SM Punch
  Club, 14; 2SM Uncle Tom's
  Gang, 14
2UE, 8, 81, 128, 130
2UW, 10, 11, 16, 51, 54, 55, 83,
  84, 88; 2UW Children's Radio
  Birthday Club, 10; 2UW Fox
  Movietone Radio Club, 30
2WG; 2WG Women's Club,
  33, 35, 41
2WL, 9
2WS, 136
2XL, 9
Ratings, 60, 112, 113, 116, 118, 121,
  132, 135, 137, 139–141
Ray, Johnnie, 63
Raymond, Betty
  'Aunty Betty,' 19
Read, A.T., 116
Read, Leonard L.
  'Uncle Ben,' 8
Reality television, 128, 141, 142
Reed, F. Wilbur, 115–118
Reeve, Goodie, 10, 57
  'Auntie Goodie,' 10
Reg Grundy Enterprises, 132
Regulation
  *Australian Broadcasting Act
    1942*, 81, 108
  *Australian Broadcasting Act
    1948*, 83, 109
  *Broadcasting and Television Act
    1956*, 87, 93, 94, 109

Reisesjekken, 142
Request Hour, 59
Returned Services League of Australia
  (RSL), 106
Roberts, Eric, 33, 35
Roberts, Ida Annie
  'Aunty Nan,' 33, 35
Robertson, Jessie
  'Aunt Judy,' 17
Robertson, Stuart, 135
Robinson Crusoe, 13
Romantic Hour, The, 128
Rosenthal, Newman, 109
Rudd, Steele, 82
Russell, Julie, 54
Rutherford, Ruth, 52

S
Saddle Club, The, 42
Saunders, B.F., 32
Saunders, George
  'Uncle George,' 8, 52
Sayre, Jeanette, 58
School of the Air, 107
Scott, Elizabeth, 62
Scott, Keith, 139
Searle, Malcolm, 131
Sellars, Ross, 39
Semmler, Clement, 111, 120
Seven Network, 90, 132, 136,
  140, 141
Shead, Isobel Ann, 13
Sholl, E.K., 116, 118, 120
Simmons, Norman W.
  'Uncle Cuthbert,' 9
Simon Townsend's Wonder World, 63
Singleton, John, 136, 154
Six O'Clock Rock, 111, 121
Skippy, 63
Slogans, 34
Smart, Jeffrey, 38
Smith, George Ivan, 57

Special Broadcasting Service (SBS), 63, 154
Stanley, Charles, 13
State Broadcasting Advisory Committees, 108, 109
Stelzer, Eunice, 30, 31, 35
Sullivans, The, 63
Sunday Concert, 112
Superman, 38
Sutcliffe, Ken, 65

T
TAA Junior Flyers' Club, 36
Talkback, 91, 130, 154
Tarax Show, 39
Tarzan of the Apes, 79
Teen Time, 112
Television commencement in Australia, 109
Television clubs, 2, 30, 154
  See also Television stations
Television stations
  ADS7, 37
  AMV4; *Cohns Cobbers' Teleclub*, 39
  ATN7, 36, 111; ATN7 Captain Fortune Club, 36
  ATV0, 93, 131; Channel 0 Viewers' Club, 40
  BCV8; *Cobbers' Teleclub*, 39
  BTQ7, 63
  BTV6; BTV Channel 6 Juniors Club, 39
  CBN8, 93
  GTV9, 39, 62, 88, 95
  GTW11, 41
  HSV7, 37, 62
  MTN9; Channel Niners' Club, 40
  NWS9; The Channel Niners, 36
  QTQ9, 63
  RTN8; RTN8 Juniors Club, 39
  RVN2; Channel 2 Children's Club, 40

SAS10, 41
SEQ8; *Teleclub*, 40
TCN9, 36, 63, 91, 111
TEN10, 93, 130, 140
TVT6, 117
WIN4; Ace Club, 41; *Channel 4 Club*, 39
Temptation Island, 141
Ten Network, 41, 63, 127, 131, 141
Terry, Jocelyn, 62
This Day Tonight, 93
This Sporting Life, 65
Thomas, L.R., 107
Thompson, J. Walter, 53
Thrillers, 78, 79, 81, 85
Tiny Tots, 10
Tonight, 63
Triple J, 65
Tupper, Fred ('Tuppy'), 17
Turner, Charles 'Hal, 41
Turpie, Ian, 66, 140
TV Review, 40
TV Times, 36
TV Week, 62, 63, 87

U
Uncles, 7, 8, 52
'Uncle Bas' (2BL), 10
'Uncle Ben' (4QG), 8
'Uncle Ben' (7ZL), 13
'Uncle Bert' (5DN), 16
'Uncle Dan and Dusty' (6KG), 17
'Uncle Jack' (2UW), 10
'Uncle Radio' (5CL), 8
'Uncle Vim' (3KZ), 32
United Associations of Women, 89

V
Varley, Gwen, 31
Vautier, Dorothy, 55
Vietnam War, 91

Violence, 32, 79, 83, 91, 92
Voice of Youth, The, 57

W
Walker, Clint, 63
Walshe, Keith, 39, 154
Walt Disney Productions, 37
Warburton, Margaret, 34
Ward, Diana, 120
Ward, E.J., 84
Webb, Ada, 33
Webb, Graham, 131
Wells, Harold
  'Uncle Rag,' 17
West Coast 63, 119–121
West Coast 64, 119
Western Australia, 11, 16, 19, 30, 32, 41, 53, 60, 65, 79, 81, 85, 106–108, 115, 116, 118–121, 135
Western Stores, 34
Whelan, Olga-Mary, 39
Whiteley, E.A., 117, 118
Whitta, Clifford Nicholls ('Nicky'), 17, 20, 85
Willesee, Michael, 136
Williams, Sir John, 37
Wilshire, Brian, 132–135

Win, Jack, 51, 52, 56
Winter, A.J., 114
Wireless Weekly, 8, 10, 14, 16, 30, 32, 33, 51, 54, 55, 76–78, 128
Withers, Tony, 130
Woman's World, 111, 114, 117, 121
Women's Christian Temperance Union, 80
Wood, Ivy
  'Cousin Joy,' 13
Wood, Robin, 120
Wooley, Bert
  'Uncle Bert,' 13
World Champion Wrestling, 91
World War II, 2, 7, 19, 34, 79, 130, 154
Worrall, David, 82
Wright, Claudia, 92
Wright, Myles, 92, 93

Y
Yeldon, Russell A.
  'Uncle Bob,' 8
You Can't See Round Corners, 91
Young Men's Christian Association (YMCA), 113
Young Women's Christian Association (YWCA), 114, 115

Printed in the United States
by Baker & Taylor Publisher Services